The Complete Guide to Getting a Grant

How
to Turn
Your Ideas
into
Dollars

The
Complete Guide
to
Getting
a Grant

Revised Edition

Laurie Blum

John Wiley & Sons, Inc.
New York • Chichester • Brisbane • Toronto • Singapore • Weinheim

Library of Congress Cataloging-in-Publication Data

Blum, Laurie.
    The complete guide to getting a grant : how to turn your ideas
into dollars / Laurie Blum.—Rev. ed.
        p.   cm.
    Includes bibliographical references and index.
                                            —ISBN 0-471-15508-X
(pbk.: alk. paper)
    1. Fund raising—United States—Handbooks, manuals, etc. 2. Proposal
writing for grants—United States—Handbooks, manuals, etc. I. Title.
HV41.9.U5B58   1996
658.15′224—dc20   96-16543

Printed in the United States of America

10 9 8 7 6 5

To Gerald Howard for inspiration;

to Laura Demanski, PJ Dempsey, Chris Jackson,

and Elaine Pfefferblit for invaluable editorial assistance;

to Alan Kellock, without whom none of this would have been possible;

and, of course, to Robert Withers.

CONTENTS

INTRODUCTION

The *Guide* is intended for the average American beset by rising costs and a dwindling bank account. You hope to put your kids through college but are horrified by the expense; your elderly parent's health insurance will not cover home nursing care; you have a great idea for a business or perhaps need some expansion capital but your bank, if it still exists, has turned you down. I think it's high time that you were privy to what we fund raisers have known for years: that five billion dollars—that's right, *five billion*—exists in grant monies for individuals. With times as tough as they are, the nonprofit world is the last frontier of untapped money for the average American.

Over the years in my fund-raising practice, I have raised millions of dollars for hundreds of individuals and projects. My fees are quite steep. *The Complete Guide to Getting a Grant* will reveal my fund-raising secrets so that you too can tap into the billions of dollars available from the nonprofit sector.

An old axiom goes, "Knowledge is power." My axiom is "Knowledge is wealth." Remember, the advice that I am offering you here is exactly the same advice that I follow myself. It is the culmination of years of experience. I have organized this book in a way that's both easy to follow and fun to read. By the time you finish reading *The Complete Guide to Getting a Grant,* you will know as much about the grant process as most professional fund raisers and will be well on your way to getting yours.

You, the person for whom this book is written, have little or no experience with the grant-seeking process. I will therefore take you step-by-step through each stage, so that even if you are a first-time grant seeker, you can successfully win a grant. This book also contains many instructive examples of individuals for whom I have raised money.

Anyone can learn fund raising, and I'm the best example. I didn't go to school to learn to be a fund raiser, I learned fund raising by doing it. Now I am considered one of the foremost experts in my field. The point is that *anyone* can get a grant for an idea they really believe in, and *The Complete Guide to Getting a Grant* is the best place to learn how.

1

IT STARTS WITH
AN IDEA

You probably already have an idea—or several. If you're thinking about getting a grant, it's likely that you're interested in certain kinds of ideas—ideas that lead to action, that have the potential for causing change, for creating something that didn't exist before, for solving a problem, for making discoveries. Or you may simply have a compelling personal need, or see a need in your community, and have the idea that there must be a way to meet this need. You may want to develop your own career or interests, or pursue a project that will help your local community, your city, or a larger interest group. Your vision might reach out to the nation or even the world.

Everyone has ideas for projects, ideas for solving problems, or ideas for fulfilling needs. Some you can act on immediately—it's just a matter of making the decision, setting aside some time, and going ahead. Others require more time and resources, and that's why you're thinking about getting a grant. You may already have a very clear idea of what you want a grant for: you're a teacher and you want travel funds so that you can study Moorish architecture in Spain, or you're a mother and want to set up a day-care center in your community, or you're an inventor/entrepreneur and you want to develop a new kind of low-cost shelter that can help the homeless and put your own company on the map at the same time. Or you may have only a general idea of an area you want to work in—you want to work in documentary film, or do something in your community to help with AIDS education—but you haven't yet come up with a specific project that you want to pursue. In either case, it's worth considering what makes a good idea, for the purpose of getting a grant.

WHAT MAKES A GOOD IDEA?

What kinds of ideas attract funders? Some kinds of grants come in standard packages—they're given out for set purposes to people with very specific needs and credentials. Other grants go to people with good ideas that have never been tried before. In my work as a fundraising consultant, I've had the opportunity to help raise funds for a variety of good ideas, and I've seen certain factors that many of them have in common. Let's look at some of the qualities that can interest funders in a new idea.

- *Originality.* Funders are looking at a vast number of proposals from year to year, have already funded many, and have some firsthand knowledge of which kinds of ideas have been tried and which have succeeded. A truly original idea is certainly going to attract attention and stir interest, especially if it seems like a fresh approach to an existing problem.

I know of a scientist who came up with what is probably one of the more original ideas I've ever come across. After much study, he had developed the theory that a specific bird living in the rain forest pecked at the bark of a certain tree, releasing a liquid secretion that the Aztecs, believe it or not, used as a form of cement in putting together structures and buildings. He'd done his research, he knew his field, and his idea was so provocative that he was able to get funding for a field trip and further research.

By originality, though, I don't mean that an idea should have no historical precedent or reference to established invention or creation. In fact, some of the most solid ideas are reactions to (or improvements upon) existing concepts. Take, for example, my own idea of "free money." Although the concept of philanthropy has existed since the time of Ben Franklin, no one before me had thought to make fund-raising information available to the general public. I discovered that there was an incredible demand for this kind of information, and wrote a series of *Free Money* books that listed sources of grants for different needs—from day care to health care to business and the arts. These books were wildly successful—a total of over 500,000 copies have sold at the time of this writing. This is one kind of originality: recognizing unexplored applications for an existing concept, and exploring them yourself.

In fact, it's always important for your original idea to have some point of reference, so it doesn't seem to be coming out of left field. Funders are looking for the relationship between your idea and what's been tried or explored before.

- **Problem solving.** Certain problems seem to be always with us: poverty, hunger, social and racial tensions, the need for more effective education. Other new problems arise with each decade, and different communities may have unique problems. Funders are always looking for fresh solutions to these problems, on a small or large scale. Originality plays a part here, too; good ideas often take a fresh approach to the problem at hand, and present a nontraditional solution.

One of my earliest clients, Jack Jackson, was a successful African American playwright who had won an Obie for his play *Fly Blackbird*. He was also a committed civil rights activist. After the Watts riots in the sixties, he decided that he wanted to use his expertise and experience in the arts to try to make a difference in this community, and developed the idea that the arts could be part of the solution to some of the social problems in this country.

Jack enlisted the help of Gregory Peck and others in the Hollywood community, and set up the Inner City Cultural Center in Los Angeles, where he not only trained playwrights and actors but also really started the whole idea of multiculturalism in the performing arts. He produced what was probably the first multicultural and multiracial *Hamlet*, and a number of former students of the Center are now successful members of the entertainment community.

Jack was a visionary, who saw a problem and drew on his own experience and expertise to come up with a fresh solution. Of course he didn't single-handedly solve the problems of the inner city, but he did help change the climate of the arts in this country, and provide training and opportunities to many individuals.

- **Timeliness.** This is another important factor in attracting funders to an idea. Times change, perceptions change—in the social and politial arenas as well as in the worlds of the sciences, arts, and humanities. Ideas and attitudes come into and fall out of favor. Current events can influence perceptions of social needs—just think of the effect of Sputnik on science education, or of the success of Japanese industry on workplace management theories. Funders change, too, and may shift their areas of interest to deal with perceived social problems or issues of the future. An idea that catches onto a wave of change can ride that wave to successful funding.

One organization I worked with that found its interests changing was Volunteers of America (VOA), which has had a long and distinguished record as a traditional charity with a small-town sensibility, engaged in such worthy pursuits as delivering meals to housebound senior citizens. In the early nineties, the Los Angeles chapter of VOA wanted to address what it perceived as the increasingly desperate situation of children in urban ghettos. This was at a time when the policy of the federal government was increasingly to look to business for assistance with social problems. Some officers of VOA came up with the idea of helping children in the inner cities start their own small businesses—they called it the Midas Touch Program. Kids might start a video delivery business, or decorate and sell T-shirts. The program was meant to pull kids away from the attraction of gangs, involve them in the world of work, and help them develop a sense of independence and initiative. It often made the difference between whether a child had one good meal a day or not.

We were able to enlist a good deal of support for this program. It was timely on two fronts—not only in addressing a pressing social need but doing so in a way that took into account reduced federal spending and the new emphasis on the business and private sectors.

- **Compelling need.** Funders do respond to what they see as the most compelling needs, whether on a social or an individual level. On the level of broad social concerns, both public and private funders try to help with what they see as the most pressing social problems and needs—poverty, education, health care, medical research, or what have you. On the individual level, many programs support very specific kinds of individual needs, whether it's educational scholarships for Native Americans, or health care for people with heart diseases.

This is not to say that every individual need can be fulfilled, but there are many private funders who have experienced hardship or difficulties either themselves or within their own family, and who have generously donated funds to help others with similar problems. On the broad social level, funders often shift priorities and funds to address what are seen as the most pressing social needs. In the early 1980s, little funding was available to deal with AIDS research or medical assistance. As funders began to realize how compelling the problem was, they channeled more funds into these areas, and into related areas, like pediatric AIDS support, as the need became evident.

Funders' perception of need shifts to some extent with the times, following current events or well-publicized issues. At the same time, many funders remained concerned with some of the basic social needs, such as education and support of the arts. If you have a specific project, you will try in your research to locate the funders who are interested in addressing that particular need (more on this in Chapter 3). Rather than changing your project, one of the best ways to match your idea to a funder's interests is to show how your project will help serve the needs that the funder finds most compelling. When Jack set up the Inner City Cultural Center in Los Angeles, he saw that this was a community with a real need to be connected to career opportunities and the cultural mainstream of our society. He decided to address this need in a specific way by creating a program for the theater arts.

- **Outreach.** Though some funders are specifically interested in individuals and individual projects, many are looking for ideas that will affect a large number of people, whether a community or a population group. The effect could be indirect, as in certain education or arts outreach programs, or direct, as through hiring or teaching a number of individuals. The bottom line is: you are asking someone, the officers of a nonprofit entity, to give you free money to execute a project. Naturally, they want to know not only that the project will come to fruition, but also that it will reach the people it's intended to reach.

Back in the fifties, Joseph Papp had the idea that the people of New York City—the public, ordinary citizens—should be able to see more theater, that good theater shouldn't be limited to those who could pay Broadway ticket prices. So he started a program of presenting free Shakespeare in Central Park, which in turn became the New York Shakespeare Festival, which became a major cultural influence in New York, producing innovative avant-garde and multicultural work, as well as shows like A Chorus Line that did wind up on Broadway. Papp had both a great love for the theater and a great respect for the public. He felt the public *deserved* good theater, affordable or free, and that was the essence of his mission.

Another example: A client of mine who owned an architectural landscaping firm needed funds to hire additional workers and buy new equipment. He allied himself with a local rehabilitation center, which was trying to place recovering alcoholics in reentry jobs. Through the center, we were able to raise quite a bit of money for him to hire recovering alcoholics, and to buy some equipment as well. He found assistance for his own individual needs by reaching out to a larger group and helping meet their special needs.

One of my favorite clients was a gentleman who had become handicapped and found that while swimming and even going underwater as a scuba diver, he could function very much like everyone else. He did not feel handicapped in the water, which gave a great boost to his damaged self-esteem. So he founded the Handicapped Scuba Diving Association, which reached out to give handicapped people a renewed sense of self-esteem, as well as a great deal of pleasure.

What if you have an idea that seems to involve you alone—you want to travel, to study, to make a film or write a play? Even here, funders will be looking for outreach. If you're a high school or college teacher, wouldn't you love to spend the summer touring exotic locations, or a year teaching abroad? There are funders who will support you, not to give you a great summer vacation but to promote international educational exchange or to enrich the quality of your teaching upon return. If you want to make a film, maybe an art film or a specific documentary, you'll find that funders are concerned not only to give you a chance to create, but also to see that you will somehow share your artistic endeavor with other people—that you have a detailed plan to get your work shown on television, or tour it to community centers.

- **Multiplying factors.** As you've probably guessed by now, the factors listed above can build on one another to make a good idea even stronger.

If you come up with an idea that takes an original, fresh approach to solving a problem, is timely, and will reach out to affect many people, you may have a project that will seem almost irresistible to funders.

THE PERSONAL FACTOR

Aside from the qualities that can make an idea attractive to funders, there's one crucial factor that can make or break a funding idea. That factor is you: who you are, what experience or knowledge you possess, how you present yourself, and perhaps most significant of all, how much you care about your idea. Let's look at some of these aspects that will have a direct bearing on your success in getting a grant.

- **Your personal knowledge and expertise.** Clearly, if you are a scientist or teacher and you want a grant to do research or further study in your field, you will already have some kind of background and experience that can begin to convince a funder of your worthiness. However, this isn't the only kind of expertise that counts. Many good ideas come out of personal need and personal experience, whether from observing a need or having experienced it oneself.

You may belong to a community or a group, and be in a better position than anyone else to help solve certain problems because you know them with an insider's knowledge. My client who started the Handicapped Scuba Diving Association had a personal experience and knowledge that led him to make a unique contribution.

Or you may simply understand a need, or see an opportunity, more clearly than anyone else. Joseph Papp wasn't trained as an actor or producer. He didn't get a degree in theater, or train to be an arts administrator. But he saw a need that he believed he could address. What he had was a *vision* clear enough and strong enough to carry him through to success.

- *Can you, will you, follow through?* You must have the perceived ability to carry out your proposed project, and to follow it through to completion or fulfillment.

A funder that is giving away either public or private funds has a mandate to do so responsibly, and a commitment to do social good. When funders give grants, they expect to see the money being put to effective use. It is an honor both to apply for and to receive this money. Funders are wary in some cases of individuals who seem to have no previous experience that relates to their idea, or who may seem to lack the ability or experience to manage funds or a project. However, don't give up if you think funders might question your experience. Enthusiasm, zest, and passionate belief can count for a great deal. If you can provide a proposal that conveys a sense of true excitement about your idea and the conviction that you can carry it out, lack of experience can be overcome.

If you know you are able to carry out your project, that you are a follow-through person, who plans to be organized and responsible, there are things you can do to make your application stronger, which we'll cover in future chapters. If you've successfully managed funds or any kind of project, whether in the workplace or in your private life, you already have some evidence of your ability to follow through. If you're insecure about your abilities, you might consider collaborating on your idea, or working with an organization that can provide support in terms of financial management or other resources. But we'll return to this later.

One of the best ways to start convincing funders of your capability is to present a top-quality proposal package, containing a clear mission statement, an outline of the project that shows you've thought of every angle, and a professional and businesslike budget. We'll go over the details of this part of the process in Chapter 9.

- *Faith, conviction, and enthusiasm.* Whatever you call it—self-trust, instinct, or belief—there are certain intangibles that have more to do with your success in grant-getting than perhaps any other personal factor. You really do have to have conviction. You have to infect funders with your enthusiasm and your vision; you have to have the faith to keep going when the funding process seems endless and discouraging; you have to be able to deal with criticism and use it or reject it; and you have to believe so strongly in success that no obstacles will stand in your way.

If you do not believe in an idea 200 percent, do not pursue it. I used to work at Carnegie Hall with the Concert Artists Guild, which sponsored the debuts of young musicians. I could always tell which ones were going to make it professionally and have a career in performance and which ones were going to end up doing something else. Those who had the drive, the need, the burning desire to realize their dream were the ones who would end up doing it—no matter if they were a little less or a little more talented than other performers. This is the kind of conviction you have to have.

This is not to say that you can't have insecurities or doubts, but you must always believe in what you're doing, be prepared to carry it through, and be able to communicate your enthusiasm. There are exercises, books, and resources to help you focus your interests—and overcome negative thinking—and we'll mention some of them in the course of this book. If you're not an extrovert by temperament, don't despair: quiet conviction works just as well as the more flamboyant kind. But however you demonstrate it, commitment to your idea is one of the key factors that make funders take notice.

It's also one of the factors that can help you overcome lack of experience. One of my more successful clients in recent years was an African American television engineer who wanted to start a school for minority, inner-city kids in Los Angeles to teach them radio and television production. Now, this man had not the slightest clue about how to run a school, or how to raise money (which was why he came to me). All he had was a great dedication to his idea. Of course, as a cameraman for ABC he certainly had some qualifications, and he himself had grown up as a member of a minority group in the kind of neighborhood he wanted to target, so he also had a point of reference. His greatest asset by far, however, was his passionate belief in his idea. He was a missionary for the cause. And if you have that kind of faith, your project will succeed no matter what. The more qualifications you have the better, but a sense of passion and commitment to your idea is essential.

WHO ARE THE FUNDERS, AND HOW CAN YOU APPEAL TO THEM?

Although we'll discuss the different kinds of funders in greater detail later in this book, it's worthwhile taking a quick look right now at who the funders are and how they may react to your idea, so that you can start from the very beginning to think about how to develop your idea for funding.

WHO ARE THE FUNDERS?

Funders are actually business people looking to make an investment in a success story. They are not "ideas people" themselves, but it's their business to review, evaluate, and support ideas. They want to give money to projects that seem likely to succeed. Most funders have specific areas they are interested in; they specialize. If your idea is well thought out, designed to meet an existing need, and related to an area they are interested in, chances are funders will look favorably upon it.

Still, different types of funders will react to your project in different ways. What are these types? There are three important ones.

The Private Foundations.   The most well known foundations are what I call the "Big Daddy" foundations, like the Ford Foundation, the Rockefeller Foundation, the Guggenheim Foundation, the Hearst Foundation. These have been set up by major philanthropists and wealthy business people who have created foundations to do very broad-based good. They are highly sophisticated. They give away huge amounts of money every year. The Big Daddy foundations have broad interests and many different types of funding areas. They give to education, to health, to the arts, and to many other areas. They are staffed by program officers whose job it is to deal with grant seekers in various areas. They are professionals, and usually very accessible.

The other type of private foundation is the small family foundation. The funders may be still alive, or they've died and have left their estates to be set up as foundations. These usually give much more specifically, in particular areas. For example, my ex-husband and I set up such a foundation. We gave primarily in the arts because that was my passion, and within that area we particularly gave to classical and contemporary music. We funded new pieces by composers, we funded a documentary film. We were able to support projects that we were personally interested in, which is the beauty of a private foundation.

Private foundations are usually administered by attorneys, accountants, or bank trust departments. Such individuals are not specialists, are usually not as accessible as the program officers of the Big Daddy foundations, and are often terribly overworked. The small family foundations, as a general rule, are very understaffed, and they do not have time to sit down and help you hash out or develop an idea. Often, they are set up as trusts, and are not even listed publicly, in order to avoid public solicitations. On the other hand, for these very reasons, there is usually less competition for their resources.

Corporations and Private Businesses. Corporate funders are, as a rule, much looser, and much more entrepreneurial than private foundations. They can respond to needs faster, and aren't afraid to shoot from the hip. They can often take monies out of their discretionary, marketing, or advertising budgets.

Corporations give money primarily for public relations and advertising value. This is why you see names like Mobil and Exxon on the big public television projects. They like the prestige that comes from giving to projects that will be in the public eye. Local businesses, too, will give to projects that they think will bring them some good publicity.

Businesses may also offer technical services and advice, in place of or in addition to money for your project. They can help you do a business plan, help you do budgets, or offer facilities. For example, a corporation may make space available for art exhibits at some of its buildings.

Government Agencies. Government funders may seem much more aloof. They have the responsibility of giving away taxpayers' money. As with other areas of government spending, many checks and balances have been set up to protect these public funds. So, if you apply, you'll have to adjust and conform to very specific, detailed procedures. If you follow the rules and fit into the guidelines, then you do stand a chance of government funding.

The good thing about federal dollars is that the grants are usually much larger than either private or corporate grants. The government will often give what's known as multiyear grants, which provide a predictable source of funding for several years in a row. Whereas you might need to apply to several different private funders to get all the money you want for a big, extended project, or have to reapply year after year, a decent-sized government grant might fund your whole project by itself.

Besides private foundations, corporate funders, and government agencies, there are two other kinds of funders that occasionally support individuals or organizations, though usually on a much smaller scale.

Nonprofit Organizations: Prizes and Awards.   Although they do not usually give grants (they actually receive them), some nonprofit organizations give prizes and awards to individuals. There may be little or no money involved, but a prestigious award can add to your credentials, and thus contribute greatly to your fund-raising efforts. Some organizations, from local churches to rotary clubs, may offer small amounts of money or other assistance to people or projects in their local community.

Individual Donors.   Individuals actually contribute the largest share of all philanthropic donations, but they often give primarily to churches and religious organizations and are not a very useful source for the individual. Some nonprofit organizations do receive support from individual donors, but they really have to dig for it, through mailings and active fund-raising campaigns. Individual donors are just not a significant source of funds for individuals, except for the extremely rare individual artist who may find a wealthy patron.

How Can You Make Your Idea Attractive to Funders?

This is the fundamental question, and in a way, my whole book is about this process. Still, you might be worrying at this point that your idea is too offbeat, too vague or personal, or even too conventional to attract funding. Or you may have started to think about how you can change your idea to match what funders want. Don't be too hasty. The key is to be flexible, but without compromising your dream. Let's consider some of the questions that might come up as you think about matching your idea to what funders want.

What Areas Are Funders Interested In?

There are over 34,805 listed private foundations in this country, and this figure does not include government agencies, which have their own distinct interests, or countless corporations and businesses that can give directly from their operating budgets to whatever projects interest them.

Because of these numbers, it's nearly impossible to summarize all the various areas of interest that funders may give to. The Big Daddy foundations, as we saw, have very broad interests. The smaller family foundations give in many areas as well. Some funders tend to support organizations and large, complex projects, while others will support individuals with unusual ideas. The conclusion? You can probably find some funder who will support your idea, but you may need to do some digging to find the precise foundation or corporation whose areas of interest coincide with yours.

It's worth mentioning that funders' priorities do sometimes change. For example, several years ago the Rockefeller Foundation was doing a fair amount of arts funding. Now it seems to be focusing more on population and hunger problems in developing countries. This reflects the changing vision of the foundation's managers and is the kind of shift that grant seekers need to be aware of. (In Chapter 3, you'll find tips for keeping up with these changes.)

Should you think about changing your idea, or even trying to come up with a new one, to fit the guidelines of a particular funder? I advise against it. I have seen too many clients, mostly nonprofit organizations, who have decided to trash a good idea and create a new program to fit a funder's existing guidelines. For an organization, it may make sense to pursue its mission in a different way. A group might give up on a job-training or education program for single mothers, and support them with a more fundable counseling program, for example, but it's always a shame to see a good idea go down the tubes. For an individual, it rarely makes sense to switch your plan.

I do think that it is very important to know the funding landscape and have some points of reference before you sit down to decide how you are going to apply for funding. Nevertheless, if you are clear in your vision and conviction about what you want to do, you should not change the focus of your project just to suit a particular foundation. There is enough variety in the nonprofit sector so that you should be able to find something that will suit your needs without altering your vision.

HOW TO ADJUST TO THE FUNDING LANDSCAPE

You will always need to take into consideration the interests of the funding organization itself. If a foundation has certain fields of interest, such as women's issues or family violence, you'll need to show how funding your idea will further this mission. Such a foundation might consider funding the operating expenses of a rescue van for a battered women's shelter, for example.

The key to the process is to stick to your vision and your convictions, while responding flexibly to the funding that exists by gearing your presentation to the interests and requirements of each funder you are approaching. I had a client a number of years back who was rather a colorful figure, an ex-CIA man who decided that he wanted to develop a low-cost geodesic dome shelter that could be used for disaster relief. He had targeted the Red Cross as the group he'd like to work with. It was a wonderful invention—it was all in one piece, it was easy to clean, it was very cost-effective to build, it could be airlifted into an area of need. The first thing we discovered, though, was that there just wasn't strong enough interest in disaster relief housing among funders.

So, what we decided to do was to go after the funding for transitional housing, and we targeted homeless organizations. We were very successful in getting seed money for a pilot project to build these geodesic domes, which we coordinated with several projects serving homeless families in Los Angeles. My client was off and running. Although he clearly went into this with a social purpose, he also started a very profitable business manufacturing low-cost housing for first-time homeowners. Though he did shift the target of his fund raising, the important thing was that he did not give up on his idea; he maintained his sense of social purpose in providing inexpensive and emergency housing, even though the recipients were different from those he had first imagined.

WHAT IF AN IDEA SEEMS JUST TOO DIFFICULT TO FUND?

It is not very often that an idea is so original that funding does not seem viable because of its novelty. If you have an invention—or an arts project—and after doing your research and putting your ideas down on paper it seems unlikely that you'll be funded, it then becomes a matter of principle whether you choose to revamp the idea to fit potential funders. But I still advise against it. The Zelig complex, as I call it, does not work in philanthropy. Your belief in your idea and its integrity are terribly important.

Still, it may seem that your idea's time has come and gone, or perhaps you are really on the cutting edge and the funding world has not yet caught up with your vision. In these cases, it's important to develop points of reference, to refresh an overfamiliar idea or educate about an unfamiliar one.

One example of the latter situation is the earliest period of funding for AIDS projects. I have done a fair amount of raising money for AIDS. Back in the early 1980s, it was next to impossible to get any money for AIDS research and even more difficult to fund support services; we simply had to keep trying to educate funders about the problem. But it took several years before the issue was enough in the public eye that more funders became open to it.

One of the more difficult projects I've raised money for was the Fund for Psycho-Neuroimmunology, which supports research into the effect of mental attitudes on physical health and the immune system. At the time, the notion that the mind and body are intimately connected was a novel one. People like Norman Cousins had helped give much wider credibility to this idea, but the scientific and medical community still looked askance at it. So I felt it was important, in writing up the proposal, to present very pertinent scientific case studies. I knew I would be submitting proposals to foundations with directors who had strong medical and scientific backgrounds, so we did careful research. We provided many points of reference, including research material from the Soviet Union, where the medical establishment had explored this idea in far greater depth. This was a case where the idea was indeed unusual, and we had to provide extra points of reference in order to raise the money.

HOW TO DEVELOP YOUR IDEA

So you have an idea, or the germ of an idea, or at least the idea of a field in which you want to work. You may have a clear sense of a personal need, or of a social problem that needs to be solved. You have some sense of how the nonprofit funding sector works, and how funders respond to ideas. How can you develop your idea, flesh it out, focus it, and polish it so that it will appeal to funders? No one gets nonprofit funding without a fully developed idea. Remember that you're not going to be calling someone on the phone and pitching your idea to them. Eventually, you'll have to fill out an application or write a letter of request. You may have to prepare a detailed three- to ten-page proposal outlining what your idea is, how it will be developed, and how it will be implemented, along with the associated financial and outreach components. So it's crucial, if you're going to do effective fund raising, to develop your idea as fully as possible, showing exactly how it will work.

Although you will need to develop a fairly specific idea to get funding, the exploration process that leads to it can begin with vague thoughts. Maybe you want to travel through Europe and you need money to do it. That's a good starting point. From there you can talk to friends or associates who have done some traveling themselves. Think about the places you'd like to visit, and what unique resources or opportunities can be found there. Talk to people in your field, and see if you can combine travel with a business, educational, or research purpose. Is there a problem in your work or profession that you could solve by making a trip?

In my work with numerous clients over the years, I've used a number of exercises that have proved very successful in helping people develop their ideas. If you've just started thinking about your idea, these exercises can help bring you to the point where you're ready to do funding research and a proposal. If you've thought through your idea pretty thoroughly, and maybe even written some form of description or proposal, these exercises can still help make your project stronger. You may have been concentrating on one aspect of your project, say, the need, and skimping on another, such as implementation.

What if your idea is already very well defined? Perhaps you even have an idea of where you're going to apply for funding. Say you want to get a Fulbright Fellowship to teach in India, and you already have an institution picked out; is there a reason to go through with these exercises? Actually, they may still help you, either in supporting your original plan or in suggesting alternative ways to realize your goals.

If the Fulbright to India—for example—is your ultimate goal, then the exercises can help you develop arguments to support your proposal. They can help you answer the questions that the Fulbright committee is sure to ask sooner or later. Why India? Why the Fulbright? How are you qualified? What are your ultimate goals? How do this specific fellowship and this specific country combine to help you accomplish those goals?

If, on the other hand, your goals are more general (you want to travel, you want to make a spiritual pilgrimage, you want to take photographs at the Ganges), then these exercises may help you come up with alternative approaches to reaching your goals. The Fulbright, after all, is a one-shot chance. Your odds are better if you apply to several different programs or funders.

What if you're involved in creative artistic or scientific work, and what you really want a grant for is the time and resources to develop an idea, write a novel, research an invention? You can't develop your idea in great detail because that's what you need the grant for. Many artistic endeavors work this way, and so do some entrepreneurial ones. I've helped raise money for numerous projects like these—visual arts projects, sculpture projects, books. In most cases, the people have credentials and have done previous work, either as artists or as business people. There are foundations that will fund work in progress and artists' colonies where you can spend time working and fleshing out an idea. Jay McInerney wrote his best-selling novel *Bright Lights, Big City* in a three-week period at the MacDowell Colony. These programs are competitive, though, and you have to have past success, or the promise of success, in order to work this out. You're not going to get $20,000 to take off time to develop an idea unless there is already interest in it, or the idea is fairly well fleshed out and what you really need is R&D money to take it further.

In any case, you'll usually need a working outline. You may not know exactly what you'll find in your research or creative process, or which direction you'll take, but you should have a logical idea of what issues you're going to deal with, what problems you'll explore, what elements you'll be working with. You'll also need to have some samples of your thinking and research to date. When you get into the project itself, obviously you'll decide exactly how you'll proceed.

YOUR CREATIVE JOURNAL

Most writers, artists, inventors, keep some kind of creative journal, where they sketch or jot down ideas on a daily basis, formed or half-formed, as they come to mind. The notebooks of Leonardo da Vinci are a famous example; he sketched and wrote notes on all his areas of interest, from fine arts and painting to engineering, military devices, and flying machines. Such a journal can be invaluable in helping you develop your ideas. Get yourself a blank notebook, and make it one that seems physically effective for you—whether spiralbound, sewn, or looseleaf, with lined or unlined pages, or maybe an artist's sketchbook. I like to use index cards in a box. Use whatever you're comfortable with. Just keep notes on ideas as they occur to you, and try to write something every day, if you can.

Start with the idea that you're already thinking about, or with the problem or issue that you want to work on. Try defining the problem—and think about how you might go about creating a solution for it. Often, the very act of writing reinforces creative thought processes, and your pen takes off with new, interrelated ideas. One of these off-the-top-of-your-head notions might be worth developing. And when you are ready to seek funding, you can use the initial notes in your Creative Journal to help shape the funding proposal. Also, you can come back to the journal later, to explore undeveloped germs of ideas and to take early thoughts in new directions.

Keep anything relevant to your idea in the journal—names of people you'd like to talk to, kinds of research you'd like to do, lists of steps that will need to be completed along the way. Just keep filling up the notebook, and be sure to look back over what you've written from time to time to recall ideas that may be worth following up on.

BRAINSTORMING—THE POWER OF FREE ASSOCIATION

Set aside some time to work with your Creative Journal, or just get a fresh legal pad, sit down, and let your mind wander freely. Take a vague idea and just free-associate—jot down everything that occurs to you in relation to that idea. No matter how silly the thought, write it down. Don't limit your thinking in any way. This is the time to be purely creative. Get rid of your internal censor; there will be more than enough time later on for you to question, evaluate, and criticize. But for now, don't be shy—no one else has to see your mental meanderings. And remember: don't be afraid to write about your personal needs and experience; this is the source of many good ideas.

If ideas are slow in coming to you, be patient. Wait for them. Meanwhile, write down everything that does come to mind, no matter how trivial it might seem. And who knows, a really crazy idea (such as using radio waves to create light) might just pay off (the E-lamp).

I've found this exercise especially valuable for those of my clients who have come to me with a general idea of what they want to do but without the specifics. I just ask them to free-associate, write page after page of whatever comes to mind. Out of this, we can usually get the material we need to prepare a detailed outline.

UNCONSCIOUS MIND

The power of free association comes from the power of the unconscious mind. You can let this power work for you, even when you're not actively focused on your idea process. If you're feeling blocked, keep using your Creative Journal and jotting down attempts to define the problem you're wrestling with. Repeat it over and over, reword it, define it, but don't worry—you can't *force* an idea or solution into being. Let your unconscious work on the problem: when you're idle or daydreaming, or just when you're falling asleep or waking up. Your brain is still working on an unconscious level even when you are not actively concentrating. Many scientists have had this experience—you wrestle with a problem, define and redefine it, analyze it ten different ways, then the solution suddenly flashes into consciousness when you least expect it. Sometimes your mind just needs a chance to see the problem in a new way. Sir Isaac Newton needed an apple falling on his head to lead him to the concept of gravity.

POSITIVE IMAGE

This is another kind of free association that is useful if you have trouble getting past your fear of failure, or if you're all too aware of the daunting obstacles you may have to overcome. It will help you if you have trouble turning off your internal censor, the little voice that says, "This will never work." Imagine that you've already gotten that grant, that you have all the money you might need to carry out your idea. Imagine that your friends and colleagues have nothing but praise for your idea, admiration that you got the grant, and faith in your ability to carry it out. Let yourself free-associate all the steps in the process—exactly how you'll begin, what you'll do next; imagine your project well under way, what it's like on a day-to-day basis. This is a good way to get down to the details of how the project will really work.

VISUALIZE THE END POINT

The best way to start from the beginning in developing your project so that it can be funded is to visualize the end point, to see clearly where it is you want to wind up. What will be the result of actually putting your idea into practice? Say you want a travel grant to write a book about Balinese music. Think about how much time you're going to spend in Bali, what you'll do when you're there, where you'll go, who you'll talk to. Write down all these details in your Creative Journal. Or say you want to start a day-care center. How many children will you take care of? What will make your center different from others that you know of? This is a visualizing process that many creative people use.

DO A "GOOD IDEA" CHECKLIST

In this chapter we've discussed a number of qualities that good ideas and viable projects have in common: originality, problem solving, answering needs and providing goals, timeliness, outreach, points of reference. We've also talked about the personal aspects: experience, faith, and conviction, ability to follow through. Make up a checklist, and write about each of these topics as it relates to your idea and your own capabilities. Write positively; find the special, unique qualities in your idea and your background. Be sure to ask yourself: Who is the audience, or who is the intended beneficiary of your project? What makes this project different from others, and at the same time, how is it related to existing ideas? What makes *you* qualified to do this project?

How to Get Your Idea into Shape for Funding

Your Creative Journal and the other exercises should have given you plenty of material to work from. Now you can begin refining and shaping your idea so that you can start the fund-raising process. There are several stages in this process. You'll need to develop a mission statement and a preliminary outline of your project, and you'll need to make the mental transition from your private dreams and brainstorming to the public sphere. You probably want to get some initial feedback and response to your idea, as part of the preparation for doing further research and writing a formal proposal.

The Mission Statement

You are now preparing to present your idea to potential funders. You need to get that idea into clear, concise language, so that it will be easy for the funder to comprehend. Funders will have limited time to consider your proposal (they'll be looking at many), so your initial statement must be strong, to-the-point, and convincing. This is called a *mission statement*—a very simple statement of the purpose of your project, which conveys the essence of your idea in a few sentences or a short paragraph. (Some nonprofit professionals call this the *statement of need*.)

The mission statement is of crucial importance. It is the first step in selling your idea to a funder, and will create the vital first impression of your project. Writing it also helps you to focus your own thoughts about your idea, and the finished statement will serve as the jumping-off place for writing your proposal. Here are some samples of mission statements from successfully funded projects:

- To obtain funding for a special scholarship fund to enable minorities, women, and disadvantaged students nationwide to attend a special one-week media education program in Los Angeles.
- To obtain funding for the implementation of an activated oxygen technology that measurably improves the quality of water in lakes and ponds without using chemicals.
- To obtain funding for a multiyear professional electronic media training program that will use the highest quality equipment to teach young people—including ex-offenders, gang members, and at-risk youth—how to use and maintain the electronic facilities utilized in the production of radio and television programming.
- To secure funding for the reproduction and publication of lithographs, limited editions, and serigraphs of at least twelve pieces of my artwork.
- To obtain funding for the writing of a book based on a seminar that I have been conducting for four years. The seminar deals with the use of live pets and stuffed animals in the therapeutic and curative treatment of ill individuals.

Notice how brief the mission statement can be, as long as it effectively conveys what the project is and why it is unique. As we'll see later, you'll use the body of your proposal to explain your project in detail, how you will implement it, the timeline, costs, and so on. But the mission statement is the log line. It says where you're going. It should grab the readers at the foundation or corporation and set them up to be receptive to your proposal. It also forces you to be clear about your own ideas. You will find that you cannot write a proposal until you have a mission statement.

How can you boil down all those notes in your Creative Journal into a few sentences? Start by looking over your original notes on the idea, then explore possible statements on the page. Work on getting down to the heart of your idea—say what you wish to do, and include the details that make your project unique and specific. Try different wordings; figure out which words are absolutely essential in getting your idea across. Don't worry, you'll have the chance to explain in detail later on. The goal now is clarity and brevity.

MAKING A PRELIMINARY OUTLINE OF YOUR PROJECT

Once you have a clear mission statement, you are ready to write the first outline of your project. This is a working document that you may revise many times. It will help you in several ways. First, it will force you to think through the actual steps of your project clearly, from start-up to full implementation. This should enable you to begin your own evaluation of your project, so that you can see what the strong points and weak points are and which areas require further thinking. You'll begin to have your own sense of whether your project is really viable. You will also be able to show the outline to professionals or potential collaborators to get feedback and response. And it will serve as the draft document from which you begin to build your actual proposal.

What should you include? Here's a check list.

- Go back to what you know about the kinds of ideas that interest funders. Ask yourself, Do I have a unique way of solving a problem? This is one of the most important points. Not that every project is going to be unique, but you should consider what may be special about yours. At the same time, make sure you have points of reference to the familiar if your project is quite original.
- Think about outreach and ask yourself: Who is the audience, or the intended beneficiary of this project?
- Ask yourself, What is the market for or potential interest in this project?, and, What are other people doing in this area? If you don't have a real feeling for this yet, don't worry. This will come as you begin to do some preliminary research, and you can add it to your outline later.
- Explain what qualifies you to do this project, whether your experience, expertise, or special knowledge of the area. (Mention here if you're going to draw on the help of advisers or collaborators, and explain their qualifications as well.)
- Make up a step-by-step chronology of your project, beginning with the point at which you are funded, or have start-up funding. Carry it through to completion or full implementation of your project.
- Include your thoughts about any additional people who may be involved in the project, what their roles will be, at what

stage they'll be brought in, whether you have names already, whether you'll do a search.

- Include your thoughts on specific locations where your project will take place.
- Include any thoughts on additional fund raising that may be part of your project, such as ticket sales for a theater series that you want to start.

You may find that you've addressed many of these questions in your Creative Journal and brainstorming sessions. This is the opportunity to put them down in order. Don't worry too much about the format of your outline; a series of paragraphs is fine. Do be systematic; address each stage of the project in a step-by-step way. At the same time, try to be succinct. The purpose of the outline is not to include every detail or thought you have about your project, but simply to plot out the basic plan. How long should the outline be? It depends on your project. It might be three, ten, or even twenty pages for a complex, long-term project.

This is where you have to start doing your homework, and it's an essential part of the process. You cannot present funders with a one-sentence idea and expect them to hand you money on a silver platter. You'll also need to have fleshed out your idea, at least in an informal way, if you decide that you might want to work with a professional fund raiser. I have turned down innumerable potential clients because they really didn't have more than a germ of an idea. In my own practice, I love outlines—I think they work wonderfully. If someone comes in with a really good working outline, a top-notch mission statement, and a good sense of what they want, as well as having done some research in terms of "What is the market out there?," "What are other people doing?," I know the person has made a real commitment, and usually find we have a good chance to get funding.

The other great benefit of the outline is that when you work from your mission statement, and you get down three, ten, or twenty pages on paper in an organized way, you will pretty much be able to tell whether your plan is going to fly or not. You'll be able to spot weaknesses, gaps that need to be filled, questions you need to answer, areas that will need more research. You'll know what you want to find out from professionals in your field, and you'll find that people will take you more seriously, and may be more generous with their time, when they sense you've done your homework. Remember, your outline is a work in progress; you'll be adding to it and adjusting it as you continue with the next stage of the grant-getting process: going public.

MAKING THE TRANSITION FROM PRIVATE TO PUBLIC

Now that you have your mission statement and your outline, you're clear enough about your idea to begin sharing it with others and getting feedback and positive criticism that may be helpful in organizing your funding campaign. This will be part of the fund-raising preparation process that we'll explore in the next chapter.

This can be an exciting time, but it can also be difficult. So far, you have given yourself lots of creative freedom and kept your self-criticism to a minimum. Sharing your idea with other people means leaving yourself open to possible negative responses. Also, you may have some fear that someone else will steal your idea for their own profit. Some people are just more comfortable playing their cards close to the chest; others are eager to share their ideas. If you are protective about your idea, take care to choose thoughtful, considerate people with whom to discuss it. Talk to people you trust, people whose opinions you respect.

Most important, don't lose touch with the source of your passion for your idea. I've always chosen to work with ideas I'm passionate about, and I think if one is not passionate about an idea or project, one has no business taking it on. However, it's important not to let your passion cause you to get emotionally tied to a set way of doing something. Flexibility is the key here. You'll find that you need input from others who have either worked in this field before or who have some specialized knowledge. They can offer you invaluable assistance in shaping your project and getting it off the ground; but you have to remain flexible enough to be open to possible different ways of doing things.

So you're ready to start talking about your idea with others—but who should you talk to? Should you start with your family and friends? Who will really be able to help, and what exactly should you ask them for? What is the best way to present your idea to them?

Your first impulse is probably to explain your idea to your immediate family or close friends. Whether you should do this depends to some extent on how comfortable you are about sharing the idea at this point. If you are still in the early stages of development and any negative feedback might discourage you, you'll want to think carefully about whom you talk to first. If, on the other hand, you are fairly confident about the idea, and other people's opinions are not likely to deter you, then go ahead. Realize that although friends and family can certainly be helpful, their comments, whether positive or negative, may not reflect the true value of your idea. They might even feel in some way threatened. In weighing their responses, take into account how well they know the field. Their suggestions may be valid, but before changing your idea to accommodate their suggestions, talk to some people with professional experience.

Talking to professionals is a very important step in going from private to public. You've spent a good deal of time thinking about your idea, and you may or may not have shared these thoughts with your friends and family. They could be invaluable collaborators, or just not that helpful. In any case, I do suggest you approach a professional in the field to get feedback that will more directly relate to the viability and originality of your project. If you want to start a day-care center in your home, talking to other day-care professionals will probably give you more valuable insights than friends or family can.

When you do consult people in relevant fields, look for those you feel you can trust, people whose opinions you usually respect, people with expertise in the field. If you're really lucky, you will find all three qualities in the same person. Avoid anyone you think may have only negative things to say; this kind of response will throw you off. Constructive criticism, on the other hand, may help you refine your idea. You will find that some individuals are better sounding boards for you than others. Keep this in mind; come back to them with other ideas. Listen carefully to their responses, weigh their suggestions against your own instincts, and make changes if you believe those changes will improve the viability or fundability of your idea.

I don't suggest you start calling up program officers of foundations at this stage. This is important, for obvious reasons. If everyone who is reading this book started doing this, the foundations would be inundated, and you can imagine the chaos that would ensue. This could mean the end of philanthropy as we know it. It's in all of our best interests that we save contacts with program officers for later on in the process, after the basic homework has been done. And there is an etiquette to contacting foundations that is important to follow.

However, I do encourage you to work with resources in your community. So, for example, if you want to start that day-care center in your home, talk to those who are operating other day-care centers in your area. You'll find that many people really like to share their expertise. That's the nice thing about the nonprofit community: it's a real community, and not as cutthroat as some commercial fields. A more gracious and more honorable style of behavior operates here, and people are fairly good about sharing information.

How can you locate people who would be helpful to talk to? This really becomes part of your fund-raising preparation, which we'll discuss in greater detail in the next chapter. For now, though, let's consider two issues that relate directly to taking your idea public: protecting your idea and dealing with criticism.

PROTECTING YOUR WORK

You may be feeling protective of your idea and reluctant to reveal it to others. Still, you will have to discuss your idea openly if you're going to pursue funding; and you'll have to get past the fear that someone might steal it. You should be careful about certain ideas, especially if a patent or copyright is involved, but you really shouldn't worry too much about theft in the nonprofit world—this is not Hollywood. I can talk about this with some assurance. My brother is a head of production in a division of a major Hollywood studio, and my sister and my brother-in-law are both successful screenwriters. So I'm fairly well versed in the workings of Hollywood from the inside. These relatives are always shocked at the way a client comes to me and discloses his or her ideas, and then we present them to a number of different foundations. They always say, "You're nuts! Why isn't someone going to steal this? It's such a wonderful idea!" The Art Buchwald/Eddie Murphy controversy over *Coming to America* has really stirred up the issue.

But the nonprofit sector has its own traditions and its own codes of behavior, going back to the time of Ben Franklin, and idea theft is simply not part of it. In my eighteen years of fund raising, I have never seen an idea stolen, and I find that rather wonderful. My colleagues attest to the same experience. To sum up: in the nonprofit world, theft is highly unlikely.

On the other hand, if you have a half-formulated idea you may want to be careful about showing it to other working professionals. If someone hears the germ of an idea, they can't help but assimilate it and utilize it, perhaps as part of a project that they're about to do. So while I don't want to alarm you to the point that you won't show your project to anyone, I do encourage you to talk your ideas through fairly specifically but not to reveal absolutely everything. Talk about your plans in a general way rather than showing a detailed outline. If you are including groundbreaking technology or some secret-ingredient recipe, just leave out the ticklish part and discuss the basic concepts. Again, I don't mean to cause serious concern that your idea might be stolen—you just need to be a little cautious.

It's important to keep this in perspective. If you are talking with professionals, remember that you're picking their brains and asking them for *their* professional insights. You have to approach this with a certain amount of mutual trust. You can't expect people to be generous with you if you play your cards too close to the chest. A filmmaker I know once joined a discussion group of other filmmakers, who had gotten together to share ideas and experiences about raising money for their projects. When it came time for the person who had actually started the group to talk about his project, he refused to say what it was. At this point, most of the others became disgusted, and the group eventually folded. Another friend meets with a group of writers who write for audiovisual programs. These people are actual competitors, they vie for the same jobs with the same companies, yet they are remarkably open with one another, sharing everything from pricing strategies to creative techniques. They realize that they each have their own unique talents and imaginations, which is what their clients pay for, and that they have more to gain from sharing experiences than they have to lose.

There are cases when you do want to be careful, and you can take advantage of certain legal protections, including patents, trademarks, and copyrights. You can't patent or copyright an idea, but you can patent a device, a chemical formula, or a specific procedure. You can't copyright a title, but you can protect the script of a screenplay, a novel, a play, a piece of music. You can protect a business name or a trademark. It's just sound business sense to take advantage of these protections if they're appropriate for your project. You can apply for most of these protections yourself and save a great deal of money that you might spend on lawyers. If you have an invention, or a for-profit business idea that is highly marketable, you should definitely apply for a patent. See the sidebar on page 40 for specific procedures.

COPYRIGHT

Copyright is a form of protection provided by federal law to the authors of original literary, dramatic, musical, and artistic works (and certain other intellectual works). Copyrightable work must satisfy the following criteria: the work must be fixed in a tangible form from which it can be reproduced; it must be the result of original authorship; and there must be at least a minimal element of creativity present.

Copyright protects only the expression of an idea, not the idea or concept itself. Names, titles, trademarks, short phrases, and slogans are not copyrightable since they lack the minimum amount of original authorship necessary for copyright. Copyrights are not available for utilitarian or functional objects.

Ownership of the copyright in a work is separate from ownership of the work. The owner of copyright has the exclusive right to do and to authorize others to do the following: to reproduce the copyrighted work in copies; to prepare derivative works based upon the copyrighted work; to distribute copies of the copyrighted work to the public by sale or other transfer of ownership, or by rental, lease, or lending; to perform the copyrighted work publicly, in the case of literary, musical, dramatic, and choreographic work, pantomimes, and motion pictures and other audiovisual works; and to display the copyrighted work publicly in the case of literary, musical, dramatic, and choreographic works, pantomimes, and pictorial, graphic, or sculptural works, including the individual images of a motion picture or other audiovisual work.

A work is protected by the copyright laws the moment it is created in a tangible form. You do not have to register the work or place a copyright notice on the work before it is published, but it is recommended that you do so.

The proper notice for copyright is the symbol ©, or the word *Copyright*, or *Copr.*; the year of first publication; and the name of the copyright "owner." The duration of copyright for works being copyrighted now is generally the author's life plus fifty years.

If you register your copyright within three months after publication, you can recover statutory damages and attorney's fees if there is an infringement of the work. Registration is a straight-forward process that requires you to submit a registration form, deposit a copy of the work for which you are seeking copyright, and pay a $20 filing fee. You can write directly to the Register of Copyrights, Library of Congress, Washington, DC 20559, to request the necessary application forms, which are free of charge. You can also call the Hotline Number for Forms and Circulars—202-707-9100—and leave a recorded request. If you want more information about copyright, you can talk with someone at 202-707-5859. You can also request the helpful Library of Congress circular *The Nuts and Bolts of Copyright.*

PATENTS

Patents protect inventions from being manufactured, used, or sold without authorization. To qualify for patent protection an invention must be new, useful (if not a design), and nonobvious.

There are three types of patents. The first, a utility patent, is granted for any new and useful machine, process, manufacture, or composition of matter, or any new and useful improvement on these. The second, the design patent, is granted for any new, original, and ornamental design for an article of manufacture. This patent helps to protect the "look" of a particular article when copyright is not available. The third type of patent, the plant patent, is granted for the invention or discovery and asexual reproduction of a distinct and new variety of plant.

The term of a patent varies according to type: seventeen years for a utility patent, fourteen for a design patent, and an indeterminate time for plant patents. Unlike copyrights and trademark rights, you must apply for and receive a grant of patent from the U.S. Patent and Trademark Office before your work is protected by federal law. You can file a patent application with the Patent and Trademark Office, together with the filing fee (a minimum of $370 for utility patents, $150 for design patents—but both fees are reduced by half if you are a sole or independent inventor). The application is reviewed, and if all the requirements are satisfied, a patent will be issued. During the time the patent application is under consideration by the Patent and Trademark Office, the work you have applied for should be marked "patent pending." When the patent is issued, this notice must be replaced with the actual patent number, for example: "U.S. Patent No. 5,0015,089."

You can easily run up substantial costs—of several thousand dollars or more—for preparing and filing your patent application. The process can be long and it may take several years before your patent is granted. Since patent law and filing requirements are complex, it's best to seek out the advice of an expert in patent law.

TRADEMARKS

A trademark is a word, logo, or other device used to identify the source of goods and distinguish them from those manufactured or sold by others. You can create a trademark simply by adopting one and using it in connection with the sale of goods or services. A trademark can last indefinitely, provided that it continues to be used as a mark to signify the quality of products and services, and so long as the public perceives the mark as an indicator of the source and origin of the goods. As owner of a trademark, you can prevent others from using the same or a confusingly similar mark or name in connection with the sale of similar goods or services when the use would be likely to cause confusion to the public.

You do not have to register a trademark to secure protection, and can use "TM" prior to registration in order to indicate your rights in the mark. Before you can register a trademark, however, you must have a trademark clearance search made. It is advisable to hire a reputable trademark search firm, which can charge several hundred dollars for this service. Usually your lawyer, who prepares the registration application, will hire the search firm. To apply for a trademark, you must file certain forms with the Patent and Trademark Office. The filing fee is $175 for each class of goods covered by the application. You can get trademark registration forms (free of charge) by writing to the United States Department of Commerce, Patent and Trademark Office, Washington, DC 20231. You can also request their booklet *General Information Concerning Trademarks*, which provides an overview of federal trademarks and contains sample registration forms.

A federally registered trademark is valid for an initial twenty-year term and can be renewed over and over again as long as the mark is used in accordance with the registration. In order to preserve the registration period, the owner must file an affidavit in the fifth year of use affirming that the mark is still in use. Once a registration is obtained, the owner has to continue to use the mark and must police it to prevent others from using it (or a confusingly similar name), or risk losing the rights to the mark.

You can file an "intent to use" application to reserve a mark and determine if it can be registered before investing heavily in advertising, promotion, and extensive use. However, the Trademark Office will not issue an official registration until there is a "bona fide use of the mark in the ordinary course of trade." You must actually use the mark within three years after you have filed the "intent to use" application, subject to certain six-month filing requirements.

The following notices can be used on federally registered trademarks: ®, "Registered in U.S. Patent and Trademark Office," or "Reg. U.S. Pat. & Tm. Off."

What of those people who talk for years about a project but never act on it? Do they have any right to complain if someone else acts on the same idea? Not in my opinion. I've met many, many individuals over the course of my life who had terrific ideas and never acted upon them. This brings to mind a story: A man was at a Van Cliburn concert and said, "I'd give my life to play like him." The person sitting next to him replied, "He did." And I think that really sums up the necessity of follow-through on an idea. It's not always easy. It can take a lot of time, it can take a lot of work. It can mean sacrifice. Just because someone spouts an idea does not mean they own it.

Sometimes people do pursue the same idea simultaneously, and it might seem that stealing has taken place when it hasn't. However, I think this is very rare among projects pursued by individuals. When it comes to community projects, it's a different story. I have had the opportunity to work on projects when I knew there were other people pursuing similar ideas in the same community. For example, there were a number of very similar plans for the homeless going on at about the same time in Los Angeles. There were also similar parenting projects, and similar child-abuse projects. But even these are broad categories. As a general rule, projects do parallel one another in social services and organizations. It's much more rare with individual projects.

However, this brings up a good point. What if you have worked very hard on an idea, and then discover that someone else is working on the same idea and probably will go after similar funding sources? This often happens to people who are doing their doctoral dissertations. I've known several people who have worked hard on dissertations, only to find, when they're just on the verge of submitting them, that somebody else has been there first. Do you abandon the idea completely? No, I don't think you should. I do think, if you are sufficiently committed to your idea, you ought to modify it somehow, so that you can run with it in a new direction.

DEALING WITH COMMENTS AND CRITICISM

So you bite the bullet, you contact a few people to discuss your project, and you get two totally different reactions from two different professionals. One tells you it's terrific and will be a great success; the other says it's deeply flawed and you should go back to the drawing board. Or someone tells you it's a terrific idea but needs one major change, which you feel would undermine the very reason you wanted to do the project in the first place. Now you don't know if your idea is good or bad, or if you should change it, give it up, or ignore the negative criticism and forge ahead. Don't panic—this is all part of the process.

Just as not everybody is equally skilled at giving constructive criticism, not everybody is equally adept at dealing with criticism and using it effectively. Still, you can learn to improve the way you deal with comments and criticism, so that this doesn't have to be a totally confusing, soul-wrenching process.

You can start by actively managing the process of getting feedback from the very beginning. When you talk to a professional or someone in your field, I suggest you avoid bringing up questions or reservations that you yourself may have about your idea. This may convey the sense that you're not really serious or committed to it. It's probably better to stay away from asking a point-blank question about why something doesn't seem to work, unless you feel wholly comfortable with your project, and confident in it. Until you have a clear vision and a very complete vision of where your idea is going, and how it will be realized,

I suggest you just present the project and listen; let your advisers respond of their own initiative.

When you do get a response, jot down some brief notes during the interview or immediately afterward. You might even want to consider asking to tape-record your discussion. Hearing someone react to your idea can arouse strong emotions, and you may not clearly remember every point.

After you've received some comments, especially if they're in some part critical, don't feel you have to react right away. Give yourself a cooling-off period to mull things over. You can use your Creative Journal at this point to help you absorb the feedback. Write down your adviser's comments and suggestions. Then write down your reactions to them. Do so without being overly defensive. Be honest with yourself; let the ink flow. Try this immediately after talking with the adviser, then repeat the exercise (on another page) after a cooling-off period. If you find yourself agreeing with the adviser's points, then think about making changes in your plan. If your instincts tell you to stick to your guns, by all means stick.

Don't get your feathers ruffled; criticism is usually constructive. Of course, it does occasionally come from envy, and there are people who just get an ego kick from imposing their ideas on someone else's project. But you are showing your idea to professionals who have long and vital experience in the field, and they may have been through a process that you're just starting. More often than not, they will really try to share this experience and give you constructive criticism. The best, most helpful advisers I've had have not torn things apart but have taken what worked in my idea and run with it, as well as offering constructive criticism. By that I mean, not only saying, "This doesn't work," but also, "Perhaps this is how you ought to rethink this," and, "This is what works in your idea."

I always let criticism sink in for a while. I mull it over. I think the best ideas need time to gel and time to be formed. Comments and criticism can lead to a positive reworking of an idea. But it's crucial not to be hasty in changing your plan. So if you do get criticism, don't start tearing everything apart. If an architect is designing a house for you, and you have one idea of how you think the house should be, and the architect completely revamps it, are you then going to say, "Absolutely," and totally abandon your vision? Of course not. The same holds true for your vision of your idea. Sit with the criticism for a while.

How can you tell if comments or criticism are valid? Again, you have to consider the expertise of the adviser in evaluating his or her comments. Constructive criticism from a professional in a relevant field may be quite valuable. But listen to your own instincts as well. You can also compare feedback from different advisers. This can be confusing if you get comments that contradict each other, but try to figure out what different experiences or attitudes may have caused two advisers to react differently to your idea. On the other hand, if you find that several people make the same comment or criticism, you know that this is a reaction you may get from others, including potential funders.

Still, I want to stress the importance of listening to your own instincts. I once worked with a composer named Alan J. Friedman on a show that I raised money for, and he had a wonderful expression: "Trust your goosebumps." I believe in this very strongly. Instinct and your gut reaction will give you a clue as to whether a change seems right or not. After all, it was your instinct that led you to your idea in the first place. So go with it. If it seems right, then take the criticism. If it doesn't feel right, then move on. While it's important to remain open and flexible, you must also have the strength of your convictions. Nobody does anything of any interest in the world without stirring up some negative criticism along the way. Some of it you'll just have to shrug off.

If you've come this far, you're already a long way on the road to getting a grant. You have a clear mission statement and a working outline of your project, and you've started to think about presenting your idea to others. So you are in a much stronger position than when you started. What comes next? More research, more refining, and more details. In the next chapter we'll explore the whole process of organizing your fund raising, from mental preparation to research to selling your idea.

2

PREPARING YOUR FUNDING CAMPAIGN

It all starts with an idea, but an idea by itself is not enough. You've already come a long way by developing your mission statement and an outline of your project. Now you're ready to begin your funding campaign, and to start work on actually applying for a grant. I call it a campaign, because you will have to do careful planning and research, think about potential funders, think about the money. This stage is all about laying careful groundwork so that you'll be in the strongest possible position when you do apply for a grant. How organized and effective you are at this stage will have a great deal to do with your ultimate success.

To be a successful fund raiser for your own project, you'll need to prepare yourself mentally for the process and organize your funding campaign. This is not something that you can do haphazardly. Seeking grants takes time, it takes effort, and it takes organization. You'll probably want to do some research into your own project area, and you'll certainly need to research possible funding sources. You'll need to consider the possibility of working with a professional fund raiser or joining up with a nonprofit organization. You'll need to think carefully about the budget for your project, prepare and revise a proposal, build support for your project, and communicate with funders. In this chapter, we'll outline all the steps in this process, so that you will know what to expect, and we'll get you started on some of them.

Many people use the term "grantsmanship" to refer to some of the skills and techniques that you'll learn in this chapter, but I've never liked this word. To me, "grantsmanship" conveys a mysterious "knack" that certain people have and others don't. This is just not the case. There's nothing mysterious about the techniques that lead to getting grants—anyone who's willing can learn them. To others, "grantsmanship" means a dull, scholarly, academic, scientific approach to getting a grant, and that's not what this book is about. I've always found fund raising to be an exciting and entrepreneurial activity. If you have a wonderful idea, and you really believe in it, there will be funding out there for you, no matter how quirky your project. There's nothing academic about it.

MENTAL PREPARATION

Preparing to get a grant isn't all organization; it's also important to put yourself in the right frame of mind for getting funded. This means both having a positive attitude about your ideas and abilities and having a realistic sense of the kind of commitment that's involved.

GET IN A POSITIVE FRAME OF MIND

Nothing can provide a more powerful boost to your grant getting than having a positive attitude about the value of your project and your ability to carry it out. This is the kind of intangible asset that will keep you going through the long stretch, will motivate you to pursue every lead along the way, and will ultimately infect funders with your own enthusiasm. *It's essential that you be able to think of yourself as a serious prospect for a grant.* How can you do this? How can you build your self-confidence about your project, and sustain it when the going gets tough? I'd like to suggest two approaches that are directly linked to the actual grant-getting process.

Positive Brainstorming. First, use the brainstorming techniques of Chapter 1 to focus directly on your confidence and abilities. Go back to your Creative Journal and write down every reason you can think of why you are the person to make this idea become a reality. Write down anything at all that's positive. Write about your skills and character traits. Write about past successes, of any kind. Don't censor, don't be modest, don't be shy. Don't leave things out because they're too trivial, or because you'd be embarrassed to mention them to anyone. No one is going to read this but you. If you're terrific at organizing your closets and you've categorized your CD collection by subject *and* alphabetically, then you have a skill that can certainly help you manage a research project *or* a day-care center. If you have a special rapport with kids, if you can sense their feelings and talk about their concerns, then you have another skill that will help you operate a day-care center *or* communicate with people you will need to talk to for a research project. Most people are all too good at criticizing themselves for things they don't do effectively. Instead, take some time now to look closely at the things you do well. Remember how you've succeeded in the past, and think about how these skills and experiences can support your present endeavor.

When you do this exercise, write for at least five minutes, and do it on several occasions, on different days. Go back to things you've already written—a fresh look may give you a new understanding of how this can help you. This exercise can give you a new look at yourself and help build a feeling of self-confidence that will inspire funders to place their confidence in you as well.

Just Dive In. A second approach is to throw yourself into the project. You often hear that even the most successful artistic people— actors, musicians, filmmakers—suffer from personal insecurities about their work. So what do they do? They abandon their fears by throwing themselves head first into a performance or a project that has its own momentum—playing a role, learning a piece of music, starting a new film or other project. No matter how much stage fright you have standing in the wings, once you're on stage, you've got to act. Suddenly, you realize you're doing it, and the moment of fear has passed.

I've experienced insecurities, like anyone else, but once I commit to a project that I believe in, I throw myself into the work, and my self-confidence shoots right up because I'm concentrating on the project instead of my own fears. When you have actually started doing your project, it almost takes on a life of its own. You become a servant of the project. It's like a calling: it's your duty and privilege to be the one that will make the dream come true.

Throw yourself into the work. Forget about the money for the time being, and look at what the project itself demands. Write out a timeline for the different stages. Go back and work on your outline, thinking about the steps. For example, if you want to produce a play, do you first have to get the play written or do you have to option the rights to a script that is already completed? You have to find and rent the theater, you have to hire a director, you have to help audition and hire the actors, and so on, all the way on to placing ads and getting an audience. Now, this might give you a daunting realization of the size of the task you have before you; but at the same time, it will clarify what it is you have to do. And having this down on paper will bring you one step closer to your goal. The more tangible you make your project in every way, the more it will take on a life of its own.

- **TIP:** There are countless personal-development books that promise to help you with building self-esteem and developing an optimistic attitude, self-motivation, and the like. Many can seem like gimmicks, but some have practical techniques or good psychological insights that many people have found useful. Four of these are listed below:
  - *The Seven Habits of Highly Effective People*, by Stephen R. Covey. New York: Simon & Schuster, 1990.
  - *Flow: The Psychology of Optimal Experience*, by Mihaly Csikszentmihalyi. New York: Harper & Row, 1990.
  - *Learned Optimism: How to Change Your Mind and Your Life*, by Martin Seligman. New York: Alfred A. Knopf, 1991.
  - *Wishcraft: How to Get What You Really Want*, by Barbara Sher. New York: Ballantine Books, 1983.

HOW LONG WILL IT TAKE?

One aspect of fund raising that not everyone is familiar with—or prepared for—is the amount of time it can take to get a grant. Part of your mental preparation should be devoted to readying yourself for a long-term, sustained effort. How long will it take to get funding? It can take as little as a few weeks or as long as several years; usually it's somewhere in between. Three to six months is not unusual, from beginning your funding research to making applications to waiting for a response. If you have a large project that will involve a number of people, the fund-raising process will be more complex and take more time. If you have a simple project that involves only yourself, the process will be shorter and simpler. Funders have their own time frames. Some funders make grants on a continuous basis; others have funding cycles and make grants only once or twice a year. You'll have to research these funding cycles, and key your proposals to the funders' timelines.

Research, writing proposals, and following up all take time. If you are not willing to commit time and effort to this process, then you are not likely to follow through and execute the project even if you do get the funding. I don't mean to discourage you from applying for money, because it *is* available, and if you believe in your idea, you can get it. But your willingness to devote the necessary time to the grant-seeking process is one test of how much you really want to make your idea happen.

To go after funding effectively, you can't just target one foundation, and wait for the big yes or no. To improve your odds, you may have to submit a number of proposals or applications. You may have to build up support gradually, getting limited support from several sources to fund your idea. You will have your work cut out for you. But if you do it, someone may be willing to underwrite your vision and invest in you. It's a long haul, though, and you'll need a good amount of persistence to see you through.

There's another reason why persistence is a major virtue in fund raising. Some foundations are funny: Many will almost automatically reject a grant proposal the first time out but accept it the second or third time a revised proposal is submitted. If an idea is fundable, if it is a good idea, and if funders see you are committed to the project and likely to carry it out, sooner or later your passionate belief will make an impression.

Of course, there will be ups and downs along the way. Are you going to run into people who do not understand your idea? Yes. Are you going to meet people who think your idea cannot be realized? Yes. But you can't let this stop you. Not everyone is going to understand your vision. Funders are human beings, with personal likes and dislikes, prejudices and enthusiasms. Not everyone is going to jump up and down and think your idea is the greatest thing since sliced bread, and you have to know that going in. But if your project is well defined, and if you follow the correct procedures in applying for grants, you will surely get some positive feedback along the way that will help spur you on.

Since the grant-seeking process can stretch over a long period of time, you may find it hard to keep the ball rolling. If you're a busy person with many daily demands or distractions, you may have trouble staying focused on the process. It can be difficult to keep in touch with your long-term goals and make them a priority when short-term obligations are pressing. But there are some practical, organizational things you can do to keep up the momentum and stay focused. We'll cover them all in this chapter. One thing you can do—and I'm indebted to Barbara Sher and her excellent book *Wishcraft* for this—is keep a daily journal. She calls it an "Actions and Feelings Journal."

A Daily Journal

Get a spiralbound notebook, or whatever kind you prefer, and at the end of every day simply write down whatever you did to further your project. If you didn't do anything directly related to your project, write down what you *did* do. Maybe you did something to earn money, or you took the afternoon off to go to a movie. Don't feel guilty if you don't act on the project every day—people do have to earn money and relax. But you do want to keep your attention focused on the project for at least this one moment every day, and be able to see how work on your project continues on a week-to-week basis, even if you do take a day off here and there.

Also note down in this journal what your feelings are at the end of the day. Are you optimistic, depressed, satisfied with your progress, anxious to do more? As you look back in this journal, you'll find that some days you did a lot to further your grant seeking, other days only a little, some days you felt up, other days you felt down. But you will get a sense of steady progress. You'll see that week after week, little by little, you are moving closer to your goal. And you'll see that although your feelings can change daily, you are always pursuing your long-term desire.

How do you cope with rejection or discouragement along the way? Keep your long-term goals and inspiration always in sight. Remember that this is a labor of love. Keep visualizing what you want to achieve. If you're trying to produce a theater piece, *see* that opening night and the rave reviews. If you're trying to produce a film, picture yourself accepting that Oscar. This is not childish fantasy—it's your long-term vision, which will give shape to your project and make all that hard work worthwhile. And remember, anything you do today that furthers your project is really part of that project. A filmmaker I know says, "Raising the money for a film is just like preparing the canvas for a painting. It's really part of the process, part of the work." Just by reading this book and doing the exercises, you've already begun to make your idea a reality.

STEPS IN THE PROCESS

By now, as you fire up your grant-getting campaign, you realize that it's not just a matter of getting an idea, finding a possible funder, and writing a letter. You'll need to plan for many steps along the way. You'll need to do some research, both into the area that relates to your idea and into which funders are interested in this area. You'll need to consider whether you should be affiliated with an organization in order to get access to more funds. You'll need to work up a "marketing plan" to sell your idea to funders. You'll need to develop a realistic sense of how much money you need, and you may have to prepare several versions of a budget. You'll need to get comfortable with communicating with funders—by telephone, by letter, and in person. Let's look at these various steps.

- *Subject or "market" research—getting feedback on your idea.* When you present your idea to funders, it's important to show that you know your subject area well. You need to be aware of what else is going on in your field and what other people are doing. You may already be well versed in your field of interest, or you may have to do some research. You may also want to talk to some professionals to get comments or feedback on your idea. We'll discuss ways you can do this kind of exploration later in this chapter.

- *Funding research.* Funding research is one of the basic steps in getting a grant. It's essential to make your applications to the correct funders, the ones that will be predisposed to take interest in your type of project. There's just too much work involved in preparing a good proposal to waste time with inappropriate funders. The next chapter—on Finding the Right Funder—will get you started. Besides researching funders, you may want to do a little bit of additional research into the fund-raising process itself.

- *Your marketing plan.* Testimonials, endorsements, and supporting documentation can all contribute to the success of your grant application. You will want to start gathering these well before you sit down to write an actual proposal. Collecting them will be part of the ongoing process, just like working on your outline and doing research.

- *Budgeting and financial planning.* Grants are based on need, and realistic budgeting is very important—not only to persuade funders to give you the grant but also so that you'll be able to put your plan successfully into effect once you get it. While some people ask for too much—and getting grants is *not* a way to get rich—it's more likely that you may ask for too little money. You should start making up a budget based on your outline, which may require some additional research. You also want to have a clear sense of your abilities for handling money, especially if your project is large and complex.

- *Affiliation.* There are thousands of foundations that make grants directly to individuals. You can apply to these directly, be approved, and receive a check. However, there are several reasons why you might want to consider affiliating yourself with a nonprofit organization. One big advantage is that you can then apply to more funders than you could as an individual. Many foundations prefer to grant funds to organizations, which pass the money along to individuals. (This is called *fiscal sponsorship,* and you can learn more about it in Chapter 4.)

  There are other advantages to affiliation. If you are working on a large and complex project, you will be able to tap into the resources and expertise of an existing organization. Even if you choose not to affiliate, there are nonprofit groups you may want to turn to for advice and assistance. Affiliation is an issue that you should consider carefully; we address it later in this chapter, and in Chapter 4.

- *Professional fund raisers.* A related question is whether you may want to turn to a professional for help with some part of your grant seeking. Can professional fund raisers guarantee that you'll get a grant? Of course not. Can they help you?

Certainly. Would it be worth it? That depends—on how organized you are, how much you can afford to spend, and how much money you are trying to raise. As someone who has worked in this field for many years, I assure you that you *can* do it successfully yourself. That is what this book is for. However, if you do want to think about working with a professional, we'll offer some tips on the subject later in this chapter.

- **Communicating with funders.** This is a big topic, which covers everything from your initial request for information (write a letter, *don't* telephone), to the way you connect your idea to the funder's mission, to possible meetings with funders. There is an etiquette to communicating with funders, and the worst thing you can do for your cause is to harass an overworked foundation officer. There are also some good reasons why you may not want to tell too much about your project right away. On the other hand, personal contact can sometimes help.

- **Your proposal or application.** In the end, it all comes down to an actual proposal or application. Different funders require different types—they can range from a simple letter to a preprinted application form to an elaborate proposal package with lots of supporting material. Nearly all of them require some of the same basic elements, such as a mission statement and a budget. When you have finished your basic outline and budget, and have done your funding research, you'll be ready to tackle your proposal. (Chapter 10 will take you through this process.)

Now that you have an overview of the whole process, let's look at some ways you can get organized to make your preparation more effective.

GETTING ORGANIZED

It's very important to be systematic about the fund-raising process. You'll need to work at it a little each week, keeping track of prospects, maintaining files, keeping a watch on deadlines, and so on. Bear in mind that when nonprofit organizations do fund raising, they have full-time staff people to do this. You will probably be applying to a number of foundations, which may have different deadlines, requirements, and application forms, and you will have to stay on top of all this. Since this is a long-term process, with many details to take care of, it's very, very important to be organized. People always ask me, What's the key to getting a grant? I think you have to learn how to be organized, and to follow through. These are two of the most important attributes of a good fund raiser.

DEVELOP A GAME PLAN

If you're going to coach a football team, you have to have a strategy. If you're starting a business, you need a business plan. If you're building a house, you need a blueprint. And so it is with the grant-getting process. You have to plan. Now that you have an outline and a timeline for your project, start to do one for your entire grant-seeking process. After fifteen years in the business, I still do this. First, draw up an outline of how you envision the process. Ask yourself how much time you'll need for research and for preparing and sending out proposals. Where are you going to do the research? How are you going to compile and keep track of what you find? Approximately how many proposals do you think you'll have to send out? Of course you won't have all the answers at first, because you're new to the game. This chapter will help you get started, and as you begin doing the research, you'll develop a better sense of how to fill in the details. You will probably revise your working plan as you go along, but you should start to develop it now.

As you begin to work up a fund-raising schedule or outline, your major steps will be (1) to do subject and funding research; (2) to request application guidelines from funders; (3) to write the proposal and the budgets; and (4) to track the results of your applications. You're not going to have any actual deadlines until you do your research and contact foundations. So say to yourself, "I'm going to allocate the next month (or the next three weeks) to accomplish my research. Then I'll spend one week writing for guidelines, and expect to get replies during the following two weeks." Try to set aside a block of time for accomplishing each stage of the process. You can fill in the details as you learn more.

Obviously, the first step is research. If you're going to do some research into your subject area, think about where and how you will actually do it—at the library, by conducting interviews, or going to seminars—and allocate time for this. You may want to combine your subject research with your funding research. As a first-time grant seeker, you will probably need at least three to four weeks of research time, and you will have to spend some hours in the library, on the telephone, and perhaps in meetings. Get started by allocating an amount of time per week that you think you can devote to your project. Then try to block out specific time periods when you can go to the library, make calls, or work on your budget or outline. You can make a lot of progress by spending even a few minutes a day on this work, in addition to one or two larger blocks of time each week. Make appointments for yourself and enter them in your personal calendar or appointment book.

MAKE A TIMELINE CHART

At the library, you'll identify potential funders and see what their deadlines are. At this point, I suggest you draw up a timeline chart, as most professional fund raisers do.

Probably the most useful chart for you to get started with is a timeline that is divided vertically into blocks of time, usually weeks. Stationery stores sell large plastic-coated charts that you can write on with erasable colored pens. They come in different styles, some with preprinted weeks or months, but I recommend the blank charts that allow you to fill in your own time periods and categories. Block off the weeks on the chart, write in the dates, and note in each column what you plan to do that week: research, requesting guidelines, writing a proposal, and so on. You may want to divide the chart horizontally into several sections, so you can keep track of separate categories of the process—one for research, one just for proposal deadlines, one for follow-up calls, or whatever categories suit you.

At first you may just be scheduling research, but as you proceed you may find yourself filling in names of grant programs or foundations you want to apply to, along with deadlines, application requirements, and so on.

In my own work, I use a chart that is keyed to individual proposals rather than to the overall process. Once you get farther along with your grant seeking, you may want to convert your chart for this purpose or start a new one. On this kind of chart, you will list the individual foundations that you're applying to, assigning columns for the different steps in the application process and the deadlines. Column 1 might list the dates when you send off a request for guidelines, and when you receive them. Column 2 could schedule when you will write your proposals and prepare your budgets. Column 3 lists information about each proposal, such as the amount of funds requested and the expected notification date. Column 4 marks the date when you completed a proposal and sent it to the foundation. Column 5 is used to schedule a follow-up call, perhaps three to four weeks later, and to check off that follow-up call after you have made it.

I love working with charts. There's something about having your process all laid out in a big chart on the wall, with color codes and special categories, that makes it more real and more accessible (and harder to escape). It's easy to glance up and see exactly where you are in the process, what needs to be done right away, and what comes after that. You can add new information daily, and it's a good idea to set aside a time each week when you go over the whole chart, make any revisions necessary, and bring it up to date.

USE A TO-DO LIST

Buy a large week-at-a-glance appointment book, or a weekly appointment calendar, and start working with a daily and a weekly to-do list. Set aside a time each week when you will plan your weekly fundraising tasks. During this planning session, make up a to-do list for the week, and then enter the items in your appointment book or on the calendar, so that you have a specific day and time for each of them. Check the items off the weekly list as you complete them. If you find yourself spending a lot of time on fund raising, set aside a period each day to make up a daily to-do list and check off the items as you finish them.

It's natural to want to do the easy tasks first and leave the disagreeable or difficult ones for later. If you find you're falling into this habit, make a point of doing the most disagreeable task first, each day and each week. Everything will be easier from that point on. Another seductive habit is to fill up your to-do lists with easy tasks that just aren't that important, at the risk of missing the essentials. To avoid this, you've got to set priorities.

Divide your to-do list into an A and a B list, even a C list. Put the essential items on the A list, and make sure they go at the top of your daily and weekly to-dos. A deadline for a foundation is definitely an A-list item. Finishing a proposal in time to get it out for a funding deadline is an A-level priority. Perhaps getting back to someone in the community about your project is an A-level priority, while organizing your files is a B-level or a C-level priority. Of course, if you start having trouble finding things because your files are in chaos, this is going to move up to A level. You are going to have to determine which are the priorities; but if you are in business, or a homemaker, you're used to managing various demands, juggling many activities and making them all work—and this is no different.

USE A CARD FILE

I like to use an index-card file as a flexible way of keeping track of ideas and information. You can use either a large one or the smaller kind that you keep recipes in. Get a number of index tabs so that you can make separate categories for ideas, referrals, contacts, budget information, etc. Try any categories that seem useful; whenever an idea occurs to you, or you get some useful information from a telephone call, a newspaper article, or wherever, jot it down on a card and add it to your file. Keep accumulating these cards, then make time once a week to go through them and activate ideas that seem useful, or discard information that is out of date. I find this easier to use than a journal, or even a looseleaf, which fills up with obsolete material and keeps you constantly flipping back and forth. It's simple to discard and add cards, and the index tabs make it easy to find what you're looking for.

DEVELOP A RESOURCE LIST

In Hollywood, and in other lines of business too, you hear people say, "I've got a great Rolodex—I've been building it up for years." They're not talking about the little brand-name wheel that holds name and address cards, of course. They're talking about their list of contacts, names, and references—the people they know and can call on in the course of business. When you're working to get a grant, a contact list can be one of your most effective tools. This is your personal universe, the platform you'll be building from. It's important from the very beginning, when you're developing your ideas and game plan, all the way to the end, when you get your grant money and start to put your plan into effect.

It doesn't much matter how you keep your list of names and resources. You can use a Rolodex—it's convenient, with replaceable cards, and you can get one in a stationery store for about ten dollars. Or you can start with a little index-card file with alphabetical tabs.

If you're into computers, you can use an address or mailing-list program, or a database. However you store your list, it's the names you put into it that make it valuable.

SET UP A FILING SYSTEM

As you get into your research, and start writing outlines and proposals and budgets, you'll definitely need some kind of filing system. This doesn't have to be an enormous file cabinet. You can begin with one of those large plastic portable file boxes, or a cardboard file box or drawer.

You will need a box of manila file folders. You should open one file for what I call "market research," or investigative research in your field. Keep another file for funding resources. When you find relevant articles in newspapers and magazines, drop them in the appropriate file. Open a file for supporting material on your own work, including endorsements, quotes, newspaper clippings, and ideas, and a separate file for each individual funder that you're going to target, sorted alphabetically. When you write to a foundation, you'll receive a set of guidelines, perhaps an application form, an annual report, or a brochure about the funder or grant program. Drop these into the new file you've opened. You may have a dozen, or even up to twenty of these funder files, with everything you need readily accessible. You can also keep additional files for your outline, for budget information, and for your master proposal. The point is to have ready access to all the information you collect.

SET UP A HOME FUND-RAISING CENTER

If you don't have an office to work from, make sure you have all the basics at home: a desk, a telephone, your Rolodex or card file, your file box, a few basic reference books, and a typewriter or whatever you're going to use to generate your proposals.

What kind of reference books are useful to have? Well, you certainly need a good dictionary. You're going to find most of your research material in libraries, but you may want to have a few basic fund-raising references at home. You may also want to have your own copy of *Foundation Grants to Individuals*. This is put out by The Foundation Center, which is a national organization that gives information on private foundations. It may not be in your local library, as it is expensive (about $40), but there may be ways you can get access to it (see the discussion on page 96). There is also my own series of *Free Money* books, which are less expensive references and are keyed to specific subject areas. You may want to own one or two guides that are directly connected to your subject. And of course you will gradually accumulate your own collection of journals, articles, and pamphlets. (See below, Chapter 3, and the Appendix, for more details on these and other references.)

What kind of office equipment will you need? A calculator for working on budgets, and a typewriter for proposals and applications. (Of course you can always write longhand and work with a typist.) Even if you're not into computers, you may want to consider buying an inexpensive word processor. There are several models available that don't cost much more than a good electronic typewriter, and are easy to use. The advantage of a word processor is that you can save your outlines, proposals, and budgets on magnetic disks as well as on paper. In this form, you can easily revise and rework them to fit the various formats that funders may require, or to incorporate new ideas. You can write a generic request for guidelines and print out ten or twenty different copies, each personalized with its own address and greeting. You can take a proposal that you've written, add a paragraph that will address a funder's particular concern, and print it all out as a perfect original. You can use a spelling checker to make sure your proposals are letter-perfect, or even a grammar checker to clean up your writing. If you do work with a word processor, make sure that you can print out your letters and proposals on good bond paper, with type that's really "letter quality." Fuzzy, poor-quality printing will turn off funders in a hurry.

I'm not saying that you should go out and spend a lot of money on office equipment. This is not necessary if you're going to apply for a few grants and won't be preparing lengthy proposals. On the other hand, if you think you are going to be involved in a long-term process, sending out many applications, or especially if you're going to be raising quite a lot of money, good equipment can greatly increase your efficiency.

The next step beyond the simple word processor would be some kind of personal computer. These offer more sophisticated word processing, as well as special programs to help you make up budgets, organize mailings, keep track of names and addresses, and the like. Most nonprofit organizations use personal computers to assist their own fund raising. You can even use a personal computer, and a modem (a telephone communication device) to get access to computerized databases of funding information. Computers are a big subject, and you could use up a lot of time exploring it. But you could start with the reference listed below:

- *Introduction to Personal Computers,* by Peter Stephenson. New York: John Wiley & Sons, 1991.

TAKING YOUR IDEA PUBLIC — AND RESEARCHING YOUR FIELD

You are going to be doing three different kinds of research: (1) market research into your own field; (2) funding research to find out what kind of grants might be available to you; and, possibly, (3) some additional research into the grant-seeking process. As you start on the market research, you can also begin to get feedback from professionals about your idea. You may find it easy to pursue the different kinds of research simultaneously—doing the market research in your field leads you naturally to possible funders. In fact, you'll find that researching your own field may influence how you think about your project, and how you end up doing it.

The most important reason for doing market research is to confirm or evaluate the feasibility of your idea. You may be able to get some professionals to give you their thoughts and suggestions; it's also extremely important to know what other people have done that's different from your idea, or similar, or exactly the same. This will help you to evaluate and refine your own project, and to support it when you present it to funders—you can refer to specific success stories and failures. It will also help you to get a more realistic idea of how you will actually execute your plan when you receive funding. Remember that getting funded is only the beginning. You will want to acquire as much information as you can about how projects in your field have been accomplished, in order to have the best shot at completing yours successfully.

Researching your subject can also lead to new ways of thinking about your idea and how you will see it through. One important aspect of this is how your project relates to your immediate community: you need to know what already exists and have a realistic sense of what can still be done. For example, let's say you want to produce a play locally. The first thing you're obviously going to have to do—if you are not already familiar with this, and you have not previously applied for a grant—is to find out what other theater companies have done in the last few years in your community. You need to know what the community wants and can support. For example, if you live in Haverhill, Iowa, which has a population of 198 people, you obviously are not going to be putting on a major musical piece, because you won't have a theater to work in or the audience to support it. On the other hand, you might think of doing something in the local school, for the surrounding communities. If you live in Chicago, there will be a number of other competing theater companies, but at the same time you're going to be able to rent space more readily, perhaps from an existing theater company, and the audience is there if you can reach it.

HOW TO RESEARCH THE MARKET

Your first priority is to identify and contact professionals and organizations in your field who are willing to talk to you, give you their reactions to your idea, and share information about what's going on in the field or local community. How can you find these people?

Probably the best place to start is at your public library. Librarians are wonderful people—tell them what it is you are trying to research and they will certainly help. Look at the directories for nonprofit and other organizations. Use a periodical subject index, and look at back issues of the local paper. Two useful directories that you can find in many libraries are:

- *Encyclopedia of Associations,* edited by Deborah Burek. Vols. 1–3. Detroit: Gale Research Co., 1993.
- *National Directory of Nonprofit Organizations.* Rockville, MD: The Taft Group, 1996.

You can also look into regional or national publications, including professional journals, professional newsletters, and organizational newsletters. (See the Appendix, page 336, for references to some of these.) This will help you get a sense of the larger picture. Perhaps you'll learn of some very successful ideas that could work in your community but have never been tried locally. Consider joining a local or national organization that relates to your subject. Organizations not only publish newsletters that report on what their members are doing in the field, but may sponsor meetings or seminars where you can meet people and find out what they are doing on a personal basis. If you have time to participate in an organization, and perhaps even serve on committees, you'll meet others who are active in the field and knowledgeable about current trends. It depends on your available time and personal style; don't feel you have to get deeply involved with an organization unless you have the time and are genuinely interested. You may get everything you need from newsletters and a few meetings, and you can still get valuable leads from your library work.

Try to talk to the staff of nonprofits, of associations, and to those who have already worked in the field. If you do find people who will agree to talk with you, ask them to apply their own expertise. If you talk to business people, ask if they think the idea is marketable, salable, generally viable, and so on. If your adviser is a former Fulbright scholar, ask about the receptiveness of the committee to such an idea and to the format of your proposal. If your adviser is an English major, ask about your syntax and spelling, get help in tightening up your language.

It's important to have a sense of restraint and limits when talking to professionals. As a first-time grant seeker, you should take special care to avoid badgering the foundations or demanding too much from people in the community. If someone is good enough to give you an interview, don't keep calling them with follow-up questions unless they specifically invite you to. If you get a few good interviews, don't feel as though you have to talk to everyone in the business. And be sensitive to the fact that professionals have busy lives and may not always be able to speak to you. Unless you are a nonprofit professional, a well-known artist or filmmaker, or an ideas person already in the field, it can be seen as pushy or time-wasting to make too many demands. You may also find that some nonprofits are less eager than others to share information, especially when they learn you may be competing for the same funds, resources, and audience. If you have friends who work in the theater community, for example, you might be able to pick their brains, but you'll probably have to tread rather lightly. There is an etiquette to this.

WHAT'S THE BEST WAY TO PRESENT YOUR IDEA?

You've done a great deal of thinking about your idea by now, and you also have your written mission statement and outline. You can either show someone these, or pitch your idea orally. Your choice will depend to some extent on the people you are talking to, and whether they respond best to oral or printed material. Both approaches can be helpful to you. In talking about a project face to face, you have a lot of opportunity to explain and clarify (and if you come across a great phrase, jot it down for future use). By showing your written mission statement, you can assess its initial impact and possibly get a sense of how you might revise it for clarity and strength.

This being said, there's an important benefit you can derive from talking about your idea. I can't tell you how many times I've started to describe an idea and discovered that I really couldn't do it as well as I wanted. And if you can't explain an idea orally, all the written pages don't mean anything, because you haven't codified and clarified your project to the point that you can effectively convey it to someone else. The old Hollywood "pitch" really has something to be said for it. To get people's attention, get them interested in an idea, you do have to be able to summarize it succinctly, in a few sentences, and then elaborate on it in a systematic but still brief and concise way. There's no better way to practice getting your idea across than by simply telling it.

When you call or write to ask for an interview, be very specific as to why you want one. When someone agrees to talk with you, be sure to do your homework first, and go in with a list of questions. Know what you're going to ask. You can't pick someone's brain effectively until you have done some real thinking yourself. You need to have put your mission statement down on paper, worked up an outline, and formulated your project as well as you can by yourself. Only then will you understand exactly what areas you need to know more about. Many nonprofit people will be generous in talking about their work, but they won't like to feel they are handing it all over on a silver platter. Don't make them feel you want a free introductory lesson in the field. Show that you've done some preliminary investigation yourself. And take notes during the interview, so you can make the most of it.

When someone has been generous enough to share their experience and knowledge with you, be sure to write them a thank-you note. I am a fanatic about thank-you notes—I write them until the cows come home, and people really appreciate it. They don't get enough thank-you notes, and they'll remember yours. Then you may find that you're able to ask the person that you interviewed for a reference later on, or they may help lead you to funding. You will find some very generous and nurturing people in the nonprofit world. They are not in it for the money but to fulfill their own dreams and passions. So do show your appreciation.

What if you get negative feedback: someone says your idea can't work or can't get funded in the existing climate of your field, or needs major changes? Don't panic. Take it all in, allow yourself time to absorb the comments, then go ahead and talk to others in the field. If you start to get the same kinds of comments from several advisers, there's probably something about your idea that you need to reconsider seriously. But don't be too quick to change your idea, unless your own instincts lead you in this direction. You may want to go back and look again at the section on Dealing with Comments and Criticism in the previous chapter (page 44).

When you do get some interviews, or find printed material, follow up by organizing, sorting through, and evaluating your research. Obviously, you should keep a separate file or files for this. When you read through your notes, or magazine or newspaper articles, write down the most important points on a separate sheet of paper. I find this helps me to organize my thoughts. You can use these lists of key points as jumping-off points for further research and planning.

However you pursue it, your subject research should be an open-ended process. Don't plan to do it for just a few weeks and then stop. Foundation officers may or may not be up-to-date on all the current trends. It can only help you to stay current yourself, so you can educate them about your field, or simply appear more qualified and knowledgeable. Most important, when you finally get that funding and launch your project, you'll want to know everything you can that might help make it a success.

HOW TO SELL YOUR IDEA — AND YOURSELF

How can you sell your idea effectively? It's not as difficult as you might think. First, you want to convey your sense of passion and commitment. It's essential that you communicate this to funders in your proposal and in any other contact you may have with them. Of course, you also need to present your idea in an intelligent, cohesive, and logical fashion. Beyond this, you can use many kinds of supporting materials— testimonials, references, supporting documentation—to strengthen your proposal. This material can help communicate the timeliness of your idea, or the need for it, as well as conveying a sense of your talent and ability to carry it out. This is the most effective kind of "marketing" that you can do—and it's a good idea to start thinking about supporting material right from the beginning.

A word to the wise: don't feel that you have to use hard-core marketing or ingenious sales tricks to promote your project. In the nonprofit world, this kind of approach could backfire. You don't have to be a good personal salesman; this is not as important as the integrity of your idea, your commitment to it, and your ability to see it through. Don't worry if you're not used to selling yourself—it's your idea that's important. A great many original thinkers in all fields were basically shy or reserved people. It didn't stop them from pursuing their vision and putting it into action. The point is, you don't need sales skills so much as the commitment to doing the work necessary to get that grant.

SUPPORTING DOCUMENTATION

One kind of material you can start collecting right away is support documentation about yourself and the need for your project. If you are an artist or filmmaker, this would include any glowing reviews of your work and any good copy from festival programs, brochures, or announcements. If you're working in other areas, you may have copies of newspaper or magazine articles that relate to your work or mention it positively. Obviously, the more prominent the source, the more impressed the funder will be. But a glowing report from a local paper or newsletter *is* valuable. If you don't have such clippings, you might consider calling editors at a few publications and suggesting an article about you or your field. If you're a student, try your school paper. Or you might interest your hometown newspaper in a human-interest profile.

Aside from material about yourself, try to locate one or two very concise articles about the area you're working in that discuss the problem your project will solve and stress the need for a solution. For example, if you are trying to start a day-care center in your home, find one or two articles that attest to the need for one in your community. If you are at work on an invention, find an article that discusses the problem it will solve. If you want to travel, find one that describes the need for a better understanding of the place you want to visit. You don't have to depend on chance to find these: go to the periodical index in your library and look up your subject area. Don't include an article just for filler—make sure it relates properly to your project and illustrates the need for it.

If you're a good writer, you might contact a newspaper or magazine and offer to do a column or a feature. This can turn you into an "instant expert" in your field as far as the public is concerned and provide useful support documentation at the same time.

ENDORSEMENTS AND RECOMMENDATIONS

Other people in your field can help your fund-raising greatly by supporting you with letters of endorsement or recommendation. They can support you in two ways: they can testify to your talent, skills, and abilities; and they can approve your idea and affirm the need for it. Try to get some of both kinds of support.

An endorsement is a statement from an individual or an organization that supports your idea. These don't have to be long or exhaustive—a brief statement from a well-known source can be very supportive. Do stick to sources in your field, and don't be shy about contacting prominent or well-known people. They may really get interested in your idea and give you the most effective endorsements. However, if you sense that someone is not that interested, and won't give you a glowing endorsement, don't bother. A lukewarm endorsement is not that helpful, no matter how famous the source.

This is not to say that you need a world-class authority to endorse your idea. It can be just as valuable to enlist the support of someone who is known and respected in your community, or who has solid professional credentials. If you have a theater project, contact a local theater critic. If you have an invention, try to find someone with professional credentials who can testify to the need or the feasibility— that the product could really be manufactured and widely used. Write some letters, make some calls. When you do get an endorsement, be sure to write a thank-you note.

It usually does help to get support that relates not only to what you are doing but also to the community you are working in. Contact organizations that work in your field, community groups, state or local government officials, schools, colleges, or universities. Institutional endorsements show that you are really reaching out.

You can also try to enlist commitments of real involvement or practical support. If you have an invention, contact someone in manufacturing or marketing. Try to get a letter from a manufacturer saying that when your project gets rolling, they will be happy to consider producing it. If you're working on a community project, get an organization to say they will help you do outreach by publicizing it among their members. If you're making a film, get a distributor to say they think there's a potential market, and would consider distributing it. If you're going to travel, get an organization to express interest in having you give a lecture on your return. You don't need a contract; a letter of interest or intent is sufficient. You may want to discuss the wording of the letter with the person who is writing it, so that you can get the strongest possible expression of interest. Get them to stress not just that they'll look at your project when it's done, but also that it sounds like an interesting idea, with real market potential. The more they write, the better.

Personal recommendations and testimonials are also important. If possible, get these from working professionals in your field. Letters from prominent people can be effective, but usually only if they really know you or get interested in your project. Someone who knows you well, has professional credibility of their own, and will write in some detail about your talent, skills, and integrity can give you very effective support. Ask a former teacher, employer, or business partner to testify to your organizational skills and your ability to follow through on a project, even if the work you did with them was different from your present idea. Be sure they know about your current work, though, so they can focus their comments in the right direction.

GET STARTED EARLY

You can start right away to collect supporting documents, recommendations, and endorsements. Don't wait until you are done with your funding research and are sitting down to write your proposal. It takes time to contact people and get responses. If you're contacting an organization for endorsements, a board of directors may have to approve it, and this will have to be brought up at a scheduled meeting. Starting early on endorsements and recommendations can be part of the market research in your area and may even lead to new funding ideas. It's also a way of beginning the process of outreach to your community. Remember, "outreach" should be interpreted broadly. If you're working on a solitary art project or research project, you still want to think about how and where your work will be presented.

WHAT IF YOU HAVE TROUBLE GETTING WRITTEN ENDORSEMENTS?

Some people may tell you that they like your idea but are too busy or for some other reason don't wish to provide a written recommendation. If you think they really do appreciate your idea, ask if you can use their name as a reference. Try to determine whether they are sincerely supportive or just don't like saying that they're not interested. You may run into people who seem to be phobic about writing letters of recommendation. Some may even suggest that you write a letter and they sign it. This is a tough one. You may sense that this person doesn't really want to support you, and it's possible. However, some professional people do get frantically busy, and some just hate to write. So if someone is willing to lend their name to help you, take them up on it. Ask them if there's anything they would suggest putting in the letter, and ask if they'll look at a draft, in case they want to make any changes. But get the letter.

SHOULD YOU DO A TRIAL RUN OR A PROTOTYPE?

You might wonder whether you should do a trial run of your project, or a sample of your work, or a prototype of your invention, to get funding. You may need to show some samples of previous work, but in most cases it's better not to start a project prematurely, unless you can get under way with limited resources. Trial runs, samples, and prototypes all cost money and take effort that might be better applied to your research, outlines, proposal, and budget. Do your thorough market research, draw up your detailed blueprint, and get your funding *before* you start work. Of course, if you have an invention that you're tinkering with, or a script you're writing, or a series of photographs that you've already started working on, go ahead. If you want to set up a project in your community, you might try holding a one-time workshop through an existing organization. This is all part of your subject research, and you'll have that much more evidence that you can do the project. But there's no need to do a large-scale effort before you have the resources.

DOLLARS AND SENSE — THE MONEY SIDE OF YOUR PROJECT

If you have a commitment to an idea that has been carefully thought through and developed, the money will follow. You are not going through this process just for the money but also because of your passion and commitment. Still, you do need money to put your idea into effect, so you have to think through the financial side of things as carefully as everything else. Since you are requesting money from a funder, it's important that the funder understands and appreciates not only what you are proposing but also the fact that you are realistic—that you are not asking for too little or too much, and that you have a realistic sense of what it's going to take to pay for your project.

Don't Underestimate Your Needs

I find that most people actually underestimate how much they will need for a project. This leads to two problems. First, the funders may conclude that you haven't thought your idea through; and second, if you do get funding based on a low estimate, you will be in trouble when you try to put your idea into effect.

You need to be very careful to plan on raising enough money to finish the project. You don't want to ask for too little, use up all the money, and then find you're unable to finish. *Don't ever be afraid to ask for too much.* If you're planning a complex project that will take place over a period of years and involve many people, you'll have far more credibility with funders if you show that you're doing realistic financial planning.

The main reason people underestimate their needs is that they haven't really sat down to make a point-by-point estimate of costs. Remember, you're not only going to need money for the actual construction of an invention, or the actual production of a theater piece, but for myriad related costs. You might need to rent separate office space and have enough to cover postage and mailing costs, telephone bills, copyright expenses, lawyers' fees, and so on. It's very important to make up a list of every aspect of your project that might involve expenses when you start considering how much money you will need to ask for.

What sort of things might you need to include in an expense list? It can certainly include a salary for yourself. If you are going to make a full-time commitment to your project, you need to have a salary. If you're going to be working with other people, you'll need to include salaries for them. If you want to hire an outside fund-raising consultant, put that expense in the budget. Consider the cost of space—office space, studio space, or whatever you need to carry out the project. Consider any special equipment you might need, or any travel expenses. Consider telephone costs, postage costs, office supplies. Don't forget to include the costs of printing, advertising, and publicity, if you're going to have to publicize your project. In fact, the best way to put together an initial budget is to go back to your outline and consider the costs involved in every part of the project.

You don't need to work up a detailed, line-by-line budget before you do all your funding research. But it helps to have a ballpark estimate of what your costs will be when you look at the giving patterns of funders. If your project will last for several years, you must take this into account. You can also start to accumulate budget information by getting price lists and estimates and putting them in a file, so you'll have them at hand when you're ready to sit down and do a detailed budget. I like to do the budget only after I've written the proposal. I like to start with the creative idea, and then fill in the dollars and cents. However, some people like to do the budget first, and then write the proposal from the budget. If you're the sort of person who naturally thinks about costs as you do your planning, you may find it easier to work this way. Everyone has their own style in dealing with money.

Are you good at handling money? Are you the sort of person who likes to do their own income tax, or do you have trouble every month balancing your checkbook? If you're not that comfortable handling money and your project will be costly or financially complex, you may want to consider getting assistance with this aspect. I have a friend who is very successful with her projects, but she is really not very good with money. She allows her husband to do the budgets, write the checks, and so forth. This works for her, because she wants to be more involved in the creative process rather than the day-to-day business. You don't have to have a handy spouse; you can include a bookkeeper's or treasurer's salary in your budget. You can also get help in preparing the budget. If your project is not too large, you may be able to find help from a service or membership organization in your community. There are plenty of nonprofit service organizations around, depending on your area of interest, and you may be able to contact officers who will offer consulting help, often free of charge. Some membership organizations make this part of their service, as well. For example, the Independent Feature Project, a filmmaker service organization, offers its members a certain amount of free consulting time with industry professionals.

How can you find out about these organizations? Some of this information will come out of your market research. You can also consult the *Encyclopedia of Associations* and other references to organizations given in the Appendix (page 323). Depending on your area of interest, you may be able to find reference books that will help you prepare actual budgets and financial plans.

If you do decide to affiliate with an existing nonprofit organization, you can certainly seek out the advice of the development officer or executive director. In fact, if your project is especially complex, if it will take place over a long period of time, or if many people will be involved, you may want to seriously consider affiliation. A fiscal sponsor can not only assist with the budget but also actually handle the funds for you, and do the bookkeeping and financial reporting. (More on this in Chapter 4.) If you're planning a big project but don't want to affiliate, you can certainly hire a professional to help you here.

But don't be too insecure about your own abilities. Say you're a homemaker who has a wonderful idea for a home business. You are probably already balancing your household budget, and believe me, that's no mean feat in these times. So if you do feel comfortable handling money, you can certainly manage a grant.

We've been talking about complex budgets, and the risks of under-estimating costs. Should you worry if your budget actually seems to be rather small? Not at all. There are plenty of funders who give grants in the range of a few thousand dollars or less. Still, raising grant money does take time and effort. If you don't need to raise more than a few hundred dollars, it might not be worth trying to get a grant.

THINK ABOUT MULTIPLE SOURCES

What if you come up with a budget that is really quite large, and you're afraid you won't find any funder willing to contribute that much? Should you scale back your project? Not at all. As a general rule, you're not going to find a single funder to underwrite your project completely; you're going to have to get money from several different sources. Some funders may give grants only in specific amounts. Others may want to assist your project but can't or don't wish to fund it completely. Some funders are happy to grant general "operating funds," the money you need to cover ongoing expenses, while others prefer to fund a specific part of a project, such as salaries or equipment purchase, or to contribute supplies or facilities instead of cash.

These are some of the reasons why you'll probably be applying to multiple funding sources. Try to be creative about this. For example, think about asking for basic operating funds from a foundation, or a donation of office equipment or supplies from a business. Ask a corporation to lend you use of a space or facilities. (This kind of donation is termed an "in-kind," or "noncash," contribution.) Perhaps you can get a city agency or a public radio or or television station to give you ad space on a bus, or air time for a public service announcement, as part of your outreach. Maybe you can get an advertising agency to make up a poster.

Funders are used to the idea of multiple sources. In fact, they even encourage it with such things as challenge grants and matching grants. A *challenge grant* is an initial grant that must be matched by another funder. It's not unusual for a foundation, a corporation, or a government agency to offer a gift that is contingent on a matching gift from another funder or funders. They might expect a match on either a one-to-one or a two-to-one basis. For example, a funder might give you $5,000, contingent on your getting a matching grant of $5,000 from another source. Or they might ask for a two-to-one match, which means you would have to raise an additional $10,000. The funder's original $5,000 gift might thereby inspire or initiate total funding of $10,000 or $15,000.

Donors like to do this for several reasons. It helps them stretch their own funding, by allowing them to assist more projects. It also lets them support a project that they can't fund completely. They do want to know that if they give you money, you will eventually raise all the funds you need and make the project actually happen. So if you get a challenge grant, you won't have access to these funds until you have raised the matching money. The great thing about a challenge grant is that it gets you started and it works as a kind of testimonial. Once a funder has given you its "seal of approval," so to speak, you'll find it easier to get other funders to contribute to your project.

Another similar grant is *seed money,* or *start-up funds.* This is money given by a funder to get your project started, perhaps on a limited scale, with the idea that you'll continue to raise funds for the full project. The big advantage of seed money is that you can use the funds right away, and it gives you a boost in your fund raising because someone has already seen fit to make an investment in you.

In some cases, funders like to see a promise of income generated by the project itself. For example, if you're putting on a play and you're going to sell tickets, then you can include an estimate of box-office receipts as income in your budget. Of course, many types of projects will not generate income. This is not a problem; don't try to invent income if it's not naturally part of the picture.

You Don't Have to Go It Alone

If you're undertaking a fairly simple project, you can easily manage all the details yourself, from the fund raising all the way through to putting your idea into effect. If you're planning a complicated project, though, you may feel the need for some kind of help with the grant-getting process, even if it's just calling on a friend for encouragement or moral support along the way. You may realize that you are going to want to collaborate with others when your project gets funded. You don't have to go it alone—you can turn to others for help with both the fund raising and the actual project. You can develop your own personal support group, or perhaps work with a collaborator. Or you can consider affiliating with a nonprofit organization, for support in both the grant-seeking process and managing your project. Or you can turn to a professional fund raiser for help in getting the grant. Let's consider some of these options.

Your Personal Support Network

If you have a family member or a personal friend who is very positive about your project, and who has some useful skills or a sense of the field that you are working in, they may be able to offer you a great deal of support. They can certainly provide moral support and encouragement. They can look through the various drafts and stages along the way, and serve as a sounding board for your ideas. However, a family member or an old friend is not always the best person to turn to for this kind of help. First of all, you need to have 100 percent positive support. If someone you are close to turns out to be lukewarm about your project, or expresses doubts, they are not going to be able to help you very much. More probably, they may simply not be familiar enough with your field, or the grant-seeking process itself, to be of much use. You may want to avoid leaning too much on friends or family, if only because they are not professionals in the field.

You may find much more valuable support by getting in touch with other professionals or groups in your field, to trade information, experiences, tips, and so on. Probably best of all is to develop a friendship with someone who is working in your field or a related one, perhaps pursuing similar goals but with a different project, and who is familiar with the general landscape that you are working in. This is not always possible, of course. Still, you may be able to turn to different friends and acquaintances for support with different aspects of your project. One friend may be good with fiscal matters and budgets, while a second might help you with organizational ideas, and a third may have a way with words and be able to help you edit or revise your proposal. Whatever you do, try to turn to people who show positive support for your idea. If they don't, they could drag you back instead of boosting you forward.

- **TIP:** If you're interested in other ideas about developing a personal support system, take a look at Barbara Sher and Annie Gottlieb's books. In their first excellent book, *Wishcraft*, they offer lots of useful tips for getting support for your long-term goals. They talk about networking, group brainstorming, overcoming family resistance, and developing a "buddy system" where you and a friend support each other with weekly "business meetings." Their second book, *Teamworks!*, describes a system of support groups that you can create or join to advance your long-term goals.
  - *Wishcraft: How to Get What You Really Want*, by Barbara Sher and Annie Gottlieb. New York: Ballantine Books, 1983.
  - *Teamworks! Building Support Groups That Guarantee Success*, by Barbara Sher and Annie Gottlieb. New York: Warner Books, 1989.

WHAT ABOUT THE COMPETITION?

If you do start networking and trading information in your field, sooner or later you're going to have the feeling that maybe you shouldn't be sharing absolutely every piece of information you come across. It's worth considering whether you might be sharing information too comfortably and giving a competitor access to something that's really perfect for you. Be aware of what you are revealing, and don't feel guilty about it. Remember that funding sources are not hidden. They're there to be found by anyone who does the research. So if you have a personal contact with a likely funding source and they are interested in your project, don't feel that you have to pass this along to someone who is looking to fund the same type of project. On the other hand, you shouldn't become paranoid about this. If a source is being widely publicized anyway, there's no harm in passing on the information to someone who hasn't heard of it yet. Generally, the more open you are with people, the more they will reciprocate by passing along tips to you.

DO YOU WANT TO COLLABORATE?

You may be thinking about the possibility of collaborating on your project, or taking on a partner, especially if it's a long-term, complex project. There are many advantages to collaboration—you can bounce ideas back and forth, you can share the work and the pleasures of fund raising and fulfilling a dream. If you and a collaborator have complementary talents or experience, this can make a grant proposal look stronger and a project more likely to succeed.

In fact, even if you're not going to undertake an equal collaboration, one of the best things you can have going for you when you ask for funding is a commitment from a few key people who have good professional credibility. This makes your project look solid, like one that is really taking shape. Of course, these commitments will be tentative, because you can't really have anybody clear their schedule or start work until you have the funding. But funders understand this and will appreciate your efforts.

On the other hand, you may feel more comfortable taking total responsibility for pursuing your personal vision. You don't necessarily have to work with a partner, even if you're planning a large and complex project. Remember, you can include salaries and fees in your budget for the backup and support people you might need. You can get funding to pay for a manager, a money person, even for other creative personnel. As you work on your project outline, keep thinking about what kind of support you'll need, and factor that in.

If you are thinking about collaborating, you are likely to have some possible partners already in mind—perhaps someone you have already worked with or whose work you know. You should have a sense of how your talents and skills complement each other's. You want to know that you and your partner will both keep going when the going gets tough. And of course you must have complete faith in your partner's integrity. A partnership is like a marriage—it has to be based on trust and a shared commitment. It's essential that you and your partner share the same passion and vision. You both have to feel that the project itself is more important than your individual egos.

THE AFFILIATION OPTION — WORKING WITH AN ORGANIZATION

There's another way that you can get substantial assistance with a project, but still retain a great deal of autonomy and control. That way is to affiliate with an organization. We'll examine this option in detail in Chapter 4, but you may find it helpful to begin thinking about this even before you start researching funders.

Thousands of foundations and government agencies will fund individuals directly, but many more will fund only nonprofit organizations. Many funders prefer to give money to organizations—it makes them feel more secure. These organizations can then act as *fiscal sponsors* and funnel the money to individuals. So one reason to consider affiliation is simply to get access to more possible funding sources. There's a second important reason to consider affiliation: you can draw on the expertise and resources of an organization to support your grant seeking and your project. Remember, it is not always necessary to have institutional affiliation. However, it is something you might want to think about because of the possibilities it opens up.

HOW IS THE APPLICATION PROCESS DIFFERENT?

Many funds that give individual grants use printed application forms. This is why it's easier for an individual to apply for a grant directly. The forms are much like college scholarship application forms, and you can sit down by yourself and fill them out. They are usually fairly straightforward.

If you work with an affiliate organization, you will have to spend a good deal of time with its officers or staff. First, you'll have to sell them on your project and convince them to work with you. You'll have to spend some time working with different staff members, learning the organizational guidelines, and sharing information about your project. When you get down to writing a proposal, though, this may be a little easier. Instead of filling out many different forms, you can make up a generic proposal that can be modified slightly for each funder (though if you're applying for government grants, you'll still have to fill out an elaborate application form). Still, there's no doubt that the overall application process will probably be more involved and take longer if you affiliate.

WHEN SHOULD YOU AFFILIATE?

Institutional affiliation does not even apply to many funding areas—for example, to undergraduate scholarships. If you are a painter and want to create new work, or if you are writing a book, or want to get a small-business-association loan, you will generally apply directly to the funders, and institutional affiliation will not be an issue. You'll be making a very simple, matter-of-fact application, and if you are applying only to foundations that fund individuals, then you can do the fund raising by yourself. Just follow the guidelines in this book.

However, even if you do want a grant to paint, or a postgraduate grant to do research, or if you want to develop an invention, you can pursue both individual funding and funding through institutional affiliation.

The more complicated your project and the more money you have to raise, the more you ought to think about affiliation. For example, if you have a scientific invention and will need laboratory space or specialized equipment or facilities, you may want to think about affiliation with a university, or perhaps a hospital. In certain areas, you will almost certainly have to have institutional affiliation. There are types of projects where funders really prefer to deal with an organization. If your project will involve a number of people working as more or less independent contributors—for example, when you are running a dance company or a large school—funders will usually want to see an organization involved.

This brings us to the second reason for considering affiliation: the kind of support it can provide for your project. One of the great advantages of institutional affiliation is that you can tap into the resources and pick the brains of the staff and officers of a nonprofit organization. This is a very important consideration, particularly for a first-time grant seeker. Nonprofits can offer resources and advice at every step of the way. They have experience with budgets, fund raising, managing grant money, and outreach. They may have a staff fund raiser or "development officer" who can assist you, or you may be able to work with the executive director, who runs the organization on a day-to-day basis.

When you do affiliate, there is generally some kind of trade-off or exchange between you and the organization. Usually they will take a portion of any grants received to cover their administrative costs for supporting your project (normal fees run from 3 to 7 percent of monies raised). Often they will want to involve your project in their outreach and their programming, but this is all to the good for you. They may also ask you to do a special workshop or performance for their membership.

HOW CAN YOU FIND A SPONSORING ORGANIZATION?

How you find a sponsoring organization depends on what kind of project you are pursuing, and what kind of connections you may already have. If you are in the educational field—as a student, graduate student, or instructor—you may be able to work through your academic institution. If you're working independently, you can check out the service organizations in your field—some make it part of their mission to act as fiscal sponsors. If your project does not compete directly with the work of an existing nonprofit, you might ask if they will take you on as part of their overall program. If you have a community-oriented project, you could ask around in your community—talk to local United Way agencies and other local nonprofits. You can talk to people at your church or at a local school.

Affiliation is a big subject, and there are many types of affiliation agreements. If you think you might want to pursue this further, you'll find more details in Chapter 4, including tips on how to locate an appropriate sponsor.

PROFESSIONAL FUND RAISERS

There's another way you can get help with your grant seeking: you can hire a professional fund raiser or a fund-raising consultant. In general, you should be thinking about this only if you're planning a very complex project and need to raise a large amount of money. As an individual artist, writer, inventor, or for a small start-up, you should be able to take care of things yourself. Remember, you may be able to get some of the assistance you might need at no cost through a service organization or an institutional affiliation. However, even for a smaller project, you might want to consider working with a freelance consultant on a limited basis. As a rule of thumb, the more money you want to raise, the more you should think about working with a consultant.

People often ask, "Can a fund raiser guarantee that I'll get a grant?"

The short answer is no. No good fund raiser would ever promise specific results, any more than a lawyer would guarantee that you'll win a case. However, what a professional fund raiser can do is offer his or her experience and expertise in doing good foundation research, analyzing your project, helping you to structure a well-written grant proposal, doing budgets, and so forth.

WHO ARE THE FUND RAISERS?

Most professional fund raisers work for nonprofit organizations, either on staff or on a consultant basis. They do what I call the bread-and-butter development work of raising money from private, corporate, and government sources. If they are on the staff of a nonprofit, they are called "development officers." If they are independent, the professional term is "fund-raising counsel." Professional consultants, as a general rule, prefer to work for organizations, though some will occasionally work for individuals on a for-hire basis. They will then bill on an hourly basis and usually charge fairly healthy fees. Many professionals avoid working with individuals, only because they simply cannot expect to make as much income as they can working for an organization. But there are professionals around that you can work with.

Professional fund raisers usually maintain a staff of researchers and assistants and are accustomed to conducting an entire funding campaign, from start to finish. Most work with all kinds of projects and all kinds of funders, though there are a few who will specialize, for example, in government grants.

Another kind of professional is the freelance consultant. These are people who have extensive background in one field and may offer their expertise, on a limited basis, to individuals. Usually, a freelance consultant will evaluate your project based on his or her experience with funders in your field and will help with preparing proposals and budgets.

WHAT A PROFESSIONAL FUND RAISER CAN DO FOR YOU

The professional fund raiser has good access to research materials and experience with funding sources. You would certainly save research time by hiring a professional. However, unless you want to invest a substantial amount of money in order to raise an even more substantial amount, I would suggest you think of using the professional fund raiser as a consultant only. It's going to get very, very expensive to use a professional for every stage of the process, and I would recommend against it.

Professionals may bill anywhere from $35 to $150 an hour for their time. If they are doing extensive research and putting together twenty or thirty individual proposals, you're looking at a lot of dollars. If money is no object, then of course you can hire a professional. I have worked with a number of individuals over the years, but I've often discouraged individuals from hiring me, only because it's so costly in billable hours, and that's how most fund raisers will work. No good professional will want to work "on spec" and wait for payment when funding comes through.

So, again, you can probably best use a professional fund raiser on a limited basis as a consultant. Get them to analyze how your campaign or your proposal should be structured, to critique what you have aldready done, and to guide you toward your next steps. You should be the one researching at the library, consulting with organizations, net-working, writing up those proposals, and typing them out. *You* should be the one doing the legwork. If you work with a professional this way, you'll be investing a certain amount of money in your fund raising, and you'll be getting in return a good professional evaluation of your work. The more preparation you do before consulting a professional, the less of their time you'll pay for, and the more useful the results will be.

What a Freelance Consultant Can Do for You

An alternative to hiring a fund-raising professional is to work with a freelance consultant. This might be a professional in your field who has had some experience with fund raising and proposal writing, or it might be a development officer with a small nonprofit service organization in your field. The going rate for this kind of consulting is much lower, probably in the range of $35 to $75 an hour. If you use the person for a couple of hours—to look closely at your proposal, evaluate how funders may react to it, and make suggestions—this could well be worth the investment. If you know that writing is not your great strength, you might hire a freelance consultant to put together the whole proposal for you, in a form that could be easily changed or adjusted. (Of course, you will have to provide them with detailed notes and a project outline; no one will be able to conjure up a proposal out of vague ideas.)

How Can You Locate a Fund Raiser or Consultant?

The best way to locate a fund raiser is to talk to people in nonprofit organizations or people working in your field. Personal references are really ideal.

Evaluating Fund Raisers and Consultants

How do you know if a fund raiser is legitimate and good at what they do? First, talk with them, meet with them, and consider your own impressions. If you're going to be working with someone, you want to feel that you can communicate easily with them, that they understand your project, that you can understand their approach. So it's important to meet with the person and interview them as much as they're interviewing you. Even though they're the professional, you're the client, and the old adage says, "The client is always right."

If you do like someone and the chemistry seems good, ask for references and follow up on them. A slick brochure and a stellar list of clients is no guarantee of success. Find out what these former clients liked or didn't like about the fund raiser. Ask what the fund raiser offered that was especially valuable. Ask how much it ended up costing. And of course you'll be interested in what kind of results they got, what kind of funding the former clients did or didn't receive.

OTHER SUPPORT SYSTEMS — THE SERVICE ORGANIZATIONS

You may be able to find service organizations in your field that will offer fund-raising seminars, for varying fees; community colleges and other community organizations sometimes offer these as well. There are also a few organizations, like the Foundation Center, that have been set up to aid nonprofit organizations. Sometimes these can be of use to individuals as well. (See the next chapter for more on researching the fund-raising process itself and on service organizations.)

APPROACHING FUNDERS

Market research, getting endorsements and recommendations, collecting support material, writing an effective proposal—these all contribute to a good funding campaign. But none of them will help if you do not communicate well with funders. You want to approach funders in a way that is efficient both for you and for them. There is an etiquette to dealing with funders, and you want to observe it. In fact, you may need to take different approaches when dealing with different types of funders, and we'll talk about these in the chapters that follow. Above all, you want to avoid sending any signals that you are not a serious prospect, that you haven't done your homework, or that you're going to waste a funder's time with inappropriate requests. This isn't difficult, but you must always keep it in mind as you go about your funding research.

THE FIRST CONTACT

First impressions are important, and so is your initial contact with a funder that you've targeted—usually to request guidelines or an application. I strongly discourage initial phone calls to most foundations, since they are often terribly understaffed. Unnecessary phone calls can be very annoying to staff members and program officers. So, after you've done your research, I recommend simply writing to request application guidelines and an annual report.

The "Big Daddy" foundations—a Rockefeller or a Ford Foundation—will have adequate staffing, so it's okay to call them and request their guidelines and materials. Government and public agencies are also usually set up to handle phone calls.

You don't need to say too much about your project. If you send a letter, just request the guidelines and annual report—you don't need to add anything at all about your project. If you do speak to a staff member by telephone, don't go into detail. If someone asks you, be very general; say, "It is a project for visual arts support," or, "It is a project for scientific support." Or use a phrase from their mission statement, which you've looked up. It's best not to say what it is that you want money for until you submit your formal proposal.

There are several reasons why you should avoid giving out information at this stage, whether in a letter or a phone call. First, you don't want a staff member making a snap judgment about whether your project fits within their guidelines. Second, there is the risk that if you start to describe your project, no matter how briefly, this may be misread by a foundation as a mini-proposal without your having been able to plan and submit a formal proposal. Finally, you want to present your idea in the best possible way, and first impressions are usually lasting. Submitting a preliminary idea either verbally or on paper before you've been able to refine it and work out all the details may create a weak impression that will haunt you when you make your formal proposal.

IF YOU HAVE QUESTIONS

After you receive the guidelines and application form, you'll be able to make a more informed judgment about whether you should continue to target this funder and actually submit a proposal. You may find something in the guidelines that contradicts what you found in your research, or indicates a change in funding patterns that might rule out this funder as a prospect. If this happens, go on to the next one on your list. However, after reading the guidelines, you may have some questions about the application procedures, or even about whether this is an appropriate funder for you. If your question is about procedures, and the funder is a Big Daddy foundation or a government or public agency, go ahead and call the staff. Government funders can be real sticklers about procedures, and you will want to follow their instructions to the letter. Smaller foundations, and especially family foundations, are usually not so picky about procedures, so it's better not to bother them on the phone about this. Just make your best guess of what they expect from you, and send in a good, strong proposal and budget. (Use the guidelines given in Chapter 9 to help you prepare a standard proposal and budget.)

If the funding interests or restrictions for any foundation seem ambiguous, you have to tread carefully. You don't want to make a judgment yourself that your project might not be appropriate, or have a staff member make the same snap decision. In this case, it's probably better *not* to ask for clarification of the funding interests or restrictions. If there seems to be a real possibility that your project might fit the funder's interests, go ahead and send in a proposal. You should add a paragraph that will slant it in the direction of their mission statement. I'm not suggesting you change or misrepresent the essence of your idea; just be sure to show clearly the connection to the funder's interests. For example, there's a small foundation that gives grants to "emerging filmmakers." Well, you could interpret "emerging" in many different ways, and wonder how much or what kind of past experience might rule a candidate out. The best approach would be to explain in what sense you are emerging. Perhaps you are switching from documentary to fiction, or you've done some shorts that have been shown, but never a feature. Give the funder the chance to make the decision. Let them make the final interpretation of their guidelines. Give them the opportunity to see a project that they might really be interested in, as long as it's not clearly ruled out by their stated restrictions.

So as a first-time grant seeker, stay away from initial telephone contact. Put in writing your request for guidelines, any application forms, and an annual report. Send in your written proposal. You will probably get a form letter sent out to all applicants that says something like, "We have received your proposal, it is under consideration, and we will be in touch with you about this at a later date." So just sit tight. If a funder contacts you after this and expresses interest, then you may start to have some phone contact with the foundation staff or program officer.

WHEN SHOULD YOU MAKE PERSONAL CONTACT?

As a rule, there's no need for any personal contact with funders unless they initiate it. And it's not appropriate for you to try to initiate it. Funders follow the old rule, "Don't call us, we'll call you"—it really does work that way. You usually won't hear from a foundation unless someone there is interested in your idea. They will get in touch if they want to speak to you. There is only one exception to this rule, and that is if you made the application on the basis of a personal contact—if someone introduced you to a funder, who told you to feel free to keep in touch about your proposal. Otherwise, unless someone says, "We would like you to call," or, "We've set up an appointment for you to call," don't do it. When they are interested in your work, some funders will be very accessible; that is all the more reason not to take advantage of the situation, and not to contact a foundation officer unless it is appropriate.

Once you've sent in a proposal, it's best not to bother the funder. Let them do their work. I once came across a funding source, in doing research, that I had never heard of before. We requested the guidelines and sent in a proposal. We had no phone contact, no meetings—and they gave $140,000 to the organization I was representing! So I do want to emphasize that personal contact is fine if you have it, but it's certainly not essential.

IF THE FUNDER CONTACTS YOU

If the funder is interested in your project, or wants to learn more about it, they may get in touch with you. (Though the fact that they don't does *not* mean they're not interested.) You may get a letter that says they are going to give your proposal serious consideration, or that the proposal is being forwarded to their Board of Directors or Trustees. (You do want to distinguish this from the form letter sent out to all applicants, saying the proposal is under consideration.) Once the funder has expressed this kind of interest, it is appropriate to make a phone call and talk to the person who signed the letter or the program officer in charge of the project. Foundations usually prefer personal contact by phone. They are inundated with requests for grants, and probably won't feel the need for a face-to-face meeting; further, they may be located in a distant city. There are exceptions, though. If your work is on display at a specific location, or if you're doing a public performance or theater piece, or if you have a scientific invention or research project with a special laboratory setup, then the funder may decide that they want to see your work on location. But if there's no compelling reason for a visit and you want a grant to fund work in progress or the beginnings of a project, a phone call is usually sufficient.

Again, try to read between the lines. If it seems that personal contact is not being offered or is discouraged, pay attention. You have to strike a balance between being persistent and being pushy. Don't call constantly, or think you have to maintain contact. As a rule of thumb, one call is sufficient. Let the funder take the lead in terms of how much contact you should have.

It's a good idea to keep a log of all your calls to and from funders. Just jot down the date, the name of the foundation or corporation, the name of the person you spoke to, and whatever information you learned from the call.

HOW TO PRESENT YOURSELF

If it does turn out that you will meet directly with a funder, don't be too anxious about how to present yourself. I remember one client who came to me with a marvelous project that is now doing very, very well. A funder wanted to meet her, and she called me and asked, "What should I wear? I mean, how should I dress?" And I always smile when I think of this. Foundation people are basically interested in the project. Meeting with a funder is not like a job interview. No one is trying to see if you look a certain way. You are simply talking with a person who is very interested in what you have to say. If you feel you are not a good salesperson, if you are not very extroverted or aggressive, don't worry. Just talk about your project—what excites you about it, how you're going to follow through and put it into effect. Be yourself.

FOLLOW-UP

If you do have personal contact with a funder, follow-up is very important. I've seen too many people sit down for a meeting with a foundation, but not follow through and provide additional material that the funder requested. If the funder asks for additional documentation, or asks you to make a call or deliver something after the meeting, be sure to do it within a reasonable amount of time, usually a week to ten days. This is a real test of your commitment to the project and whether you will follow through if they grant you the funds. If they don't request anything further from you, be sure to write a note to thank them for their interest and their time. This not only makes people feel good, but shows that you do really care.

FUNDERS ARE PEOPLE

In my nonprofit work, I've found that funders can be very accessible, open people. They are interested in ideas, in social issues, in the arts and sciences. They like what they do, and if you think about it, it's wonderful to be able to give money to people with exciting projects who are trying to solve problems and make a difference in the world. Funders really deserve our admiration and appreciation. Above all, they are people who are interested in other people. So when you do have contact with funders, relax and be yourself. Whether or not you get a particular grant will ultimately depend on a funder's mission, policies, and interests, and not solely on your presentation. Relax and enjoy the process.

By now you should have a pretty good overview of the whole process of getting a grant. If you're not daunted by the process, if you're still committed to your idea and excited by the thought of forging ahead, then you're in the perfect frame of mind to get that grant. Let's go on to the next step: finding the right funder.

3

FINDING THE
RIGHT FUNDER

A s you realize by now, there are thousands of foundations, corporations, and government funding sources out there that can provide you with free money. Your task is to find the funders who are most likely to support you. The real key to getting a grant is to research these sources thoroughly and discover those that best match your interests. When you find funding sources that support individuals like yourself, then you can begin applying for support.

WHAT YOU NEED TO KNOW ABOUT FUNDERS

To apply successfully for nonprofit money, you need to match a specific type of purpose and project to the right type of funder. To do this, you need to know many details about possible funders—where they have given money in the past, what their areas of interest are, if they give grants to individuals or just to organizations, and what types of grants they give. You have to figure out if you do qualify for the kinds of grants that a funder does offer. Just because, for example, a funder gives to the arts will not necessarily mean that they give to theater or that they give to the visual arts. So it's important to learn more about each potential funder.

You also want to find out as much as you can ahead of time because you really can't write a proposal before you know whom you are addressing it to. You won't have to tailor every proposal from scratch for each individual funder; you will probably create a general proposal that you adapt to suit various funders. But the first step is to find out exactly what the funder is looking for.

In this chapter, you'll learn what you need to know in order to research funders: how to use the basic references to build a prospect list; how to organize your research; where to look for additional information; and how to start honing your prospect list. But first some general advice.

DOING IT YOURSELF

I always encourage individuals to do their own research, even when they hire my firm to assist with their fund raising. I believe that if you know what you want to do and how you want to do it, you will pick up on things that even a professional researcher might miss. You know your own field better than any professional, you will hear about things and get references from people you talk to.

How long will it take to do the research? Probably longer than you think. You have to be very patient and careful to be successful in your search for funders. This is the most arduous and time-consuming part of your quest for free money. You will probably need to spend between ten and forty hours of your time going to the library, poring over the grant books, taking careful notes, and keeping them organized. You will, however, save a good deal of time by using the references in this book (including the Appendix); a lot of information is right here at your fingertips. All that's left is for you to do the legwork of digging up the specific facts you need.

Yes, you can consider what a professional fund raiser might offer in terms of experience or contacts. As we saw, the more money you want to raise, and the more complicated your project, the more seriously you will want to think about this. As a result of having worked with many funders over the years, the professionals know the ins and outs, and the special interests, of various foundations and corporations. They have a rapport with these funders and an inside track on how they operate. But it just isn't necessary to hire a professional for research purposes. You really can and should do it yourself. Tracking down funders can be a fascinating process—you may even find yourself getting hooked by the thrill of the chase.

BUILDING YOUR PROSPECT LIST—A FOUR-STEP PROCESS

The first grant-seeking tool you will need to create is a prospect list of potential funding sources. This might include foundations, businesses and corporations, government agencies, even individuals. You will develop your prospect list by finding funders who have interests that match your project.

Building a prospect list is a four-step process:

1. You will need to locate lists of possible funders. There are many kinds of reference sources that list funders by various categories. Of course, you can also get names from the media, by word of mouth, and from other sources.
2. You will have to read and evaluate listings in reference sources to draw up a preliminary list of funders to write to for additional information. Since this follow-up takes additional time, you must consider carefully which prospects are really worth pursuing.
3. You will have to write to these potential funders for their funding and application guidelines and their annual reports. You may also want to do additional research on these sources by looking up the reports they must submit to the Internal Revenue Service.
4. Finally, you'll have to evaluate all this information and decide which funders to add to your prospect list and which to forget about.

HOW TO USE FUNDING CATEGORIES

The most useful way to research funders is to think always in terms of "funding categories." Foundations and other donors nearly always limit their grant giving to specific areas of interest. These may be defined by subject area, by geographic location, or by "population"— that is, by the type of individual or group that the funder wishes to support, such as students, the homeless, minorities, women, and so on. Throughout your research process, you'll be scanning lists and indexes to see which funders give grants in your subject area, in your community or region, and to your population group. Clearly, if you find a funder that matches you and your project in all three categories, this is a very strong prospect.

Subject area may be defined broadly or narrowly. A funder may simply give "to the arts," or, more specifically, "to support musical education, performances, and new compositions," or even more specifically, "to young composers who show promise and are recent graduates of a doctoral degree program in musical composition." Because of the many ways of defining subject area, you will need to read listings and guidelines very closely to rule out funders that give in your general subject area but not to your specific kind of project. Subject categories can be one of the most useful ways of narrowing your search. Many directories specifically list only the funders who give in a certain subject area, such as the arts, or filmmaking, or education.

Searching by region or geographic area can also be highly productive. A high proportion of private foundations and corporate funders prefer to give primarily or exclusively in their geographic region. Like subject area, geographic region can be defined broadly or narrowly. One funder might give in a multistate region, while another might give only to projects in eastern Massachusetts, for example, or primarily in Boston. Community foundations generally give only within a municipality, and a fund might give only to residents of a single county. So it's important to be on the lookout for very local funders. Some regional directories of funders are listed in the Appendix; you'll find geographic indexes in other directories, and geographic limitations noted in guidelines and listings.

Though this won't work for everyone, you should also try to narrow your funding search to any population group you belong to. There are grant programs directed specifically toward various minorities, women, the economically disadvantaged, people suffering from certain diseases, and so on. There are college scholarships that go to students of a given ethnic or national background, or even to those with a certain last name. Some directories list funders who support specific population groups, and you should keep an eye out for those indications in general listings and guidelines.

Finally, make sure you cover all the bases by researching each of the major funder types—private foundations, corporate funders, and government agencies. Some directories list grants available from all types of funders; others specialize in one or two. If you notice that you are only adding private foundations to your prospect list, make a special search for government or corporate funders that might also support your project.

WHAT TYPES OF GRANTS TO LOOK FOR

To do effective research, you also need to know what types of grants are available. This is a good time for some basic definitions.

A *project grant* supports a particular project or program of an individual or organization. It could fund a specific film, pay for you to travel to India for three months to take photographs, or support a six-week educational program of the Jacques D'Amboise Dance Company in an inner-city school in Detroit.

An *operating grant* is a grant made to an organization or individual to cover operating expenses for an ongoing program or project. This type of broad-based, unrestricted grant can cover anything from rent to the electricity bill to staff salaries or artist's fees—anything needed to keep the project going.

A *restricted grant* covers one specified part of a project, such as the fee for a musical score for your theater production.

A *general purpose grant* is a broad-based grant, not restricted to any particular purpose, to assist with the ongoing work of an organization. These are generally given only to organizations. An example: $10,000 to the Houston Opera to support their work.

Start-up funds or *seed money* are kinds of grants made to help an organization or individual start a new program or project. Seed money can cover salaries, operating expenses, and other expenses necessary to start a new venture, such as a new business or a theater company.

A *challenge grant* is an award that will be paid by a contributing organization if the grant seeker is able to raise a specified amount of funds to match the grant in question. For example, a foundation will give $10,000 to Joe Smith if he also raises $10,000 (or $5,000, or $20,000) on his own or through another grant.

A *matching grant* is similar to a challenge grant. A funder gives money to match funds granted by another organization. For example, the Ford Foundation may decide to match a $10,000 grant by the Rockefeller Foundation to help fund a particular research program.

A *regrant program* is an arrangement whereby a private foundation or a government agency gives funds to a nonprofit organization, which in turn administers a grant program with these funds, soliciting proposals and giving grants, usually on a local level.

An *in-kind donation or service* is a contribution to an organization or individual that might consist of materials or equipment, property, or free services of some kind. These could include computers, fax machines, other office equipment, office space, exhibition space, mailings, or any other kind of donation aside from direct cash gifts. This is sometimes called a *noncash grant*.

Technical assistance is aid in the form of free consulting services that are offered to nonprofit organizations (and sometimes to individuals). It may include fund raising or budgeting assistance, financial or legal advice, computer training, etc.

Grant periods are the time periods during which funds will be available, or during which they must be used. Grant periods vary according to the individual funding programs. A general-purpose grant might cover six months or one year of operation, at the end of which the organization or individual will generally have to report on the progress of the project.

Funding restrictions mean that grant monies may not be used for specific purposes, such as salaries, equipment, or real estate purchase. Limitations vary from program to program. A government grant might permit funds to be used for a wide range of expenses, excluding only equipment purchase. Another might give funds only for equipment purchase.

Fellowships are grants for educational studies or research, usually at the graduate or postgraduate level. They are always granted to individuals, though the funds may be channeled through a sponsor. The term "scholarships" strictly applies to undergraduates, although it's sometimes used loosely for both undergraduate and graduate grants. Although "fellowship" usually implies some sort of academic connection, several fellowships are available that support unstructured, unrestricted work. There are fellowships for writers, for example, that provide for living expenses while the person completes a novel or collection of poems. Research fellowships may permit original work either within or outside an academic environment.

Awards and prizes are grants given on a competitive basis, for specific accomplishments or achievements. They are usually initiated by the awarding organization, and individuals can't apply for them directly. However, there is often a nominating process, and an individual might be able to ask an appropriate person to nominate them.

How to Use the Basic References

The library is going to be your principal source of information, but you can adopt the right frame of mind even before you get there.

Start Thinking "Funders"

Before you open a book, you can start pumping up your awareness of who the funders are. When you read a newspaper article about a new school, or a theater, or a scientific venture, take note of who funded it. When you see an interesting public television program, notice the credit to sponsors. You may have seen a local announcement of an event or charity that included the words: "This was made possible by the generous support of XYZ Foundation." When you go to the library, look up a listing for the XYZ Foundation and see what else it funds and what its giving priorities are. If they give grants in your subject area, put the XYZ Foundation on your preliminary list of potential funders.

If you know other people working in your field, ask them what funding sources have given them grants, or which ones they have applied to. Or you might want to call some organizations in your area to get ideas. Don't be afraid to ask for advice before you even sit down at the library. The more you know about the world of foundations, the easier your research will be.

Libraries—The Place to Begin

You'll find at least some of the reference materials you need in a library. So make your first stop your local public library, a nearby university library, or other research facility. Many kinds of specialized libraries do keep funding references.

Once at the library, you can start sifting through reference guides and periodicals. Don't be discouraged by the vast number of sources that are out there, or the time you will need to spend to locate them. You can do much of your research with a few basic directories. *Remember, these references are your essential tools for getting that grant.*

You can get help building your initial list of prospects by talking to library staff members. They will point you to the appropriate reference section and to the specific books and directories you need to use. Ask about any special resources for funding research that may be available at your library, and about other libraries in your area that may have additional resources.

THE "BIBLES" FOR FUNDING RESEARCH

There are a few basic directories that you should start with. These can give you most of the information you need. Three of the most useful ones are published by the Foundation Center, the national service organization that disseminates information about private foundations (see later in this chapter, page 114, for more on the Foundation Center and what it does).

- *Foundation Grants to Individuals.* 9th edition, New York: The Foundation Center, 1995 (or latest edition). This is an extremely valuable directory that lists foundations making grants of at least $2,000 a year to individuals. It includes some smaller foundations that don't appear in other directories. It can save you lots of time by helping you focus your search on just those funders who give directly to individuals. The directory lists funders under several basic categories of awards—including educational, general welfare, arts and culture, grants to foreigners, awards and prizes by nomination, and company employee grants.

  This directory is probably the best starting point for you as an individual, and it contains useful bibliographies of other references, including all the publications and services of the Foundation Center itself. Entries give most of the details you need, including application guidelines (with limitations), addresses, contact names, and phone numbers. Unfortunately, you won't find this reference book in every local library, so you may need to go to one of the Cooperating Collections that keep Foundation Center materials (see page 115). You can also order *Foundation Grants to Individuals* directly from the Foundation Center, for the hefty price of $40.

- *The Foundation Directory.* 17th edition, New York: The Foundation Center, 1995. This is a basic reference that fundraisers have used for thirty years. It gives detailed information on about 7,600 of the largest foundations in America, including both private and corporate foundations that hold assets of $1 million or more or make total grants of $100,000 or more each year. These foundations give out nearly $7 billion per year to institutions and individuals in areas that include education, research, travel, culture, health, and general welfare.

During 1985–86, grants by these foundations amounted to 92 percent of all foundation money given out.

The Foundation Directory gives detailed information on application procedures, types and amounts of grants awarded, names of foundation staff, addresses, and phone numbers. It has several indexes that list foundations by name, geographic area, areas of interest, and types of support provided, and even by names of foundation officers and donors. You'll find it at some larger libraries, and at the Foundation Center Cooperating Collections.

- **The Foundation Directory, Part 2: A Guide to Grant Programs $25,000–$100,000.** New York: The Foundation Center (latest edition). This directory is similar to *The Foundation Directory* and provides information on 4,200 mid-sized foundations which make grants ranging from $25,000 to $100,000. Listings are broken down by foundation geographical indexes, type of support, and subject area indexes.

- **National Directory of Corporate Giving.** 3rd edition. New York: The Foundation Center, 1993. This directory has information about more than 1,500 corporate foundations and direct-giving programs. Listings are broken down by geographical location; type of charity (e.g., school, religious organization); type of recipient (e.g., youth); type of grant (endowment, seed money, cash awards, in-kind gifts); and amount of grants given. Of course it has all the necessary addresses and phone numbers, as well as a guide to corporate fund-raising techniques.

If your library doesn't have the *National Directory of Corporate Giving,* there are two other sources you can check out that also list grant-giving corporations:

- **Corporate 500: The Directory of Corporate Philanthropy.** San Francisco: Public Management Institute, 1993–94 (latest edition). This is a detailed directory that profiles 590 corporate giving programs. It is indexed by geographic region, subject, and funding areas. It offers information on application procedures, sample grants made, contact persons, corporate decision makers, giving priorities, and restrictions.

- *Corporate Giving Directory 1996.* Rockville, MD: The Taft Group, 1995 (latest edition). This is a good sourcebook, detailing 571 of the largest corporate charitable giving programs, which provide at least $500,000 in grants. It features alphabetical listings of corporate foundations and giving programs, and information on whom to contact, size of grants given, type of grants, giving priorities, and sample grant recipients.

For grants by federal agencies, there is one master directory:

- *Catalog of Federal Domestic Assistance.* Washington, DC: Government Printing Office, 1995 (published annually). This is definitely not a user-friendly guide, but it does offer invaluable listings of all federal programs, projects, and services that offer aid to organizations and individuals. It lists many programs that individuals can apply to in a great number of areas. But the sheer size and bureaucratic jargon make it difficult to work with. If you want to try, see Chapter 7 for help with using this source.

To research government funding sources, you might find it easier to start with my own guide:

- *Free Money from the Federal Government,* by Laurie Blum. New York: John Wiley & Sons, Inc., 1996.

Other directories are listed later in this chapter and in the Appendix, but these are a good place to start.

How to Organize Your Research: The Basics

Once you've located a few of these references, you're ready to get started. There's a standard procedure you can follow to come up with potential funders for your prospect list. And of course you need to organize and keep notes on the information as you collect it. Let's start with these references, and begin our research by using the indexes and the funding categories.

Working with Categories

When you use a directory, always work with the major funding categories—funding by subject, funding by geographic location, and funding by population group. Look for indexes that categorize the funders, and try to do some cross-referencing—if you find a funder that gives in your subject area and geographic region, and supports a population group you belong to, you've found a very good prospect.

Since many foundations limit their giving to specific subject areas, start by looking at the subject index or at the subject divisions. For instance, if you are applying for a grant in the arts, look for the subject heading Arts and Humanities, or perhaps even more specifically, for Music, Dance, or Theater. In the index, under each subject heading, you will find a listing of those foundations that specifically fund these areas, and where in the directory to find the expanded listing for each foundation.

In some of the larger directories, you'll also find private and corporate foundations indexed by their locations, or by geographical areas where they offer funding. So if you are only looking for foundations based in Illinois, or that fund in Illinois, you may find them listed alphabetically in the geographical index.

The most important part of your research is your ability to identify sources that match your needs. Be creative in your search and take your time as you look under the various headings. Check to see what kind of indexes a directory might have in addition to subject and geographic indexes. Be sure to look at "population" categories and at other funding types. Look for indexes or sections that list funders under additional categories, such as Education, Youth, Research, Awards and Prizes, Company-Related Scholarships, Medical Expenses, and Welfare Assistance. Check to see if any of the special categories apply to you, and look at the listings of funding sources for those that do.

By looking through various categories and subcategories, you may find alternate funding sources you might not have considered before. If you want a scholarship, you would start looking under Educational Support or Scholarships. However, you might also look under Funding for Women or Funding for Minorities to locate specific scholarships that are directly focused toward your circumstances or interests.

CONSIDER THE DIFFERENT FUNDER TYPES

Even though you're starting your research by focusing on categories like subject area, make sure you consider all the possible funder types, or at least the major ones: private foundations, corporate funders, and government funders. Don't rule out any of the types because you think they may not be appropriate—you'd be surprised at the variety of projects and needs funded by corporations and the federal government. The only category you may not want to consider at all is that of individual donors, since they usually require the most effort to find and result in the least amount of funding. Still, there are exceptions, so don't rule out any possibility if you get a bright idea.

Some of the directories you will be using are compiled by funder type. As you proceed with your research, when you find you want to know more about a specific funder type, turn to Chapters 5 through 8 in this book. You'll find more details on how most effectively to research and approach each type in these chapters. But for now, get started by looking at the listings in the main directories.

START COLLECTING FACTS

Once you've picked out some likely funders in a directory, what should you look for? Here are some details you should check on to determine whether a funder might be right for you:

- Do your needs match the objectives or mission of the funder?
- Do they give grants in your *specific* subject area?
- Do they give grants in your geographical area?
- How much money do they have to give away, and what is the average size of their award? (A foundation that gives very small grants may not be worth the pursuit, if you have to raise a large sum.)
- What types of grants have they made over the last few years? Have they given any to projects like yours? (This will give you a better idea of whether they will fund your project.)
- Do they give to individuals or only to organizations? (Remember, you can possibly affiliate with an organization to receive some types of grants.)
- Are there any limitations on their grants that might rule out your project or you as a recipient?
- What are their application deadlines? If you missed the deadline for application, when is the next deadline and/or when does their Board of Trustees or Directors next meet?

If they do look like possible candidates for your prospect list, note down the program names, addresses, phone numbers, and contact persons. If you think that you meet all the requirements, then you'll want to go on to the next step and contact this source.

Before you move on to contact a funder, however, be sure that you clearly understand their limitations and giving priorities. If you are going to the trouble to sift through pages of information, don't waste your time by contacting or applying to a funding source that is an unlikely prospect for you. The best way to build a good prospect list is to weed out unlikely funders carefully. *Be sure to look for any special limitations.* Foundations will often tell you that they do not fund certain kinds of projects or expenses. If you are looking for a grant in the performing arts, for example, a funder's guidelines must clearly state that they support cultural projects or the arts. Applying to a foundation that isn't a good match for you wastes your time and theirs.

NOTE AFFILIATION REQUIREMENTS

You will find, as you look through the various directories, that some funding sources state that they don't make grants to individuals. If a listing says this, you know that you can't apply directly; however, you might still be able to apply under the auspices of a nonprofit organization. Even though some foundations will not give grants to individuals, they may support a person who is doing work at a non-profit institution like a university. You might therefore apply under the sponsorship of the university, and if a grant is awarded, the check will be delivered to the university, which in turn will disburse funds to you.

Accordingly, you may be able to meet your funding needs by associating yourself with a nonprofit institution that will accept funds from the foundation on your behalf. When you are doing your research, look to see if a funding source you're interested in provides grants to such institutions. You can then consider whether you want to find a formal sponsor to receive and manage your grant money for you. If you are a writer, artist, or researcher, you may even be able to use space or facilities provided by your sponsor. By affiliating with a non-profit institution, you can also increase the number of grants you can apply for. (More details on affiliation in the next chapter.)

ORGANIZE YOUR FINDINGS

It goes without saying that as you start to sift through all this information, you'll need to organize your findings so that you can make good use of them later and follow up on potential names for your prospect list. Here are some rules for keeping track of all these details:

- *Keep a record on each potential funder.* If you're working at a library with a photocopier, you can simply copy each page that has an interesting listing, and drop the copy into your active research file. Or you can note down the important information about each funder on a large index card, and put these in a card file. Or you can use letter-sized paper and keep at least one page for each potential prospect in a folder or looseleaf binder.

- *Note down the essential facts for each potential funder.* Make sure you collect the same important details for each prospect. These should include:
  Name of the funder
  Address and telephone number
  Areas of interest and giving priorities
  Financial data, including assets, number of grants given, and average amount
  Whether they give to individuals or just to organizations
  Any special limitations
  Name of contact person and board members
  Application procedures and deadlines

- *Use a data sheet.* If you think it will help, you can use a typewriter or word processor to make up your own data sheet with blanks. Photocopy your data sheet, take the copies with you to the library, and just fill in the blanks with the information listed above. (See sample data sheet opposite.)

If you keep track of the information you find in an organized way, with at least one page per prospect, it will be easy to follow up when you decide to dig for more information or to contact a funder. Your note page or data sheet then becomes the start of the prospect file that you keep for each funder you actually send a proposal to. If along the way you decide to rule out a prospect for any reason, just pull the data sheet or card from your active file and put it into a reject file. (Don't throw it out; you might be able to turn to this funder in the future or pass the information along to another grant seeker.)

FUND RAISER'S DATA SHEET

Funder's name: _____

Address: _____

_____

Contact person: _____

Financial data:

Total assets: _____

Total grants: _____

Grant ranges: _____

Subject focus: (in order of importance) _____

Geographic limits: _____

Population group(s) served: _____

Type(s) of support: _____

To individuals/org's? _____

Special limits: _____

People (officers, board members, staff): _____

_____

Application requirements:

Printed guidelines, report? _____

Method of initial approach: _____

Deadlines: _____

Board meetings: _____

Information source: _____

Date: _____

MAKE SURE YOUR INFORMATION IS UP TO DATE

It's very important to know that you are working with accurate and up-to-date information. As a general rule, foundations are pretty stable, but they do change their priorities and their personnel. It's not always easy to know whether the information you have is current or accurate. The references you are working with are usually one or two years old. Try to use the most current reference volumes—check with the publisher if necessary to make sure you are looking at the latest edition. *Never rely on files or directories that are more than a year old.* You will find that many libraries, even foundation libraries, stock volumes dating from the mid-1970s and early 1980s. These are practically useless. Remember that these books took one or two years to compile, so the information was already two or three years old on date of publication, as it is for even the most current editions you are consulting.

The only way to get current information on a funder—and you should definitely do this—is to locate its current annual report in a foundation collection, or write to the funder for the current report. You may well find that the current annual report indicates a change in guidelines or focus or that a contact person has changed. But again, until you do your homework in the library and go to a reference volume, do not contact the foundation. First, see if it is likely that you fit the funding profile; only then should you go on to the second step and request an annual report and application.

You can also try to keep up by reading special philanthropy journals, doing computer database searches, or seeking out the newsletters that are published by some of the larger foundations. However, you will probably have to go to one of the main foundation centers, or possibly a Cooperating Collection, to do this (more on these resources later in this chapter). So try to be thorough in your original research, and know that you can always confirm the information by writing to the funder directly.

The truth is, it can be quite difficult to find out certain types of information about funders, such as the average amount or number of grants they give to individuals. This is because many foundations do not publish information about more than just their best known and largest grants, and these usually go to nonprofit organizations. They simply do not list the grants that they give to individuals. The Guggenheim Foundation is one of the relatively few major exceptions. To make matters worse, when a foundation gives money to an individual through a sponsor or an institution, its listings will generally not reflect this type of grant either, making it even harder to discover its true giving patterns. The rule of thumb is, if an organization doesn't specifically rule out grants to individuals, don't cross it off your list—try to find out more. If it does rule them out, try to find out if it channels funds through sponsors.

HOW TO DIG DEEPER

You cannot always determine on the basis of a listing whether you will ultimately want to apply to a specific funder, or even whether you should bother to contact them. The listings will give you an idea, but you may need to do a little extra digging. Suppose, for example, you are trying to fund a play, and you find a listing for a funder that gives to the arts, but the listing doesn't specifically say that they give to theater. You should try to dig up additional information about this funder. See if you can find out about some of their past grants. If you see that they have primarily supported painters and sculptors, and have not given to theaters in the past, pass on the listing. This will again save you the time and trouble of contacting funders that are not really right for you. However, you may find it quite difficult to learn what specific grants a particular funding source has made in any given year.

Where can you look for more information? There are two primary sources: the foundation's own publications (including annual reports) and the reports it must file with the Internal Revenue Service.

THE 990-PF REPORTS

You may be surprised to learn that the U.S. Government has made things easier for you. All foundations are required by law to file an annual "private foundation information return," called a 990-PF, with the Internal Revenue Service. The PF stands for "Private Foundation." This form must state what the foundation's assets are and how many grants were given each year. The government requires this information because foundations' funds are tax-exempt. The 990-PF is a terrific research tool, because it will list at least some examples of grants given during the year, as well as actual recipients and amounts. Even more important, it is a way to find out about those small private foundations that might not appear in any directories or listings. If you do get the name of such a foundation, you can look up its 990-PF form to find out what its giving patterns are.

If you have access to one of the Foundation Center's main libraries, you can look at copies of these 990-PF forms for private and corporate foundations. Some Cooperating Collections keep 990-PF forms for local foundations and will help you order copies of forms from the main Center (see page 115 for details on the Foundation Center collections). You can also obtain these through some state attorneys' general offices, and you may purchase them directly from the IRS. Contact the Public Affairs Officer at your local IRS office.

- **TIP:** You can order foundation returns by contacting the Public Affairs Office at your local IRS headquarters. You will need to know the full name of the foundation, the city and state where it is located, and the year of the return you are ordering.

ANNUAL REPORTS AND NEWSLETTERS

For a very good resource, you can always turn to a foundation's or corporation's own publications. Individual foundations publish their own annual reports and giving guidelines. The annual reports will usually provide detailed information about a foundation's giving policies. They may summarize the foundation's history and why it was established, then outline the major kinds of programs and projects the company has funded. They will usually list the names of grant recipients, brief histories of their affiliations, and the amounts they received. Annual reports and guidelines provide the detailed information that can help you decide if you should apply to a particular foundation.

A small number of the bigger foundations also publish bulletins and sometimes quite elaborate newsletters. You may be able to find some of these publications in the Foundation Center's main or cooperating collections. If a larger foundation gets your request for an annual report and guidelines, they will most likely put you on a mailing list for bulletins or a newsletter. Some small foundations do not publish or distribute annual reports; to research these you'll have to stick to the listings and the 990-PF forms.

THE NEXT STEP—CONTACTING THE FUNDER

When you've done all the research you can from directories and other sources, and you really think you have found some likely prospects, go ahead and write to them. Just send a short letter requesting a copy of their annual report and a set of grant guidelines. If you know from your research that they use an application form, ask for that too. That's all you need to do at this point. Particularly if it's a smaller foundation, don't ask for anything else—you'll just bother the program officer.

When the material comes in, you can immediately check the information against your own information or data sheet to make sure your facts are up to date and accurate. You will then begin looking through the materials more closely to decide whether you want to keep this funder on your prospect list and eventually submit a proposal.

In the final section of this chapter (pages 130–33) you'll find more details on how to evaluate and act on the information you've collected. But first you may wish to do an even more thorough search for potential funders, going beyond the few major directories. In fact, there are a number of specialized resources you can use to zero in on the best funders for you, those most likely to give you a grant. The next section offers details on how you can find these resources and use them.

THE LARGER PICTURE: ADDITIONAL RESOURCES

Now that you know how to use a basic directory and manage your funder facts, you should consider some of the additional reference books and resources that are available. You can use these resources to dig deeper for additional information about specific funders or to track down obscure ones. You can also turn to specialized books and directories that focus on your own particular areas of interest.

GENERAL REFERENCES AND RESOURCES

Aside from the basic directories listed earlier, there are three other general references that you may wish to consult:

- *Annual Register of Grant Support,* edited by R. R. Bowker. Wilmette, IL: National Register Publishing Co., 1995 (published annually). This is a valuable reference that offers more than just listings. It gives information on special programs sponsored by funding sources of all types, including professional associations and special interest organizations.

- *Awards, Honors and Prizes,* edited by Gita Siegman. Vol. 1: *United States and Canada.* Detroit: Gale Research Co., 1994 (11th edition). A comprehensive directory of over 22,000 awards, indexed by organizations, awards, and subject areas.

- *Encyclopedia of Associations,* edited by Deborah Burek. Vol. 1: *National Organizations of the United States.* Detroit: Gale Research Co., 1993 (published annually). Lists national organizations you may be able to affiliate with, including trade, business, environmental, government, health, athletic, etc. Includes addresses, publications of these organizations, and whether they hold conferences.

RESEARCH BY SUBJECT AREA OR CATEGORY

There is another direction you can take with your research that may prove especially efficient and productive. Start looking for specific references for your subject area, need, or "population." Many reference books deal with specific grants in various fields, such as education, the arts, company-employee grants from corporations, and grants by state.

The Free Money® *Books.* I have a written a series of *Free Money®* books which provide lists of funding sources that support individuals in many different fields—from college scholarships to grants in the arts to support for health care. Whether you use my books or others, I do suggest you pursue this idea of specific sourcebooks; it can save you a good deal of research time.

There are other specific guides on the market and in your local libraries. Ask your librarian to show you what he or she has in the reference sections. Scan the indexes of all these books to find the funding categories (subject areas, geographic areas, etc.) that might apply to your project. Be sure to read the introductions of all these reference guides for help as well. Introductions provide summaries of the various indexes and funding categories in each book.

The following is a selected sampling of some of the most useful specialized funding guides, listed by subject area in alphabetical order. You can find a more complete list in the Appendix, page 323.

THE ARTS

Free Money® for People in the Arts, by Laurie Blum. New York: Applause Books, 1996.

Guide to Corporate Giving in the Arts, edited by Robert A. Porter. New York: The American Council for the Arts, 1987.

Guide to Funding for Emerging Artists and Scholars, by Jennifer Sarbacher. Washington, DC: President's Committee on the Arts and the Humanities, 1991.

The National Directory of Grants and Aid to Individuals in the Arts, by Nancy A. Fandel. Arts Patronage Series, no. 15. Des Moines, IA: Arts Letters, 1989.

National Guide to Funding in Arts and Culture. New York: The Foundation Center, 1994.

1992 Guide to Funding for Arts and Culture, edited by James Marshall. Alexandria, VA: Educational Funding Research Council, 1992.

(See the Appendix for additional subject guides for performing artists, filmmakers, musicians, visual artists, writers, and others.)

BUSINESS

Computer Grants Directory. 4th edition. San Francisco: The Public Management Institute, 1991.

Free Money® for Small Business and Entrepreneurs, by Laurie Blum. 4th edition. New York: John Wiley & Sons, 1995.

EDUCATION

If you are looking for a scholarship and are already enrolled in or admitted to a college or university, your first stop should be the financial aid office of your school. Individual colleges and universities have many scholarships of their own for which you may qualify—for minorities, for women, for individuals with handicaps, etc. Your school's financial aid officer will be able to help you with these, as well as with information about other special scholarships, and will know about the many government grants in education. (And see complete listings in the Appendix.)

College Financial Aid Annual, edited by John Schwartz. New York: ARCO Publishing, 1995.

College Blue Book, New York: The Macmillan Co., 1995.

Financing a College Education: The Essential Guide for the 90s, by Judith B. Margolin. New York: Plenum Press, 1989.

Free Money® for College, by Laurie Blum. 3rd edition. New York: Facts On File, 1994.

Free Money® for Private Schools, by Laurie Blum. New York: Simon & Schuster, 1992.

National Guide to Funding for Elementary and Secondary Education, 3rd edition. New York: The Foundation Center, 1995.

Peterson's Guide to Four-Year Colleges. 26th edition. Princeton, NJ: Peterson's Guide, 1996.

Scholarships, Fellowships and Loans 1994–95. Detroit: Gale Research Co., 1993.

Foreign Study: See TRAVEL, below.

Graduate, Postgraduate, and Research
The Directory of Research Grants. Phoenix, AZ: Oryx Press, published annually.

Free Money® for Graduate School, by Laurie Blum. New York: Facts On File, 1996.

Graduate Scholarship Directory: The Complete Guide to Scholarships, Fellowships, Grants and Loans for Graduate and Professional Study. Englewood Cliffs, NJ: Prentice-Hall, 1993.

The Grants Register. New York: St. Martin's Press, published twice a year.

U.S. Government Support
Directory of Federal Aid for Education: A Guide to Federal Assistance Programs for Education. Santa Monica, CA: Ready Reference Press, 1982.

The Federal Educational and Scholarship Funding Guide. West Warwick, RI: Grayco, 1989.

Free Money® from the Federal Government, by Laurie Blum. New York: John Wiley & Sons, 1996.

Student Guide: Five Federal Financial Aid Programs. Washington, DC: U.S. Department of Education, Government Printing Office.

State-by-State Support: Refer to the state funding directories—a complete listing appears in the Appendix.

ENVIRONMENT
Environmental Grantmaking Foundations 1992 Directory. Rochester, NY: Environmental Data Research Institute, 1992.

Environmental Grants: A Guide to Grants for the Environment from Government, Companies and Charitable Trusts, by Susan Forrester. London: Directory of Social Change, 1989.

National Guide to Funding for the Environment and Animal Welfare. New York: The Foundation Center, 1994.

HEALTH
AIDS Funding: A Guide to Giving by Foundations and Charitable Organizations. 3rd edition. New York: The Foundation Center, 1993.

Directory of Biomedical and Health Grants. 10th edition. Phoenix, AZ: Oryx Press, 1995.

Free Money® for Diseases of Aging, by Laurie Blum. New York: Simon & Schuster, 1992.

Free Money® for Heart Disease and Cancer Care, by Laurie Blum. New York: Simon & Schuster, 1992.

Handicapped Funding Directory, by Richard M. Eckstein. 7th edition. Margate, FL: Research Grant Guides, 1990.

National Guide to Funding in Aging. 3rd edition. New York: The Foundation Center, 1992.

National Guide to Funding in Health. 3rd edition. New York: The Foundation Center, 1993.

HUMAN SERVICES

Free Money® for Day Care, by Laurie Blum. New York: Simon & Schuster, 1992.

Fundraiser's Guide to Human Service Funding, by Susan E. Elnicki. Rockville, MD: Taft Information, 1992.

HUMANITIES

Directory of Grants in the Humanities. Phoenix, AZ: Oryx Press, 1995.

MINORITIES

Directory of Financial Aids for Minorities, 1993–95, by Gail Ann Schlachter. San Carlos, CA: Reference Service Press, 1993.

Guide to Multicultural Resources, edited by Charles Taylor. Madison, WI: Praxis Publications, 1989.

RELIGION

Foundation Guide for Religious Grantseekers, edited by Kerry A. Robinson. Atlanta, GA: Scholars Press, 1992.

RESEARCH AND FELLOWSHIPS

Directory of Research Grants. Phoenix, AZ: Oryx Press, 1995.

Guide to Funding for Emerging Artists and Scholars, by Jennifer Sarbacher. Washington, DC: President's Committee on the Arts and the Humanities, 1991.

Guide to Research Support, edited by Kenneth Lee Honig. 3rd edition. Washington, DC: American Psychological Association, 1987.

SCIENCE

Directory of Biomedical and Health Care Grants. 6th edition. Phoenix, AZ: Oryx Press, 1991.

Directory of Grants in the Physical Sciences. Phoenix, AZ: Oryx Press, 1986.

Fellowships and Grants for Training and Research: To Be Offered in 1991–1992. New York: Social Science Research Council, 1991.

Grants for Research and Education in Science and Engineering: An Application Guide. NSF, no. 90–77. Washington, DC: National Science Foundation, 1990.

SENIOR CITIZENS

The Caregiver's Guide, by Carolyn Rob. Boston, MA: Houghton Mifflin, 1992.

TRAVEL

Financial Aid for Research, Study, Travel and Other Activities Abroad 1990–1991, by Gail Ann Schlachter and R. David Weber. San Carlos, CA: Reference Service Press, 1990.

Financial Resources for International Study: A Definitive Guide to Organizations Offering Awards for Overseas Study. Institute of International Education. Princeton, NJ: Peterson's Guides, 1989.

Free Money for Foreign Study, by Laurie Blum. New York: Facts on File, 1991.

Fulbright and Other Grants for Graduate Study Abroad 1992–1993. New York: Institute of International Education, 1991.

Funding for Research, Study and Travel: Latin America and the Caribbean, edited by Karen Cantrell and Denise Wallen. Phoenix, AZ: Oryx Press, 1987.

The International Scholarship Book: The Complete Guide to Financial Aid for Study Abroad. 2nd edition. Englewood Cliffs, NJ: Prentice-Hall, 1990.

WOMEN

Directory of Financial Aids for Women 1991–1992, by Gail Ann Schlachter. San Carlos, CA: Reference Service Press, 1991.

Directory of Women's Funds. New York: Women and Foundations/Corporate Philanthropy, 1988.

Grants for Women and Girls. New York: Foundation Center, 1994. This is just a sampling. More directories are listed in the Appendix, and you may come across others as you start to dig into your research.

RESEARCHING THE JOURNALS AND ANNUALS FOR YOUR AREA

Current journals and periodicals are a good source for up-to-date information about funding sources. Some magazines and newsletters have special sections on funding, including names, addresses, and deadlines. Many will run features on funding. Many organizations, and some journals, publish annual directories about their fields, with names of companies, services, organizations, etc. These can also be a useful source of information. Look into the specific publications that serve your area. (See the Appendix, page 336, for a listing of some of the major ones.)

PERIODICALS AND NEWSPAPERS

If you want to find out more about a funding source, check out the periodical index at your library for newspaper or magazine articles about the funder or the individual donor. You might run across an article on a particular foundation or organization that was assisted through a grant, or one on a business or corporation that you're interested in. You could also look for articles about your project area, to see if funders are mentioned. Also, take a look at indexes for periodicals that deal specifically with your project area.

There are a number of journals that deal specifically with philanthropy. These contain articles on such topics as who is giving, trends in philanthropy, latest grants awarded by particular foundations or corporations, and latest congressional rulings. If you can't find these in your local library, contact them directly to ask for a sample copy, or to find out which library might collect them (see the Appendix, page 336, for addresses and phone numbers). Some of the primary journals are

- *The Chronicle of Philanthropy*
- *Corporate Philanthropy Report*
- *Foundation News*
- *Fund Raising Management*

- *Giving USA (annual and update)*
- *Nonprofit Times*

THE FOUNDATION CENTER — FOR IN-DEPTH RESEARCH

We've already mentioned the Foundation Center as the source of some of the most useful funding directories. If you are having trouble finding the directories you need, or if you want to do some in-depth research, the Foundation Center could help. This is a clearinghouse for information about the nonprofit world—for nonprofit management as well as for foundations themselves. It was set up as a national service organization in 1956, supported by a group of foundations, and its mission is to assist other nonprofit organizations with their fund raising. It keeps a valuable collection of information on philanthropy and foundation, corporate, and government giving. The Foundation Center publishes a multitude of reference books, directories, and reports that can answer virtually any question about philanthropy, and provide detailed information about the kinds of grants that corporations and foundations offer.

The Foundation Center maintains five principal reference collections—located in New York, San Francisco, Washington, D.C., Cleveland, and Atlanta—but their directories are available in libraries throughout the United States. The collections are free and open to the public, and free orientation sessions are also given for nonprofit organizations (call for an appointment). Individuals can attend the orientation sessions. There are Cooperating Collections in nearly every state, and these too are open to the public, by appointment.

A word of caution, though: individuals are not turned away, but they are not really favored at the Foundation Center. It was not set up to service individuals; it exists primarily for the use of nonprofit organizations. You will not find the staff ready to hold your hand or offer you all the assistance you might get at your local library. If you do turn to the Foundation Center resources, be sure to study the orientation guides and information pamphlets about how to use the Center. Ask about the free orientation sessions, and try to take a course; this way you won't be bothering the staff with unnecessary questions.

There are two National Collections:

The Foundation Center
79 Fifth Avenue (8th Floor)
New York, NY 10003
212-620-4230

The Foundation Center
1001 Connecticut Avenue, N.W.
Washington, DC 20036
202-331-1400

And three field offices:

The Foundation Center
Room 312
312 Sutter Street
San Francisco, CA 94108
415-397-0902

The Foundation Center
Kent H. Smith Library
1422 Euclid, Suite 1356
Cleveland, OH 44115
216-861-1933

The Foundation Center
Suite 150, Grand Lobby
Hurt Building
50 Hurt Plaza
Atlanta, GA 30303
404-880-0094

You can purchase Foundation Center publications at the National Collections, and place orders at the field offices. There are also more than 180 affiliated Cooperating Collections—one or more in nearly every state—and several abroad.

THE COOPERATING COLLECTIONS

The Cooperating Collections offer free public access to the basic collection of Foundation Center publications, and some offer access to computerized fields. These collections also provide free orientation sessions; in addition, they sometimes offer funding research guidance, and special workshops and orientations, though these are usually aimed at organizations. Some have sets of 990-PF forms for their state or region. Check with the Cooperating Collection near you to find out what they offer. (For the location of the collection nearest you, call the Foundation Center's toll-free information number, 800-424-9836.)

Because collection hours and services vary, it's best to call them in advance and make an appointment if you want to visit. You can also check with the Foundation Center at the same number toll-free to find out about new locations or get updated information.

What services exactly does the Foundation Center provide?

THE FOUNDATION CENTER LIBRARIES

First, the Center provides access to all of its own publications and references. In addition, you can find valuable publications provided by the foundations themselves, as well as other materials, such as the IRS 990-PF forms provided by the U.S. Government. You'll find a core collection of references at each of the four main collections and at each of the Cooperating Collections. You can also order Foundation Center publications directly by writing to the New York office, or by calling the toll-free number and charging them to your credit card. Be forewarned: many of them are quite expensive. The major directories cost upward of $100 each. For information about any of the Center's services, call their toll-free information number: 800-424-9836.

- **TIP:** Call the Foundation Center's toll-free number, and ask them to send you their free catalogue, *Fundraising and Nonprofit Development Publications and Services.* This is a good orientation to their publication list and to the nonprofit world.

Here is a detailed listing of the core collection that you will find at each Foundation Center library:

- *The Foundation Directory.*
- *The Foundation Directory, Part 2: A Guide to Grant Programs $25,000–$100,000 (latest edition).*
- *Source Book Profiles.* New York: The Foundation Center, 1995. This directory offers in-depth information on the largest 1,000 foundations and their areas of interest and giving patterns.
- *National Data Book of Foundations: A Comprehensive Guide to Grantmaking Foundations.* New York: The Foundation Center, 1995 (latest edition). A comprehensive sourcebook on 34,000 large and small U.S. foundations.
- *National Directory of Corporate Giving.*
- *Foundation Grants to Individuals.* 9th edition. New York: The Foundation Center, 1995. Probably the best starting point for you as an individual.
- *Selected Grant Guides by Subject.* New York: The Foundation Center, published annually. These comprehensive guides break down foundation giving into many subject areas. The guides list actual foundation grants in thirty different subject areas; each guide shows listings of foundation names and addresses, the amount that was awarded and when, and who received the grant.
- *The Literature of the Nonprofit Sector.* This is a bibliography of books *about* fund raising, including those published by the

Center and elsewhere. Titles range from simple booklets to fairly technical studies on managing nonprofit organizations. The Center's main libraries have a broad selection of these books on hand, and you can find many of them at the Cooperating Collections as well.

- *Foundation Fundamentals: A Guide for Grantseekers*, edited by Judith Margolin. New York: The Foundation Center (latest edition). A concise guidebook that provides the beginning fund raiser with various information about foundations and philanthropy.
- *Foundation Giving: Yearbook on Facts and Figures on Private, Corporate and Community Foundations*. New York: The Foundation Center (latest edition). A good general data book, providing information about 33,000 U.S. foundations.
- *The Foundation Center's User-Friendly Guide: Grantseeker's Guide to Resources*, by Judith Margolin. New York: The Foundation Center, 1994. A revised edition that provides even more details about the grantmaking process to the novice fund raiser.
- *Directory of New and Emerging Foundations*. 3rd edition. New York: The Foundation Center, 1994. This sourcebook lists 1,000 new community, corporate, and private foundations in the United States, and also features information on 2,500 foundations, which make grants up to $2,500 each year.

Beyond the core collection, the National Collections, and some of the Cooperating Collections, contain other useful materials, such as:

- *Foundation files.* Annual reports, press releases, grants lists, application guidelines, and other materials provided on a voluntary basis by many major foundations.
- *IRS 990-PF returns.* The Center keeps on file the 990-PF returns of all 30,000 foundations required to file them (usually stored on microfiche). You can find a complete set of the 990-PF returns at the New York and Washington, D.C., offices of the Center. The Cleveland and the San Francisco offices hold returns for the Midwestern and Western states, respectively. Some of the Cooperating Collections also contain the private foundation returns for their state or region. If one of these collections doesn't have a 990-PF return you are looking for, they can order it for you from the New York center.

Besides the library collections, the Foundation Center offers a few additional services, although these are mostly for the benefit of non-profit organizations:

The Associates Program. The Center has an Associates Program, which it calls "the direct line to fund-raising information." This is quite expensive—it costs $495 a year to be a member—but some organizations find that it saves many hours of research time. The program offers a toll-free telephone reference service, access to selected pages and files from the Center's references, and custom searches of the Center's computerized database. The Associates Program will help an organization (or an individual) to identify potential funding sources, target information, and write effective proposals.

This is certainly a good deal for many organizations—it's like having your own research staff—but I really don't recommend it for individuals. It's oriented toward fund raising for organizations, it's too expensive, and you can do this work quite effectively on your own. I've known a few small nonprofits that liked this service very much, but I've never known an individual who had any real use for it. (If you do want more information about this program, call the Center's toll-free number, 800-424-9836.)

On-Line Computer Databases. The Foundation Center supplies information through two on-line computer databases, available through DIALOG Information Services. These offer specialized information on funders and grants. This is one way to access the Foundation Center's resources and gain specific information on funding sources—their finances, giving interests, grants given, names and addresses, and application guidelines. The great advantage of searching a database is that you can specify very narrowly the type of information you are looking for.

Here are some examples of the kinds of questions that a database search might answer (taken from *Foundation Grants to Individuals*):

- Which New York foundations support urban projects? Who are their officers and trustees?
- What are the program interests of the ten largest corporate foundations? Which ones publish annual reports?
- Which foundations have given grants in excess of $100,000 in the past two years for continuing education for women?
- Which foundation would be likely to fund a cancer research project at a California hospital?

- Which are the ten largest foundations in Philadelphia by annual grants amount?
- What are the names and addresses of smaller foundations in the 441 zip-code range?

One of the databases, called "The Foundation Directory," includes information from the following publications: *The Foundation Directory; The Foundation Directory, Part 2;* the *National Directory of Corporate Giving;* the *National Data Book of Foundations; New York State Foundations;* and the *Directory of New and Emerging Foundations.* The second database, called "The Foundation Grants Index," contains records of grants to organizations of $5,000 or more. However, it does not list any grants to individuals. For more information on how to access these databases directly through DIALOG, call 415-254-7000, or 800-334-2564. To find out about what other on-line services provide access to DIALOG, or for free help in searching the files, call the On-line Support Staff at the Foundation Center at 212-620-4230.

There's one major drawback to using these database systems: the price. It costs $45 simply to access the database, plus $1.50 *per minute* to search records and 60 cents per minute to display them. So it would be easy to spend $100 on a simple search. My suggestion? Use the directories in the library.

If you do want to pursue this resource, and you are not set up with a computer to search the on-line DIALOG files yourself, you might try going through a third party. Some large libraries and information centers can also access these databases, and so can certain corporate libraries and some of the larger nonprofit organizations. Talk to the reference librarian at your local public or academic library to find out if a database search is available and at what cost.

You may find that your local library does not have access to the Foundation Center's data because the system is so costly. In that case, ask your librarian whether your library can access a system called "Easy Net" or the "GE Network of Information Exchange (GEnie)." Bear in mind that libraries will charge a fee for the service if they do provide it.

The Foundation Center's Associates Program also offers custom DIALOG searches as part of their services. But this too is a costly program, and you are not likely to want to sign up for it as an individual.

To find a library or other third party that could help you gain access to these databases, consult one of the following directories:

- *American Library Directory*, 1995–96. New York: R. R. Bowker, 1995.
- *Directory of Special Libraries*. Vol. 1: *A Guide to Special Libraries, Research Libraries, Information Centers, Archives, and Data Centers*, 17th edition. Detroit: Gale Research Co., 1993.
- *Online Database Search Services Directory*, edited by Martin Connors. 2nd edition. Detroit: Gale Research Co., 1987.

GOING BEYOND THE LISTINGS — CREATIVE RESEARCH

The listings, indexes, and directories are your primary sources of funding prospects, but you don't have to limit yourself to these. Keep your antennae up, keep your funder awareness activated, and try to go beyond the listings.

THINK CREATIVELY

How can you think creatively about funding? Think about the details of your project, brainstorm, make connections. Who is the audience for your project, whom will it affect, who will want to see it succeed?

With a PBS project I worked on, the producer was planning a program that was basically about books but with a real entertainment twist. And so his natural funders were booksellers, publishers, and literacy foundations—people who had a real interest in reaching and developing a reading public. Another wonderful project that reached out to booksellers is Garrison Keillor's American Public Radio show, "American Radio Company." Though the show is not strictly about books, Keillor has done specials on authors like Mark Twain and Willa Cather, and he always includes monologues and radio drama in the show. I am sure that he managed to convince the American Booksellers Association, a regular funder, that people who like to listen to radio stories (just words, not pictures) are also people who like to read books.

Here's another example of thinking creatively about sources that may not appear in any of the listings. Recently, a client of mine got a very large grant from Herb Alpert, whom he happened to know through a social connection. My client runs a private school, and he operates many arts programs in partnership with some of the public schools. As it turned out, Herb Alpert cares about the teaching of music to kids, and had never been approached for a contribution before. Thinking of him was a wonderful leap of the imagination and it resulted in a six-figure grant.

So creativity as well as common sense are certainly important when it comes to identifying possible funding sources. However, a word of caution. Do your traditional library research before making those leaps of imagination. It's your library research that will get the bread buttered; the creative flashes don't come every day.

KEEP UP WITH THE MEDIA

Read newspapers and magazines on a steady basis, especially magazines in your subject area. Keep a clipping file on projects that relate to yours. Even if they don't talk about specific funders directly, they may give you ideas about how to present your own project, creative ways that other people have raised money or reached out for funding. And you will come across some specific names to follow up on.

CONSIDER DIFFERENT TYPES OF AID

Don't limit yourself to going after cash grants. Cash is certainly preferable, but you should also think about in-kind donations of space, equipment, or services. In-kind donations can sometimes mean the difference between being able to do a project or not. Some years ago I raised the entire budget for a PBS documentary on women and the Constitution. The producer—a journalist—had been tearing her hair out trying to raise the money. In the end, a third to half of the budget came from Georgia Public Television, which gave us postproduction editing time, gave us tape, and gave us a lot of equipment and services that we would have had to pay top dollar for. Even though we did raise a fair amount of hard cash, the in-kind donations made it possible for us to get the project under way much sooner than expected, which was essential, since we had to meet a deadline for shooting an event that was crucial to the project. The in-kind services really made the difference and enabled us to do the project.

Don't be discouraged if you find that a corporation you've targeted does not want to give you money. Perhaps it's because their budget is spent, perhaps you are making too small a grant request, or perhaps they just don't choose to fund you at this time. Whatever the reason, they may well consider making an in-kind donation, so it's worth asking about this.

BE A DETECTIVE

Whether by reading newspaper articles or through word of mouth, you may come across the names of individual donors or small private foundations that you think might help you. And you may find it quite a challenge to track them down. They won't be listed in the major directories—and individual donors won't be listed anywhere as such. This part of funding research is like detective work. And like actual detective work (not the TV kind), it will take some real time and persistence digging for leads, trying different angles, sifting through information. You may have to go through newspaper articles, search periodical files on microfiche, talk to a local Chamber of Commerce, or hunt down those 990-PF IRS returns. It's hard work, but it's an adventure at the same time—and in the end you may find the perfect small foundation or donor that the people who stick to the directories will never come across.

What about a funder that you know of but can't find anywhere? I've had that happen, and believe me, it can drive you crazy. There's no rule of thumb about this—you really have to look under every stone. I had a client once who ran an animal shelter organization called Paws. She took in abandoned dogs and then flew them anywhere in the country she could find good homes for them. She had heard of a small foundation in Boston that supported this kind of work, but we couldn't find anything on it. My whole professional research staff couldn't turn anything up. But my client didn't give up; somehow she found out their address, and we finally got a seed grant from them for her project. The moral is: do make the extra effort to track down those difficult leads; it may be well worth your while.

STAY ORGANIZED—RESEARCH YOUR LEADS

Personal contact and word of mouth are wonderful, but don't neglect your homework. Just because someone gives you an inside reference to a foundation board member, don't think you can call them up and ask for money. You still need to collect your hard data—through the directories, a Foundation Center collection, newspaper articles, or a 990-PF. You must get the facts before you determine whether or not this is someone you should send a request for information. Follow the same steps that you would if you first found the source in a listing. Funders are swamped with requests from people who have heard of them, haven't done their homework, and have a project that really isn't appropriate for them. Even if you get a personal reference, make sure the funder is appropriate for you.

By the same token, if you see a tag line in a theater program that says "This production was made possible in part by a grant from the XYZ Foundation," that does not mean *your* theater project will qualify for a grant. Follow your step-by-step research plan. Go to a directory or specialized listing, find out what the foundation does, and decide whether your project fits their interests. If you think it might, write away for guidelines and an annual report. Only by looking at these will you know whether it's worth applying to them.

TALK TO PEOPLE

Never be afraid to ask for further assistance. If your local library does not provide as much information as you would like, and you've looked at the specialized guides but still have questions, go ahead and contact other people. Talk to the experts in your area. If you are an artist, talk to other artists in your community or to your state arts council. Go back and look over the sections in this book on market research, prepare your list of questions, then *get in touch.*

Talk to people in your community: community organizations, church groups, youth groups, anyone you have an affiliation with who might be able to help you. They might even be potential sponsors or funders themselves. But remember, you have to let them know how assisting or sponsoring you will benefit them. Perhaps your project will be good publicity for them, perhaps it will draw in new members and help them extend their outreach. Bear in mind that you are selling a product—even though it happens to be a nonprofit project.

Talk to people who are in fund raising. If you are a scholar or researcher, talk to people in a university development office. Talk to development officers of nonprofit organizations in your community. They may be able to give you some useful ideas about funding and the world of philanthropy. The more you know about this world, the more likely you will find a funder that is right for you.

KEEP EXPLORING

As your fund-raising awareness increases, you'll probably hear about courses, seminars, and workshops that are intended to assist the grant seeker. Some of these might help you, others might not. Unfortunately, aside from the basic orientation to research that the Foundation Center offers, there is not too much available in terms of low-cost general assistance for grant seekers. In fact, reading this book and following the guidelines in it carefully will probably give you as much as most basic courses can.

You may find that some organizations active in your field offer reasonably priced workshops from time to time. You might have to pay from $35 to $50 for an evening workshop, though you usually get a discount if you join the organization. These classes can be helpful. Although they will probably repeat some of the information given here, they will orient you to the standard practices and expectations of funders for your particular field and may direct you toward some specific possible funders. Some of these organizations may offer mini-courses that take place over several days; some may even offer workshops run by the program officers of foundations, who will talk about their programs and tell you how to apply. The best way to find out about such workshops is to seek out organizations in your specific field (see the next section, page 127).

There are also a few established organizations, such as the Grantsmanship Center in Los Angeles, that offer help with fund raising. However, their courses and materials can be quite expensive—and not always helpful, since they are directed toward organizations rather than individuals. Of course, if you have an organization and you want to raise a very substantial amount of money, you might find some of these services useful. You can also contact organizations that promote or support philanthropy and ask if they know of any workshops or assistance programs in your area. Some of these organizations are listed below.

The Grantsmanship Center.   The Grantsmanship Center in Los Angeles holds training programs and workshops in Los Angeles and around the country in grantsmanship, program management, fund raising, proposal writing, and so on. Their courses are quite expensive, $400 and up, and are targeted to nonprofit organizations. This is not an organization that's going to be of much help to individuals.

- The *Grantsmanship Center Whole Nonprofit Catalog* is published seasonally, and contains feature articles about fund raising and nonprofits, as well as information about the Center's programs and other publications. (It also lists various directories and publications that you can order.) The Center will mail this publication at no charge to staff members of nonprofit and government agencies, so if you can't find it at a Foundation

Center collection, ask someone you know at an organization if they would like to get it.

- For further information, contact:
The Grantsmanship Center
1125 W. Sixth Street (5th Floor)
P.O. Box 17220
Los Angeles, CA 90017
- 213-482-9860; Fax 213-482-9863

The Support Centers of America. The Support Center of New York, which is the organization's main office, conducts management workshops for nonprofits in fund raising, human resources, finance, marketing, grant proposal writing, and so on. Again, these are really aimed at organizations and are not very useful for most individuals. However, for smaller organizations their fees are quite reasonable, ranging from $25 to $50. They offer special discounts to Latino organizations. The Support Centers of America is a network of sixteen offices throughout the country that offer similar training programs. See Appendix, page 353, for a complete list of Support Center offices.

- For further information, contact:
The Support Center of New York
305 Seventh Avenue
New York, NY 10001
212-924-6744

The American Association of Fund-Raising Counsel (AAFRC). This is a membership organization of fund-raising professionals that was founded in 1935 to promote philanthropy in the United States. Their mission is "to advance professional and ethical standards in philanthropic fund-raising consulting and promote philanthropy in general." The AAFRC also operates the AAFRC Trust Fund for Philanthropy, which works to advance research and education.

The trust publishes *Giving USA*, an annual report on philanthropy and charitable giving in the United States. It breaks down the sources of contributions in the United States according to individuals, foundations, corporations, and bequests. A second report, the *Giving USA Update*, promotes philanthropy at the undergraduate level with the assistance of the Association of American Colleges (which facilitates seminars and courses).

- For more information, contact:
American Association of Fund-Raising Counsel, and AAFRC
Trust for Philanthropy
25 West 43rd Street
New York, NY 10036
212-354-5799

Other Organizations in the Field of Philanthropy. There are
other organizations in the field that support the work of fund raisers,
nonprofit organizations, and foundation executives, or do research or
educate the public about philanthropy. If you are an individual seeking
a grant, you are probably not going to find these directly relevant to
your grant-seeking activities. Still, it's interesting to know they exist,
and if you are involved with a nonprofit organization, some of them
may be worth contacting. Here is a short list:

- Council on Foundations, 1828 L Street, N.W., Suite 300,
Washington, DC 20036; 202-466-6512. Sponsors meetings for
grantmakers, trustees, officers, and executives to keep abreast
of current trends in the various fields of philanthropy.
- Independent Sector, 1828 L Street, N.W., Suite 1200, Washington, DC 20036; 202-223-8100. Conducts research and ed-
ucates the public about the role of the independent nonprofit
sector and its usefulness to society.
- National Charities Information Bureau, 19 Union Square
West, Sixth Floor, New York, NY 10003; 212-929-6300.
Works to maintain sound standards in the field of philanthropy
and to aid sensible giving through advisory reports to
contributors.
- National Society of Fund Raising Executives, 1101 King
Street, Suite 700, Alexandria, VA 22314; 703-684-0410.
Holds periodic workshops and seminars dealing with all phases
of fund raising.
- Points of Light Foundation (formerly National Volunteer Cen-
ter), 1737 H Street, N.W., Washington, DC 20006; 202-223-
9186. Assists communities and organizations to reinforce, expand, and improve the effectiveness of volunteer activities.

CONTACT ORGANIZATIONS IN YOUR FIELD

Organizations in your subject area are probably the best source of free or low-cost assistance with your fund raising. These are usually nonprofit organizations set up to provide services to individuals in a specific field. Many publish journals or newsletters that announce grant opportunities, and some sponsor workshops and seminars on fund raising. Some organizations will channel grants to individuals, and some may themselves offer grants to individuals.

There are a number of service organizations around—more or less, depending on your area of interest—and their staff or officers will often be happy to offer consulting help, in many cases free of charge. Some will require membership for you to use their services, others will not. Some offer special consulting programs to members that enable you to consult with professionals in the field.

Every so often, an organization will conduct a *funding symposium* in a specific field, with multiple seminars and presentations, open both to individual grant seekers and to representatives from nonprofit organizations. I've gotten some really excellent funding sources through conferences and seminars. Still, you shouldn't feel obligated to attend a symposium just because you hope there'll be a potential funder there; go only if you think you'll get something out of the discussions and presentations.

HOW TO FIND ORGANIZATIONS

The quickest way to find organizations is to ask people in your field. And if you join one organization, or read one newsletter, you'll probably start finding out about others. Organizations are like people— they have their own unique characters, and you'll want to be in touch with those that seem sympathetic. If you join several organizations in a field, you may derive more benefits than from joining just one.

If you're having trouble locating an organization in your subject area or community, consult one of the following references, which are available in many libraries:

- *Encyclopedia of Associations*, edited by Deborah Burek, Vols. 1–3. Detroit: Gale Research Co., 1993. These reference books list 22,000 national and international organizations you may be able to affiliate with, covering nearly every conceivable interest area.

- *National Directory of Nonprofit Organizations.* Rockville, MD: The Taft Group, 1996. This directory lists 257,000 nonprofit organizations in the United States with annual revenues of $25,000–$99,000.

MAJOR NATIONAL ORGANIZATIONS AND PUBLICATIONS

You can also contact one of the major national organizations in your field. Many are open to individual members throughout the country, and they can refer you to regional or local organizations they are affiliated with. Here is a partial list:

THE ARTS

American Council for the Arts, 1 East 53rd Street, New York, NY 10022; 212-223-2787.

Art Information Center, 280 Broadway, Suite 412, New York, NY 10007; 212-227-0282.

Business Committee for the Arts, 1775 Broadway, Suite 510, New York, NY 10019; 212-664-0600.

BUSINESS

American Business Association, 292 Madison Avenue, New York, NY 10017; 212-949-5900.

National Association for the Self-Employed, 2121 Precinct Lion Road, Hurst, TX 76054; 800-232-6273.

National Business Association, 5151 Beltline Road, Suite 1150, Dallas, TX 75240; 214-458-0900.

EDUCATION

American Council on Education, One Dupont Circle, N.W., Suite 800, Washington, DC 20036; 202-939-9300.

Council for Advancement and Support of Education, 11 Dupont Circle, N.W., Washington, DC 20036; 202-328-5900.

Council for Aid to Education, 342 Madison Avenue, Suite 1532, New York, NY 10173; 212-661-5800.

National Association of Independent Schools, 1620 L Street, N.W., Suite 1100, Washington, DC 20036; 202-973-9700.

ENVIRONMENT

Americans for the Environment, 1400 16th Street, N.W., Washington, DC 20036; 202-797-6665.

HEALTH

Association for Healthcare Philanthropy (formerly National Association for Hospital Development), 313 Park Avenue, Suite 400, Falls Church, VA 22046; 703-532-6243.

National Health Council, 1730 M Street, N.W., Suite 500, Washington, DC 20036; 202-785-3910.

HUMANITIES

American Council of Learned Societies, 228 East 45th Street (16th Floor), New York, NY 10017; 212-697-1505.

Council for International Exchange of Scholars, 3007 Tilden Street, N.W., Suite 5M, Washington, DC 20008-3009; 202-686-4000.

National Humanities Center, 7 Alexander Drive, P.O. Box 12256, Research Triangle Park, NC 27709; 919-549-0661.

MINORITIES

National Association of Minority Women in Business, 906 Grand Avenue, Suite 200, Kansas City, MO 64106; 816-421-3335.

RELIGION

Global Congress of the World's Religions, 10 Dock Road, Barrytown, NY 12507; 914-758-6881.

The Interchurch Center, 475 Riverside Drive, Room 253, New York, NY 10115; 212-870-2931.

SCIENCE

National Research Council, 2101 Constitution Avenue, N.W., Washington, DC 20418; 202-334-3000.

SENIOR CITIZENS

American Association of Retired Persons, 601 E Street, N.W., Washington, DC 20049; 202-434-2277.

TRAVEL

Academic Travel Abroad, 3210 Grace Street, N.W., Washington, DC 20007; 202-333-3355.

Council on International Educational Exchange, 205 East 42nd Street, New York, NY 10017; 212-661-1414.

WOMEN
Ms. Foundation for Women, 141 Fifth Avenue, Suite 6-S, New York, NY 10010; 212-353-8580.

Honing the Prospect List—Getting Ready to Act

You've done your research, you've dug through those directories and files, you've written away to a list of potential funders. Now you are beginning to receive responses—your mailbox is jammed with envelopes from foundations—and you're starting to look through the guidelines and annual reports. This is an exciting moment: holding those guidelines in your hands starts to make this venture seem more real. You're at the point of making up your actual prospect list.

How to Evaluate Material for Your Prospect List

Once you receive the guidelines and reports you've requested, you can start to make final judgments about whether you should continue to target each funder and take the next step—actually send in a proposal. As you look through the material, you may find limitations or other factors that didn't appear in the directories or come up in your initial research. Sometimes, the new information may seem to rule out your project or suggest that a funder is not really for you. Don't get carried away by a glossy brochure, or by a letter addressed to you. If, after looking at the material, you're not convinced this is a potential funder, put it aside. This is the last stage of your research, and you need to be as careful here as you were in the beginning. Don't waste your time and theirs by applying to an inappropriate funder.

But if the potential funder still does seem appropriate, keep it on your prospect list; these are the funders that you are actually going to send proposals to.

What if you've read all of a funder's material and you still have a question about how to interpret the guidelines and whether your project fits? Should you contact the program officer for clarification? First, see if you can't possibly answer the question for yourself. If it's a matter of definition of terms, or interpretation, look up the item in this book or in one of the library references. Ask someone at an organization you've been in touch with, or someone you know who has applied for grants before. You do want to avoid bothering overworked program officers if you can, and you certainly don't want to convey the impression that you haven't done your homework or read the material carefully. If you still can't figure it out, and it's a larger foundation or a government agency, go ahead and contact the funder. Talk to the receptionist or the program officer, explain that you've read their guidelines but are still left with questions. If it's a smaller foundation, don't call. Write a brief note that clearly states your question, and ask for a short reply. Give your phone number and address, and let them respond to you.

FEED THE NEW INFORMATION INTO YOUR GRANT-SEEKING PLAN

There are two other ways you can use the information you've gathered by now, in addition to building your prospect list. First, look at the grant amounts that are available. If you need to raise quite a bit of money, and you see that only one or two or maybe none of your prospects can fund your whole project, you will realize right away that you can't rely on getting just one grant. Know from the start that you'll have to raise money from several sources and build this into your grant-seeking plan and project outline. There is no reason to conceal this fact from any potential funder; they like to see their money matched by other funders.

Second, take a close look at the funding deadlines and the notification times for grant awards. Some funders will notify you fairly quickly—within three to ten weeks—if you've gotten a grant. Others—including some government agencies—may take up to six months from submission of the application to notification of recipients. If your project requires you to act by certain key deadlines, you will have to take these long processing times into account.

WHAT ARE YOUR CHANCES FOR GETTING FUNDED?

It's going to be next to impossible to determine just what your chances of getting funded are. There are too many variables—the funder's current budget, shifting interests, proposals still under consideration from a previous grant cycle, other proposals that have come in. The best way to think about this is simply to prepare the best possible proposal package for those funders that seem likely, and take your best shot.

DO YOU NEED TO KNOW SOMEONE?

You don't really need to know who makes the funding decision—whether it's a board, a single program officer, or a panel. And it doesn't matter as much as you think if you know someone on the Board of Directors or Trustees. I've had quite close friendships with some board members and decision makers and still haven't gotten all my proposals put through. These are responsible people, people with integrity, and if they're doing their jobs as they should, they will make their own well-considered judgments about what projects they are going to fund. They will choose the ones they feel best serve the mission of their foundation.

WHAT ABOUT THE COMPETITION?

Usually you will have no way of knowing how much competition there is for funds. Sometimes you can get a rough idea—if you're applying to a program that tells you how many applications it received for the last grant cycle, and how many of these it funded. Still, competition is never a reason to eliminate a funder from your prospect list. You should only do this if the guidelines or limitations clearly rule your project out. So if you do fit a funder's guidelines and interests, give it your best shot. There is only one surefire way to increase the odds in your favor: apply to every good potential funder on your list, and don't rule any out because you're afraid of the competition.

IF YOU HAVE A HOT PROSPECT

You may, in the course of your research, come across a potential funder that really seems likely for you. Maybe someone has referred you, or you've spoken to a program officer who seems very excited by your project. Maybe someone has even indicated that they would like to fund you. Should you stop pursuing other prospects? Not a good idea. Keep putting your prospect list together and considering other potential funders. Never put all your eggs in one basket, and never stop your grant seeking unless you have a definitive yes and a written commitment. You can lose not only time but credibility as well. Funders like to see that you aren't waiting for them, that you are pursuing other prospects. It shows that you aren't taking them for granted, that you're serious, that you're determined to get this project done no matter what.

Should You Do a Mass Mailing?

Absolutely never. Funding officers get really annoyed when they receive mass mailings. It suggests that you haven't done your research properly. They get all too many proposals that have nothing to do with their programs, or their missions. No matter what works in the world of direct-mail marketing, this is not an effective way to raise grant money. Do not send out a mailing based on the idea that you need only one or two funders to respond.

Second, don't even do a general mailing to your prospect list. You will end up creating the same impression—that you haven't done your homework—and will alienate the very funders that are best for you. Instead, you will need to tailor your proposal and application carefully to each funder.

Prepare Targeted Proposals

What you *can* do now is start planning your proposals. Build your proposal timeline, put up a wall chart with information on your likeliest prospects. Do any further market research that needs doing on the project, now that you know very specifically who your targeted prospects are. Gather your supporting materials and endorsements. If you're planning on working through a sponsor, be sure to read Chapter 4 of this book carefully. If you're specifically targeting private foundations, government agencies, corporate funders, or individual donors, be sure to read Chapters 5 through 8 on these funder types. And when you are ready to start working on your proposal, turn to Chapter 9.

4

YOU DON'T HAVE TO GO IT ALONE: WORKING WITH A SPONSOR

If the truth be told, the majority of grant-making foundations do not give grants directly to individual applicants. Instead, they award grant monies to nonprofit organizations, which, in turn, provide individuals with grants. This is what I call "flow-through" funding—it is indirect in that the money originates with a grant-making foundation, passes through a nonprofit organization, and ends up in the hands of individuals. It may be that the individual targeted the foundation with the help of the nonprofit organization. Or the original funder may have set up a "regrant program" and given funds to a local or regional organization, which then conducted its own grant-making operation to give money to individuals. Call it the trickle-down theory of grant making.

So how do you position yourself at the receiving end of this cash flow? You have two options: create your own nonprofit organization and seek incorporation and federal tax-exempt status; or establish a sponsor relationship with an organization that already has these things going for it. Let's examine the sponsor arrangement first.

THE IDEA BEHIND SPONSORSHIP

There are several different terms for the sponsorship arrangement— "institutional affiliation," "organizational sponsorship," "fiscal sponsorship," "fiscal adoption." They all mean essentially the same thing. Although there are various forms of sponsorship (each of which will be discussed later in this chapter), the basic idea is that an individual and an organization get together in order to raise funds for the individual's project. This mutually beneficial (and primarily financial) relationship usually lasts for the duration of the project's life, whether that is one month or ten years.

WHY AFFILIATE?

Why should you bother to affiliate with a sponsor organization? The most obvious reason is to give yourself access to funding sources that do not award monies directly to individuals. If you can raise all the funds you need for your project with grants made directly to you, then you probably don't need a sponsor.

But there are other, less obvious reasons for institutional affiliation. Your project may require special equipment, laboratory facilities, or trained support personnel. In such a case, a sponsor organization (ideally a university or research institute) may be willing to provide you with access to its own facilities and staff. This is usually a much more efficient arrangement than trying to purchase expensive equipment and hire qualified staff members yourself.

One more reason for lining up a sponsor is that in the eyes of potential funders, the involvement and approval of an established organization lend credibility to your case. The fact that you have gotten a sponsor to agree to work with you means that others in your field think your idea is a good one.

This is especially valuable if your project is highly technical or on the cutting edge of your field. If you have an innovative, breakthrough idea, some funders may mistrust or fail to understand it, and will be unwilling to award grant money for it. But the same doubtful, uncomprehending funders will often respond favorably to the recommendations of established experts in relevant fields. And that is what a well-chosen sponsor organization can do: shift funders' dollars in your direction by giving your project an official stamp of approval.

THE SPONSOR'S SIDE

However, affiliation is not a one-way street. You're not going to reap all the benefits while the sponsor does all the work. This is a business relationship. The sponsor organization has its own reasons for allowing you to affiliate. To begin with, your project must serve the sponsor's overall purpose or mission. The sponsor is a nonprofit organization with specific goals; in an ideal individual/sponsor match, your project will help the sponsor meet those goals.

Along the same lines, the success of your project will bring the sponsor increased prestige. The sponsor thus achieves its own share of success through the association. A proud sponsor may boast of its support of your project in board meetings, annual reports, and media publications.

Further, your own quest for funding may bring your sponsor to the attention of previously untapped funding sources. This can be a strong motivating factor for the sponsor organization. The nature of your project, and the sponsor's support of it, may make the sponsor itself more attractive to foundations. In other words, you and your project may serve as a kind of magnet to attract new funders to your nonprofit sponsor.

As part of this business relationship, most nonprofit organizations that serve as sponsors will expect a small percentage of your grant money. This is a reasonable expectation; helping you prepare grant applications and providing support services during the course of your work can cause the sponsor to incur some additional administrative costs. Giving the sponsor a small share of your award helps defray their expenses.

WHY FUNDERS LIKE ORGANIZATIONS

So there are many ways in which institutional affiliation is good for you and good for the sponsor organization. What benefit does it offer the funder? Why are some foundations unwilling to award grants to individuals, yet eager to fund nonprofit organizations for the very same projects?

It stems in part from a congressional amendment in 1969 to the U.S. Tax Code, Section 4945, which set up the ground rules that private foundations must follow. The basic intent of the law was to ensure against arbitrary, whimsical, or personally motivated grants and to guard against people setting up self-serving foundations to give money to their relatives. The IRS code required that foundations must obtain reports at least annually from those they give grants to, and they quickly found that it was much easier to do the necessary monitoring and paperwork when they were giving to organizations than when dealing with individuals. So it became the general practice for foundations to deal only with organizations, simply in order to avoid headaches with recordkeeping and reporting.

Besides the recordkeeping issue, working with organizations is more efficient for many foundations. For a large foundation giving away millions of dollars, it would be an administrative nightmare to try to evaluate a flood of individual applications. And a small foundation may find that it simply costs too much to dole out the money in many small increments. Remember, this is business. It requires less administrative staff time to give a few large awards to nonprofit organizations, which can then turn around and share the wealth with individual grant seekers. By structuring their giving in this way, the foundations pass the administrative costs and some of the responsibility (along with the money) down to the nonprofit grant recipients.

I mention responsibility because there is a bit of risk involved. The individual grant recipient may abscond with the money and never actually begin his or her proposed project (it's been known to happen). An individual artist may use grant funds to create a sculpture that someone considers obscene. By funding the nonprofit sponsor rather than the individual, the grantmaking foundation protects itself from direct association with such problems.

But the foundation's reasons for preferring the sponsor arrangement are not all so selfish. More than anything, the foundation wants the projects it funds to be successful. In some cases, the involvement of a sponsor organization can improve a project's chances for success. For example, if your project requires specialized equipment, trained support personnel, or built-in technical evaluation processes, that project has a better chance for success if you have access to a sponsor's existing facilities. So especially when considering highly technical or scientific projects, foundations are predisposed toward funding nonprofit sponsors, which can provide adequate resources for the completion of the project.

TYPES OF AFFILIATION

There are several forms of fiscal sponsorship. I discuss them here in terms of levels of involvement. The greater the level of a sponsor's involvement, the more control it has over your access to the grant money and even the course of the project itself. I recommend that you seek a sponsorship arrangement that gives you the minimum level of affiliation necessary for you to obtain adequate funding. Retain as much control over your work as possible.

The Basic Fiscal Sponsor.   At the low end of the affiliation spectrum is the individual working alone. If you are an artist, a researcher, an inventor, or a traveling scholar, you might use a nonprofit organization simply as a "conduit" to funnel grant money to you. You are essentially doing the project by yourself, and the organization you are affiliated with simply handles the money for you. For example, you are doing graduate work and a funder gives money to your university, which applies it to tuition fees and perhaps gives you a check for living expenses.

Umbrella Organizations.   The next level of affiliation is umbrella sponsorship, which is well suited to short-term, seasonal, or one-time projects. This level of active, but not meddlesome, participation on the sponsor's part is often appropriate for educational projects, festivals, art shows, or theatrical performances. You conduct your project fairly independently, but the umbrella organization may handle things like bookkeeping and assist with publicity.

Institutional Sponsorship.   This is a long-term arrangement requiring give and take on both sides. The sponsor gives you use of the resources you need, and in return you give the sponsor some degree of management power and a greater role in the project itself. This level of affiliation is appropriate for a scientist needing a laboratory, a researcher needing access to materials, or a television producer needing studio facilities and broadcast distribution.

Employment.   The highest level of involvement is direct employment by the sponsor organization. This requires a surrender of autonomy, but the rewards are regular deposits into your bank account.

How the Different Types of Sponsorship Work

Sponsorship arrangements can be set up in many different ways. You might work with an umbrella organization that exerts a high degree of control over your project, or through an institutional affiliation that is rather loose.

Basic Fiscal Sponsorship—The Individual Working Alone

If your project truly is an individual pursuit, you should investigate sources of individual grant funding first. If you find you need additional support, however, then institutional affiliation may help you. Affiliating yourself—even loosely—with an educational institution or fellowship program can open up new funding opportunities as well as give you access to research facilities, libraries, rare-book holdings, special collections, and so on that can prove useful once you get started.

How It Works.   Look into forming a loose affiliation with a university, fellowship program, research institution, or other nonprofit organization appropriate to your needs. What you want is an organization willing to serve as a simple conduit for funding. You apply for funding through the organization and include a nominal administrative fee in your budget. Many universities and fellowship programs allow you nearly complete autonomy; they hand the grant check over to you and require only occasional reports on progress. Often, they even provide you with letters of introduction, giving you access to facilities that are off-limits to the general public. Another possibility is an existing "re-grant program" through a local service organization. Many arts and cultural organizations offer support to individuals by channeling money from a government agency or large foundation. If you find such a program, you apply for funds from the local organization.

Even with this loosest form of affiliation, you might benefit from some form of written agreement with your sponsor, addressing how the grant money will be handled and putting a time limit on the sponsor's involvement. In cases of established fellowship programs, you should clarify with the fellowship committee or representative just what is expected of you in the way of follow-up and financial recordkeeping.

The Fund-Raising Approach.   Once you have established a relationship with a sponsor organization, meet with that organization's fund-raising staff to discuss the financial requirements of your project and work out a grant-seeking strategy. Depending on the organization, you may be responsible for creating your proposal package, or the organization's staff may draw up the proposal for you. You may be responsible for researching potential funding sources, though the organization's staff may also give you some guidance here. In any case, you will be applying for project-specific funding through the sponsor's general fund-raising apparatus. This is because funding sources (those that do not fund individuals) require some hefty paperwork from the nonprofit organization that is submitting the application for you. At the very least they will want the IRS certification of tax-exempt status and audited financial statements—probably more.

When grant money is awarded for your project, the funder makes out a check to the sponsor organization. The sponsor at this point becomes your "fiscal agent" and will distribute the money to you, either as a lump sum or in installments. This fiscal agent may also keep track of your expenses, for eventual reports to the foundation granting the money. However, this is the extent of the sponsor's involvement. With this loose type of affiliation, the organization serves as a sponsor "in name only," exerting no control over your project itself. Bear in mind that it is still important for you to keep good records of your expenditures. This is not your money; it is public or private money that is given to you for a project, and you may be asked to account for it.

SPONSORSHIP BY AN UMBRELLA ORGANIZATION

An umbrella sponsor is a nonprofit organization that acts as your sponsor only for the duration of your project. This type of sponsorship is strictly short-term; it is most appropriate for seasonal or one-time projects, such as film productions, summer art fairs, theater festivals, or educational workshops. Projects that do involve some kind of community outreach require or benefit from an umbrella sponsor. If you want to do something in the community, such as setting up video workshops for young people, the very fact that a community group offers you space and assistance will strengthen your proposal and lend credibility to your project.

Any nonprofit organization can serve as an umbrella sponsor for fund-raising purposes, but it is best to choose a sponsor with federal tax-exempt status. Local groups such as church and school groups, arts councils, self-help groups, nonprofit clubs, and community organizations are ideal, especially if your own project is local in scope or promises to have some local impact.

How It Works. The umbrella organization is more actively involved in your project than a basic fiscal sponsor and may assist you in outreach to the community and presentation of your work. They will want to work closely with you and may have some requirements of their own concerning management or direction. The relationship with the umbrella organization can take many forms, depending on their interests and the nature of your project.

In establishing that relationship, be sure to discuss all aspects of the arrangement up front. You and the sponsor should both state your expectations. Will you work on the sponsor's premises or your own? Will you have use of the sponsor's administrative staff and equipment? Will you have to make regular progress reports? Who is responsible for purchasing your supplies? Who will keep track of your project-related expenses? How is the money to be handled—is it to be given over to you in a lump sum or doled out as your work requires? What is the time limit on your financial relationship with the sponsor? What is the percentage of grant received or the amount due to the organization for administrative costs? Who is to have final artistic and administrative control? Who will own the finished work, if there is one? Will you or the sponsor have the option to renew or continue the project after the initial period?

All these details should be spelled out on paper, and it's a good idea to have an attorney draw up or review a contractual agreement. Both you and the sponsor should sign it and keep copies. This sounds like a lot of trouble, but stating your expectations up front can save you many headaches later on, and it is well worth the money to have an attorney look over your agreement. Remember, the umbrella organization is going to be receiving and handling the money for your project. You want to be as careful about this arrangement on your end as they are on theirs.

A few organizations that do re-granting may already have sponsorship guidelines, but most don't, or will be new to this, so you will still need to draw up an agreement in letter form. If the nonprofit organization has done this before (or even if they haven't), you can ask them to draw the letter up, but I do believe it is a good idea to have someone else look at it. You don't necessarily have to have an attorney draft the entire agreement, but you should have one review it and make comments. The more complex the project and the greater the sponsor's involvement, the more input you need from an attorney. If you are going to be using an organization's facilities and staff, if an original product will be produced, if ownership or use of a project name is involved—these circumstances all call for careful thinking. You'll want to establish how much freedom you are to have in directing your project, and just how much control or oversight the organization will have. Try to find an attorney who has some experience with nonprofit organizations, or in your own field.

- **TIP:** Call some of the law firms in your area, and ask if any of the partners do volunteer or pro bono work for nonprofit organizations. If you are working in the arts or a cultural area, contact the following organization, which offers free, arts-related legal assistance to those who can't afford private counsel and keeps lists of attorneys and volunteer groups around the country that do the same:
  Volunteer Lawyers for the Arts
  1 East 53rd Street (6th Floor)
  New York, NY 10022
  212-319-2787

Remember, you should have a comfortable, cooperative relationship with your sponsor. Don't let the process of putting the details down on paper throw you off. If certain things, such as the project start-up and ending dates, cannot be pinpointed, just make an estimate. Use the process to improve your communications with the sponsor; you both may find that creative ideas come out of it. Ultimately, your positive relationship with other individuals on the staff of the organization is what is going to make the sponsorship work and render your project successful.

The Fund-Raising Approach. To do successful fund raising, you'll need to make a cooperative effort with the organization's staff. You should meet to determine who will be responsible for creating the proposal package, and for researching potential funding sources. As with basic sponsorship, the proposal or application packages will be sent out from the sponsor's offices, since they have to enclose quite a bit of supportive paperwork.

Once you've received a grant, the sponsor takes on the role of fiscal agent. It's worth noting that an umbrella organization may take a more active role in administering funds, asserting more discretion and control over your use of the grant monies. You may have to justify and keep receipts for each project-related expenditure; you may also have to prove that all grant funds were spent only on the budget items for which they were intended.

So, it is very important, as always, to keep good financial records. When a nonprofit organization allocates funds to your project, they are taking on a fiscal responsibility and liability to both the original funder and the IRS. You want to be able to back them up, just as you would for your own tax return, and to provide receipts in order to prove how money was spent. And as your success reflects directly on the reputation of the umbrella sponsor, you may be under some pressure to keep the sponsor involved in and informed about your work.

INSTITUTIONAL SPONSORSHIP

When you have a long-term project, or one that requires a great deal of support in terms of staff or facilities, you might consider an institutional sponsor. As we have seen, working with an institutional sponsor means prolonged involvement and, often, some type of institutional management or control over your project. In return, you may benefit from the use of the sponsor's laboratory or studio facilities, special equipment, technical expertise, administrative services, and trained support staff.

If your idea is controversial or just brand new, your chances of funding will increase greatly if you apply through an institutional sponsor. Funders tend to look more favorably upon projects backed by established institutions; the sponsor's track record makes your project seem feasible. Funders are not usually in a position to evaluate controversial ideas within a field; they'll rely on the judgment of an institution.

Also, if your project is going to require high-tech, expensive equipment, special facilities, powerful computers, or the like, institutional sponsorship strengthens your position with funders. Funders want to know that you have access to the resources you will need to carry out your project.

And if you anticipate that your project will have significant community impact (for example, you might want to create a shelter for battered women), your funding position will be strengthened by an affiliation with a local community agency (in this case, a women's health organization or a family violence agency).

When you are looking for an institutional sponsor, you can go to some of the same nonprofit organizations that might serve as umbrella sponsors. You can also look to institutions that don't normally channel funds to individuals, and to larger national organizations, since your project may not be only locally based. Institutional sponsors include schools and universities, research institutions, professional societies, historical societies, art associations, museums, hospitals, health agencies, performing arts groups, sports clubs, community foundations, unions, veterans groups, civic leagues, Chambers of Commerce, and churches and religious groups.

How It Works.   When you do your project with an institutional sponsor, you will be in constant communication about your activities, accomplishments, and financial status. Your project begins to resemble a program of the institution itself. In fact, this is a good way to think about this kind of sponsorship: you are essentially proposing to the institution a new program, which you will manage, as part of their overall activities. Expect to be making regular progress reports.

A clear written agreement is even more important with an institutional sponsor than with an umbrella organization. You need to create and sign an agreement detailing all aspects of the arrangement. This is not so much a sign of suspicion on anyone's part as an exercise in discovering and acknowledging your mutual expectations. It allows you and the sponsor to establish the ground rules for your long-term relationship.

You may not want to specify a time period for this relationship, as you are hoping to fund a long-term project. In fact, your arrangement may be permanent. But there are other issues that should be addressed and agreed upon now. Will you work on the sponsor's premises or your own? Will you have unlimited access to the sponsor's facilities and equipment? Will you have use of the sponsor's support staff and resources? Will the sponsor have any control over the progress of your work? Will the sponsor claim joint ownership of any invention/discovery you make during the course of your affiliation? Will the sponsor take responsibility for financial recordkeeping, or is that up to you? (Many foundations and government agencies require detailed records of how their grant money is spent, especially those that disallow funding for administrative salaries.) The most basic issue to settle is whether the sponsor organization will act as your fiscal agent, giving you relative autonomy while ensuring your appropriate use of grant funds, or whether it will adopt you, taking legal control over your finances and your work. Either arrangement is possible on a temporary or permanent basis.

The question of ownership may be one that you want to look at closely. Many institutions assert ownership over products and inventions that are developed under their auspices. Some will even claim copyrights of articles and material that are written with their support. If you start a project and at some point want to stop working with an institution, they may wish to carry on with your project under its original name. At the same time, if you have your own patent, copyright, or trademark as you go into a project, it's unlikely that an institution will try to take it over. Nonprofit institutions are not in business to rip off ideas, although they do like to find new sources of income to support their activities. Many kinds of relationships are possible with different institutions; you simply need to work things out based on what the institution is offering you and what you are bringing to them. Make sure you spell everything out clearly in a written agreement and have a lawyer who is familiar with the issues look it over and advise you.

If you are entering into a long-term association with an institution, keep in mind that officers or staff may change. If a new person comes in, the tone and interests of the institution can change. New officers may have a different level of enthusiasm about your project, or wish to move the institution in new directions. Even though it's an institution and you have a concrete project, everything is based on the relationships and interests of individuals. This is another thing that you will need to consider when structuring a letter of agreement, and another reason to make sure everything is crystal clear.

The Fund-Raising Approach.   In an institutional sponsorship arrangement, the sponsor organization will probably want to be actively involved in the grant-seeking process. In fact, your project may be included in a larger, more comprehensive funding proposal for the institution as a whole. In this case, you would be responsible for supplying project-specific support material (a brief project description, biographies of the personnel involved, budget figures, etc.) for the larger proposal. If the grant-seeking process includes interviews with foundation representatives (as is often the case when large sums of money are being requested), you might be asked to participate in a discussion of your project. Be as cooperative as possible. Remember, you are in this for the long haul.

Once the money is awarded, you will either have relative freedom to pursue your project (if the sponsor simply acts as your fiscal agent), or your work will be closely watched and perhaps influenced (if you are adopted by your sponsor). If your project is being funded as part of a larger institutional grant, you may have to rely on appropriations from the institutional operating budget.

DIRECT EMPLOYMENT BY THE SPONSOR ORGANIZATION

When you go to work for a sponsoring organization, you are trading off some degree of autonomy for the institutional support and a steady paycheck. If this idea appeals to you, look for a creative environment for the work you want to do. Ideally, you can get a job at an institution already receiving grant funding, so that you are the indirect (and immediate) recipient of grant monies.

If you become an employee, there's still quite a wide range of possible involvement. At best, you might be paid to work on your project in an organization's office, or theater, or laboratory. You might also have to become a part-time fund raiser for the organization, helping to raise money for their other projects in order to get your own project off the ground. You don't have to consider the job a permanent one—there is quite a bit of turnover in some of these organizations, and sometimes people work at a nonprofit for a while, build up experience and connections, then move on to other projects. You might also consider working for a nonprofit on a consultant basis rather than as a full-time employee. You could try to get yourself hired to do a specific project—running poetry workshops in the schools, setting up a research lab for a university, and so on.

There are some potential drawbacks to the employee relationship. There's the issue of autonomy—how much control the organization will want to exercise over your work. It is likely that you will have responsibilities in addition to working on your own project. There's always the possibility of getting so caught up in other activities or projects that you are deflected from the work you want to do. You should weigh your eagerness to get your project done right away—maybe you can afford to proceed at a more leisurely pace as a nonprofit employee. You do want to make sure that you are going to work for an organization that is closely enough involved with the kind of work you want to do that you won't be permanently deflected. If you want to produce theater, for instance, you should work for an organization that does productions, or would like to, not an organization that only does research or provides information services.

The potential advantages, besides the steady paycheck, are several. For one thing, you will have easy access to and comfortable use of the facilities, because you are a part of the organization. You will also— and I think this is very important—enjoy the camaraderie and inter- action with other professionals in your field. There is a great deal to be gained from this kind of day-to-day experience. And of course, it is a good way to establish credibility in your field. Funders will now consider you a professional.

Getting Hired, Getting Paid.   If you have limited nonprofit ex- perience, you will probably find that you have a better chance with a local, grass-roots organization. They will probably be more interested in hiring you if you can offer them services that they may not have other means of fulfilling. Perhaps they don't have a fund raiser, and you can offer to help with their other projects. Perhaps you have a particular idea for an outreach program that fits with their mission. If they like the idea and see that you have the expertise and passion to do it, they might be willing to hire you.

Now the catch is money. Often if you propose to work for a nonprofit organization on a project that they are really interested in, they will ask you to find the funding in order to pay your salary. They may have all kinds of institutional support they're happy to offer you, but no money in their budget for your salary. If you are going to have to raise the funds to pay your own salary, do think through the reasons you want to affiliate with the organization, and whether this still seems to have advantages over working independently.

If you are interested in pursuing the possibility of working directly for a nonprofit, see the references below for some books that may offer you guidance.

- *Careers for Dreamers and Doers: A Guide to Management Careers in the Nonprofit Sector,* by Lilly Cohen and Dennis R. Young. New York: The Foundation Center, 1989.
- *Internships: On-the-Job Training Opportunities for All Types of Careers,* by Kathy Jobst. Cincinnati: Writer's Digest Books.
- *What Color Is Your Parachute?,* by Richard Nelson Bolles.

How It Works.   Here again, you may need a contractual agree- ment. Many nonprofit organizations do offer contracts to their regular staff members. If you are going to work on a temporary, project-related basis, it's still important to spell things out in writing. If, for example, you will be working as an artist-in-residence for a nonprofit theater, you should lay down some ground rules as to what is expected of you during your tenure. This might take the form of an employment contract. Perhaps you will be required to direct one show during the course of the season. For the rest of your tenure (the remainder of the six-show season, let's say), you have an office, a computer, free access to the theater's support staff and resources, and unstructured time for the pursuit of your own project—writing a new play. In exchange for its generosity, the theater might want right of first refusal on the premiere production of your play.

If you and the theater can agree on the terms, then by all means draw up a formal agreement and sign it. Have a lawyer create the agreement or at least read over any standard agreement that the theater offers.

Do consider what could happen to programs you've been involved with if you should leave the organization. It's possible that the organization may want to keep using your idea or the names of your programs. After all, they have made an investment in these programs. Anything is possible; it all depends on the written agreement.

The Fund-Raising Approach. If you have the best of all possible arrangements, the organization is hiring you to do a project under their auspices, and already has funds, or will handle the fund raising. If you are coming to them with a new project, they may expect greater involvement. If the organization already has a development officer or a fund-raising staff, your involvement may be similar to independent affiliation with an institution or umbrella organization. You may be expected to do some funding research, write the basic draft of your proposal, and provide a budget and some supporting materials, while the staff prepares the additional paperwork.

If you are really coming in on the ground level, there is no development staff, and the organization is looking to you for some basic fund-raising assistance, you have your work cut out for you. In fact, you are almost in the position of someone operating their own nonprofit organization, except that the basic organization already exists. You are going to have to get familiar with a lot of bureaucratic details, and work closely with the secretary and treasurer or bookkeeper to come up with the various documents, budgets, and financial reports required by the IRS and by funders. If no one on the staff is familiar with all the procedures, you could ask the organization to send you to one of the seminars conducted by the Grantsmanship Center or the Support Centers of America (see pages 124 and 125). There are also some useful references available on management and fund raising for non-profits (see page 160).

HOW TO FIND A SPONSOR

When you have figured out which level of affiliation best suits you and your project, it's time to pinpoint those organizations you want to approach. Where do you look for names of potential sponsors? How do you even get started?

The best starting point is your own clubs, societies, and other affiliations. Think about all the organizations in which you are involved. Are any of these groups appropriate for sponsoring your project?

What about your friends' clubs and organizations? Ask around about their personal connections. There's nothing like a close friend's recommendation to get you in the door for sponsorship affiliation.

Research local nonprofit groups. If you've been doing market research in your field, you probably know of some of these already. Ask the organizations you know about for references to others in the field. To search further, see if your public library has a directory of local nonprofit groups in its reference collection. Larger, broad-based non-profits, such as the United Way, may be able to direct you to organizations whose goals and interests are in line with your own.

Also check into citywide, consortium-type associations, such as arts councils, if they are appropriate for your project. Your local Chamber of Commerce may be able to give you some leads in this area.

On a wider geographical scale, investigate national or regional organizations in your field. Look at the listings in Chapter 3 and in the Appendix, page 326, for some of the major ones; local professionals in your field may be able to refer you to others. A comprehensive list of national associations (arranged by subject) can be found in the *Encyclopedia of Associations*, a multivolume reference work available at most public libraries.

You can contact some of the major national organizations in your field to ask for references to similar local or regional groups. You will find a partial listing of these in Chapter 3, and a more complete listing in the Appendix, page 326.

At each step of your search, be sure to ask for referrals to other organizations that might serve as sponsors. Word of mouth is a powerful tool in nonprofit circles.

CHOOSING THE RIGHT SPONSOR

Begin by making an exhaustive list of potential organizations. As we saw in the section above, the best ways to create this list are through brainstorming and research. Think creatively. During this initial step, you will want to give yourself room to explore every possibility. Don't rule anything out yet; write it all down. You will thin out your list soon enough.

The second step is to evaluate the organizations on your list in order to determine just how helpful an affiliation with a specific organization would be in your search for funding. To make such an evaluation, you'll probably have to do a little research into each organization on your list, and we'll discuss ways to do this. First, however, let's consider the specific things you need to know about each sponsor:

1. Is the potential sponsor organization a nonprofit that is incorporated and designated as federally tax-exempt by the IRS? If the IRS considers it a bona fide tax-exempt organization, it will designate it as a charitable organization under Section 501(c)3 of the Internal Revenue Code. This arcane grouping of figures and letters may seem absurdly technical, but it's all-important for nonprofits. You'll hear nonprofit people freely talking about whether this or that organization has "501(c)3 status." If so, the organization is eligible to receive restricted foundation funding, and an affiliation would give you access to a new tier of funders; 501(c)3 status also means that individual donors can claim a tax deduction by contributing to your project through the organization. If the organization does not conform to this description, cross it off your list. You are best served by a sponsor that can lead you to new funding sources.

   You really do have to be a stickler about this. Not all nonprofit associations will have the tax-exempt status; although a community orchestra or a sports club probably will, a bird watchers' club probably won't. You *must* go through an organization that has a 501(c)3 tax-exempt status. Not a (c)4, not a (c)9, but a (c)3—this is essential. Even if an organization has applied for the tax-exempt status and the application is pending, they don't have a history of funding, so they're really in the same boat as you and probably could not offer you much more than you could get on your own. Most important, they will not be able to receive funds until their tax status is established. So don't waste your time. *Only go to an organization that has a 501(c)3 status.*

2. Do the activities and purposes of the organization reflect your own? If so, the organization is likely to be a good match for your project. Funding sources will perceive that your sponsor has a logical, fundamental interest in the success of your project. If your project doesn't seem to fit the purposes of the sponsor, you will confuse potential funders and weaken your proposal. Be sensitive to conflicts of interest in choosing a sponsor organization. If you do approach an organization that hasn't traditionally worked with projects like yours, there is probably a reason why not, but you might be able to convince them to work with you if your project relates closely to their overall purpose. If they are sincere and enthusiastic about moving in a new direction, they will have to do some extra explaining in their section of the proposal for your project.

3. Is the organization equipped and willing to support you in fulfilling your goals? This willingness may not be something you can determine before meeting with representatives. If you're looking for more than a simple fiscal agent, however, you should consider your support needs for the project. Will you need fund-raising assistance, facilities, office space, staff support, or equipment? You should have some sense of whether the organization will have the ability to meet those needs. It is as important for you as for the organization to determine whether this might be an appropriate marriage. The ideal sponsor will be able (and willing) to provide whatever you need to complete your project successfully.

4. Does the organization have a good reputation in the fund-raising world and a positive record of accomplishments in its field? This may be difficult to determine up front, but the organization's history and track record can make or break a grant request, especially where money management is involved. An organization that has mismanaged funds, failed to make regular progress reports, or otherwise disappointed fun-

ders will not help you make a favorable impression on grant committees. Worse, an organization that does not manage funds effectively may cause you problems with your own project if you do get funds and they become your fiscal agent.

Investigating Potential Sponsors.   How can you find out more about a potential sponsor? See if they have a good local reputation, if people like working with them, if they have community support. Talk to members or constituents and ask how they like dealing with the organization.

How can you find out if the organization has done successful projects? That's easy—they'll be telling everybody about them. They might not be publicizing the failures—but you can usually find out about this by talking to others in your community or at other organizations. Even national organizations may have regional offices or some kind of local presence.

Whom should you talk to in the community? The Chamber of Commerce is always a good place to start. Talk to the staff of other nonprofits who work in the same area, but realize, of course, that they may not say the most favorable things, since they are in competition. For the most part, though, nonprofit people really do cooperate with one another and form a community. Depending on the organization, you might also talk to the United Way. They can give you a good handle on what is going on with a nonprofit organization in your local community.

You can also talk to someone at your local Better Business Bureau if you have doubts, and ask them to look at an annual report or an audited financial statement. This doesn't have to be a federal investigation—you just don't want to walk blindly into a complicated situation.

APPROACHING A POTENTIAL SPONSOR

By doing a little investigation, you should be able to narrow your original list of organizations down to just a few. You may also be able to rank them in order of preference. Now, starting with your top-rated organization, set up meetings with representatives from each of the best, most appropriate organizations still on your list. Here is the best way to arrange such a meeting:

1. Send a letter outlining your project and requesting a meeting to discuss a sponsor affiliation.

2. Make a follow-up phone call (after you are sure the letter has been received) to schedule the meeting. If you plan to bring core project group members with you, mention this during the phone call. Their presence can help make you look serious and organized, but their unexpected arrival could be overwhelming. If possible, tell the representative how many people you will be bringing; he or she can then choose an appropriate meeting room.

3. When the time comes for the meeting, be prompt and professional. Bring support materials to help explain your project and demonstrate your serious commitment.

You can use this initial meeting as an opportunity to find out more about the organization, but don't start by asking what they are all about. You want to show first that you have done your homework and read their brochures and newsletters. Then discuss all aspects of the sponsor relationship. What would be the daily work arrangements? What administrative fees would the organization require? How would the money be handled (a lump-sum payment to you or cash as required)? What time limit would you set on the sponsor relationship? Has the organization participated in similar sponsor relationships in the past? How were they handled?

Be as specific as possible, especially about the items that most concern you. But don't commit yourself to anything yet. Both you and the organization are in a process of exploration and consideration. In fact, an organization will often have to present a new project to its Board of Directors or Trustees and get approval for supporting it. When you've discussed everything, you should have some sense of what their interest is and what they have to offer. Thank them for the meeting and say that you appreciate their time and consideration of your project and that you are exploring several possibilities; if they seem interested, suggest a time when you will be in touch again.

One of the most important things you can gain from a meeting like this is to get the feel of an organization—whether it's formal or informal, whether you have a rapport with the director or staff, whether communication is easy or difficult, and whether they seem genuinely interested in your project. This is important even if you don't end up affiliating with a particular organization; if they appreciate and respect your project, they may be able to help with an endorsement or a referral to other possible funders. Most of all, though, you want to have a sense of whether or not you could have a comfortable and effective working relationship with them.

After you have met with all the organizations on your short list, you should have compiled enough information to make a well-informed decision. Your best choice would be the organization that not only serves your needs but also shows real enthusiasm for your project. Call up the person you met with at that organization and tell them you would like to work with them. They may give you their decision immediately, or they may suggest another meeting or give you a time when they will let you know their decision. They may need to present your project to their Board of Directors for approval. Don't be disappointed if things don't work out with your first choice; they may still be able to offer you assistance or referrals.

When you *do* get an organization to agree to sponsor you, it's time to formalize the details of your relationship. If it's going to be a simple arrangement, draw up a letter of agreement. If it's going to be complex, work out the details in written agreement or contract. When your lawyer is satisfied that the document protects your interests, both you and the sponsor should sign it. Your sponsor affiliation is now official.

THE ALTERNATIVE TO SPONSORSHIP: FORMING YOUR OWN NONPROFIT ORGANIZATION

I'm mentioning this option last because it involves the greatest level of personal commitment (and the most work) and is appropriate only for very long-term projects. Incorporating yourself as a nonprofit can allow you as much autonomy as you have working as an individual, and many more funding prospects. But it requires a great deal of thought, initiative, and planning—and some initial expense.

Forming your own organization can get complicated; it can be not only time-consuming but expensive as well. Further, the statistics show that a great number of new nonprofit organizations collapse within the first few years. This may be partly because of competition for funds, but it's more likely because the founders simply didn't know what they were getting into. This is a step that must be taken with an eye toward the long-term future of your project. On the positive side, nonprofit incorporation will allow you to retain autonomy and control and give you more funding options.

What do you need to do to set up a nonprofit? First, be prepared to shell out some money for legal, accounting, and registration fees. This could amount to an outlay of several thousand dollars, which is one important consideration. To do this right, you will need to file for formal incorporation. And you'll need to apply to the IRS for official tax-exempt status. You are going to need to get other people involved, put together a board of directors, keep financial records, and have monthly meetings, keeping minutes. The process of getting started can take from six months to a year. This is not something that you do haphazardly. If you do not plan to continue this project for an extended period of time—several years, at the minimum—don't bother. I really recommend that people work with an existing nonprofit organization, or umbrella organization, before setting up their own. Working with an existing organization for a one-time, short-term project can save you a great deal of administrative work, time, and expense.

If you cannot find an existing organization that is really a good fit with your project, you may need to create a new entity. Remember, you do still have options other than the nonprofit mode. You should think about which would be better for you: a nonprofit, tax-exempt organization, or a for-profit business. If you have a marketable idea, product, or project, you may be able to turn it into a profitable business. You can pursue investors and loans and you can build up income and equity. It's important to think about this at the outset, because once you've started a nonprofit organization, it will not be able legally to transfer any assets, title, patents, or ownership to you as an individual or to a for-profit business.

Of course, a nonprofit corporation can earn income. It just has to plow any earnings back into its programs, to help serve its mission. It cannot distribute earnings to its directors or staff as bonuses or stocks. It can hire directors and staff, pay reasonable salaries, purchase health insurance for its employees, reimburse expenses, pay for advertising, and build up its facilities. The Children's Television Workshop, which produces Sesame Street, is a good example of a nonprofit organization that earns a good deal of money in the profit sector—in their case, by marketing toys and games. All these earnings then go back into the furthering of the Workshop's mission—to produce educational programs for children.

The relationship between an individual owner and a nonprofit organization can be complex. Individuals can sell goods or services to a nonprofit organization. A nonprofit can commission a writer to write a play, pay the writer's salary, and put on a performance, all while permitting the writer to retain copyright of the work. An individual may lend a trademark or patent to a nonprofit organization for its limited use without giving up ownership. At the same time, the government does not want individuals using nonprofit corporations as devices to build their individual careers. There has to be some kind of public service involved.

So if you do have an artistic, scientific, cultural, or social project that you would like to extend into the indefinite future—and it is not really a profit-making idea, and does not match any other existing program—then consider setting up your own nonprofit. Although the laws governing nonprofit organizations vary from state to state, there are two principle types: the unincorporated association and the nonprofit corporation.

THE UNINCORPORATED ASSOCIATION

Few legal requirements apply to the unincorporated association. There's no need for detailed articles of association—just some simple rules about procedures. This kind of organization is useful for neighborhood or community groups, such as a block association or a local homeowners' group. It has no legal identity separate from the individuals who make it up; the individual members share all financial and legal responsibilities and liabilities. This kind of association is easy to set up, but it's not very useful for grant seekers. Funders may perceive it as unstable, since the laws governing it are often vague. There can be problems with organizational credibility, and it can be difficult to do banking and establish ownership of property. A lawsuit or government inquiry will target the individual members.

Worst of all for the grant seeker, it can be difficult for an unincorporated association to establish its credibility with the IRS and gain the coveted 501(c)3 tax-exempt status. Although you can get limited funding without it, the 501(c)3 certificate is essential. Most funders require it; they won't give to nonprofits who don't have the IRS certificate (they would endanger their own tax-exempt status by giving to unqualified organizations). And of course, without the tax-exempt status, individuals cannot deduct their donations to such groups from their own income taxes. For these reasons, I do not recommend working through this type of nonprofit structure.

THE NONPROFIT CORPORATION

Unlike the unincorporated association, the nonprofit corporation is an independent entity, legally separated from its founders or board members as individuals. This offers several real advantages:

- *Limited liability.* This means that board members or directors are not individually liable for any lawsuits or debts that the nonprofit corporation may incur. This is especially important if the organization is operating in the public sphere, or managing large sums of money.

- *A greater sense of stability.* Board members, staff, and the community itself will have a stronger sense of commitment to the enterprise. Funders, government agencies, banks, and others will perceive the nonprofit corporation as more predictable, reliable, and likely to be around for a long time. This leads to the third advantage.

- *A greater likelihood of winning grants.* It's easier for a nonprofit corporation to earn the essential tax-exempt status, which makes it a legal recipient of foundation money and a legal write-off for individual donations. Funders will also respond to the appearance of commitment and stability.

There are many different types of nonprofit corporations, depending on different state laws. They can include business groups; political, trade, and service organizations; and charitable, educational, religious, scientific, and cultural organizations. They may include corporations established with a business purpose, such as a thrift shop set up to generate funds for a hospital or charity. If you seriously intend to set up a nonprofit corporation, you should work with a lawyer who can identify the best type for your purpose, under the laws of your state.

How It Works. Setting up any nonprofit organization involves taking a number of basic steps. (The specifics vary from state to state, so check with local authorities, and with a lawyer, before beginning the process.)

1. Choose a name and create a statement of purpose.
2. Create Articles of Incorporation and Bylaws. These should explain how the corporation may dissolve itself.

3. Form a board of directors. In most cases, the actual legal responsibility and control over the organization is held by the Board of Directors, not by an individual founder or project director. (Though the board may choose to follow this person's lead.)
4. Incorporate with the state government.
5. Begin financial recordkeeping and regular reporting to the state government.
6. Apply to the Internal Revenue Service for federal tax exemption.

- **TIP:** Call or write Volunteer Lawyers for the Arts at 1 East 53rd Street (6th Floor), New York, NY 10022, 212-319-2787, and order their short booklet on not-for-profit incorporation, *To Be or Not to Be: An Artist's Guide to Not-for-Profit Incorporation* (1986). Although this is addressed to artists and refers to New York State law, it gives a good overview of how the process is likely to work for any field and may help you decide whether you want to go ahead. The same organization can direct you to individuals and other volunteer organizations around the country that offer free or low-cost assistance with the process.

    You might also contact the Small Business Administration for free advice and guidance on how to form and incorporate a nonprofit, tax-exempt organization. The SBA is a federal organization. Its address is 409 Third Street, S.W., Washington, DC 20416.

To ensure compliance with your state's requirements, you should also contact your state's Secretary of State or state Attorney General for detailed information on formal requirements, forms, and fees for setting up charitable or nonprofit corporations. And as with any business endeavor, you will benefit from the advice of professionals, including lawyers, accountants, and bankers.

The Tax-Exempt Status. Once you are incorporated, the first thing you want to pursue is the all-important tax-exempt status. Without a copy of written notification of this, it will be hard to get contributions or grants. Apply to the IRS, and expect to wait several months for your application to be processed. You will probably want the assistance of an experienced attorney in filing your application.

You have to supply information about the goals and history of your group, your Board of Directors, and your staff, salaries, and organizational structure. You also have to give detailed financial information, including a history of finances since you incorporated, projected budgets, and fund-raising plans.

The IRS will review and evaluate the information you supply and make a determination. To meet federal requirements, your organization must conduct activities that are in the public interest and must fit into one of the categories in Federal Tax Code Section 501(c), such as educational or charitable organizations. Your group can offer to individuals no privilege or benefit derived from its earnings. If it looks like your group is simply serving one individual's private career, the IRS may deny or revoke tax-exempt status. It can take three months or more to get a response.

- **TIP:** For detailed information on how to qualify for and receive an IRS certificate of tax exemption, order IRS Publication 557: *How to Apply For and Retain Exempt Status for Your Organization.* This is published by the U.S. Government Printing Office in Washington, D.C., and you can order it through your local IRS office.

When your organization receives notification of 501(c)3 status, this means that not only will it pay no tax, but it also now has the right to receive grants from government and other tax-exempt organizations, including foundations. In addition, individuals who make donations to your organization can deduct these from their own income tax. This makes it legally possible for funders and motivated individual donors to help you.

Remember, there are different categories of nonprofit corporations, and the IRS does not treat them all the same. Some will require more stringent recordkeeping and reporting, and some do not allow individuals to deduct contributions to the organization. You should have professional help in applying for the proper category. In any case, you will have certain obligations to the government, including holding regular meetings and keeping minutes, making annual reports to the IRS and other government agencies, observing IRS regulations, and keeping up the activities for public benefit.

No Shortcuts to the 501(c)3! Are there other legal forms your group might take? Do you have to go through the whole process of getting tax-exempt status in order to be eligible for certain grants and donations? The short answer is, yes, you do. There are no shortcuts. Even incorporation is not enough—you still have to apply to the IRS.

The Fund-Raising Approach. Once you have established your own nonprofit, tax-exempt organization, you can start to seek funding for it. Your organization is qualified to seek and receive funding from a wide range of foundations. Just be sure to follow each foundation's application instructions carefully. You will have to supply documentation attesting to the tax-exempt status of your organization. (This usually means a copy of your IRS 501[c]3 certificate and audited financial reports.) Filing an institutional application can require more paperwork than filing an individual one. The added responsibility— and increased opportunity for funding—are now all yours.

Seeking funding for a nonprofit corporation is quite a bit different from seeking funding as an individual. Organizations like the Foundation Center, the Support Centers of America, and the Grantsmanship Center are really set up to serve organizations like yours (see pages 114 and 124). You can get more assistance from them and can attend seminars and workshops that are directed to you. (Of course, you may have to pay for these.) Here are some specialized references that you may find of use:

- *A Nonprofit Organization Operating Manual: Planning for Survival and Growth*, by Arnold J. Olenick and Philip R. Olenick. New York: The Foundation Center, 1991.
- *Raise More Money for Your Nonprofit Organization: A Guide to Evaluating and Improving Your Fund-Raising*, by Anne L. New. New York: The Foundation Center, 1991.
- *Securing Your Organization's Future: A Complete Guide to Fund-Raising Strategies*, by Michael Seltzer. New York: The Foundation Center, 1987.

The Foundation Center
79 Fifth Avenue (8th Floor)
New York, NY 10003
212-620-4230

The Foundation Center
1001 Connecticut Avenue, N.W.
Washington, DC 20036
202-331-1400

The Foundation Center
Kent H. Smith Library
1422 Euclid, Suite 1356
Cleveland, OH 44115
216-861-1933

The Foundation Center
312 Sutter Street, Room 312
San Francisco, CA 94108
415-397-0902

The Grantsmanship Center
1125 W. Sixth Street (5th Floor)
P.O. Box 17220
Los Angeles, CA 90017
213-482-9860; fax: 213-482-9863

See Appendix, page 353, for a complete list of Support Center offices. For further information, contact:

The Support Center of New York
305 Seventh Avenue
New York, NY 10001
212-924-6744

5

THE
FOUNDATIONS

When you started thinking about getting a grant, the first word that probably came to mind was *foundations*. As you begin looking through the directories of grant givers, you'll find listing after listing of foundations. These are a major source of free money, and probably the one you've heard most about.

Everyone has heard of the Ford Foundation, the Rockefeller Foundation, and a few other of the "Big Daddies." But did you know that there are over 34,805 private foundations in the United States that give money to worthy causes? Many of these give to individual projects or needs like yours, either directly or through sponsors. They range from the major foundations, with their national—even global—and long-range concerns, to tiny foundations that give a few grants a year in very specialized areas or to specific kinds of recipients.

But what is a foundation? A private foundation is a nongovernmental, nonprofit institution created for the purpose of contributing to the common good. Foundations support charitable, educational, religious, and other activities, and focus on important social needs—in health, the environment, the arts, and so on. Foundations do their work by providing financial support, in the form of grants, to individuals or groups. Each foundation has its own independent Board of Directors or Board of Trustees that decides what kinds of issues it will grapple with and what kinds of projects it will support.

In pursuit of the common good, foundations can make grant awards to individuals, to assist with individual needs for health care or for education or with professional or creative goals, or to assist those who are helping and reaching out to others. Foundations set up procedures and guidelines for selecting those they'll give money to, and may have staff, program officers, or selection committees to advise the founders or Board of Trustees on these selections.

A LITTLE HISTORY

The idea of a "charitable trust" is very old. Even Plato had a kind of "foundation" that supported his Academy after his death. The modern American foundation is based on the nineteenth-century English model of charitable trusts that were set up to do good works, aid the unfortunate, improve education and medical care, support religion, and generally better society. The first American foundations were set up over two hundred years ago—Ben Franklin started his American Philosophical Society, which operated like a foundation, as early as 1743.

Other charitable trusts were put in place in the nineteenth century, most of them in support of specific institutions, but the real boom in establishing foundations took place around the turn of the twentieth century. The great tycoons and "robber barons," whether for personal or charitable reasons, began to concern themselves with social issues. Andrew Carnegie in 1896 set up the Carnegie Institute in Philadelphia to support education, and then the Carnegie Corporation of New York in 1911 to support libraries and medical education. Others—like Commodore Vanderbilt, Henry Ford, and John D. Rockefeller, Sr.—followed suit. The foundations of this period went beyond the support of specific institutions and began to address a wider range of issues and to support research to solve social problems.

From the beginning, these foundations were surrounded by some controversy and suspicion; people accused the founders of trying to conceal or "launder" their wealth. Nevertheless, American society would be much the poorer without their efforts.

A second boom took place in the 1930s. Millionaires like Andrew Mellon and Henry Ford set up foundations to escape giving up their profits to the graduated income tax and to avoid massive estate taxes.

The biggest boom of all came about immediately following World War II. The desire to shield their money from taxes again motivated many wealthy people to put it into foundations. Congress had voted massive increases in taxes on capital gains and high profits, and the 1950s were a time of high profits. The result was a great increase in donations to foundations—more than 90 percent of existing foundations were set up at this time.

In 1969, Congress passed a Tax Reform Act, and one of its major provisions was a set of rules to regulate foundations and control abuses. The Tax Reform Act prohibited the use of grants for private purposes or personal gain, restricted the kinds of programs that foundations could support, barred them from political lobbying, and required public disclosure of grant programs through the IRS 990-PF forms. The act also established clear definitions of which kinds of nonprofit organizations were private foundations and which were not. It distinguished "private foundations," which give away funds, from "public charities," which are tax-exempt organizations that solicit contributions and receive donations. It also distinguished private foundations from trade associations, political lobbying groups, and phony "foundations" that had nothing to do with the public good.

The Tax Reform Act established two clear and distinct types of foundations: operating and nonoperating. *Operating foundations* are limited to the function of supporting a single institution or program, like a hospital or research institute. *Nonoperating foundations* give away money in the form of grants to programs, organizations, or individuals. There are three basic types of nonoperating foundations: independent, community, and corporate.

Under the Tax Reform Act of 1969, foundations were permitted to make grants to individuals for "travel, study, or similar purposes," as long as they got approval in advance for their criteria and selection procedures and agreed to make detailed reports on their grantmaking. Many foundations chose not to go through this process and instead began to restrict their grants to nonprofit organizations with tax-exempt status. The same act set up the IRS 501(c)3 tax-exempt classification for these nonprofit organizations, which were called "public charities."

The last major law to affect foundations was the Economic Recovery Act of 1981, which required foundations to give away a minimum of 5 percent of their assets each year in the form of grants. This was to ensure that they really would fulfill their stated function. But foundations can still receive new funds, and they have the option to reinvest any investment income in excess of that 5 percent.

FOUNDATIONS TODAY

By the 1990s, there were over 32,000 private, corporate, and community foundations active in the United States. These foundations held assets of over $137 billion, and by 1992, total annual foundation giving had reached the $8 billion mark. Those contributing include not only the larger foundations, such as the Ford Foundation, the Lilly Endowment, the Andrew Mellon Foundation, the W. K. Kellogg Foundation, and the Rockefeller Foundation, but also smaller foundations. About one-fourth of these foundations held at least $1 million in assets or gave at least $100,000 in grants annually.

Foundations are located in every state of the Union, but the greatest concentration is in the Northeast, where the oldest and largest were originally set up. Those based in New York State alone hold about 23 percent of all foundation assets. This concentration of assets is offset by the fact that some of the very large foundations based in the Northeast distribute their funding throughout the whole country. Foundations in the Pacific region and South Atlantic states have been rapidly increasing in total assets recently.

As you begin to research foundations that might support your project, you should be aware of the various types in existence, since they often consider different types of requests, and sometimes handle them quite differently. The major categories, as defined by Congress, are the private or independent foundations, the community foundations, the corporate foundations, and the operating foundations. Of these, only the first three are set up to give grants to individuals or organizations that apply to them from the outside. There are also categories that reflect how a particular foundation operates, such as the pass-through type. Let's take a look at these different types.

PRIVATE FOUNDATIONS

Private foundations constitute by far the largest group. There are more than 28,000 of them, with total assets of nearly $120 billion, and they account for nearly 76 percent of the grant dollars awarded by all foundations. These are often termed "independent," or "family," foundations, because they have usually been funded or endowed by a single individual or family. Family members may be actively involved in guiding the foundation's program interests. Private foundations may limit their support to the specific cause, charity, or interests of the founder.

Private foundations are customarily divided into two categories: the large foundations—for example, the Ford, the Rockefeller, the Guggenheim—and the smaller independent or family foundations, which are scattered throughout the country. The distinction between the two is made according to an arbitrary cut-off point—usually $1 million in total assets, or $100,000 in annual giving. There is even a directory of so-called mid-sized foundations. For the individual grant seeker, the most important differences between large and small foundations are in how they are staffed and how they deal with the public.

The large foundations are among the oldest; they were set up by the major industrialists and millionaires of the late nineteenth and early twentieth centuries. Many are based in the Northeast, and they have long experience with addressing social needs and problems. They have national, even global concerns, and are interested in projects that can serve as models for dealing with long-term problems and needs. They may have a number of program officers who deal with specialized giving areas. Because of their high profiles, these large foundations get many proposals and have to be very selective about which ones they fund. Most give to large-scale projects administered by nonprofit organizations, though a few, like the Guggenheim, do give directly to individuals.

Large foundations generally have paid staffs that can review proposals and even seek out and develop projects. They make an active effort to communicate with the public by issuing guidelines, annual reports, and sometimes newsletters. They can respond easily to requests for information. It's easy to find out about the large foundations, and the big directories tend to focus on them.

The smaller foundations may have been set up as trust funds or started during a benefactor's lifetime. They usually focus on specific geographic areas. Their giving may be very closely tied to a local community or to the special interests of the founder. Perhaps a successful business person wants to give something back to the community, or to benefit individuals of the community, or individuals who share the founder's interests. Although they hold only about a third of total foundation assets, the smaller foundations actually give a greater number of grants than the large ones. The size of grants is usually smaller—ranging from perhaps $3,000 to $15,000—but they tend to give more toward ongoing operating expenses.

Many of the smaller foundations are unstaffed, and administered by a single director or trustee, who must process requests and present them to a board. Because of this, they often cannot actively reach out to the public, and it may be hard to find out about them and contact them. They do not have the facilities to respond easily to requests for information. They won't always appear in directories, but you can sometimes find them in specialized publications. If you learn of a small foundation in your region, you can research it by getting hold of its latest 990-PF form (see Chapter 3, page 105).

COMMUNITY FOUNDATIONS

Community foundations are set up to benefit a particular city or region. Their boards of directors are often representatives of the community. Unlike private foundations, they have been established with gifts and bequests from many different sources; in 1992, there were only about 330 of these, but they held assets of nearly $6 billion. Community foundations generally limit their giving to projects benefiting the immediate community, and to local residents. For example, the Marin Community Trust awards grants only to residents of Marin County, California. Some community foundations are classified as private foundations, reporting on IRS Form 990-PF, and some as public charities, reporting on Form 990. Their total giving is relatively small, amounting to only about 5 percent of all foundation grants. Still, they may be an important resource for the individual with community residence, or a locally based project.

CORPORATE FOUNDATIONS

Corporate foundations have been set up by profit-making corporations to support a variety of interests. They may give small grants to employees for education or general welfare, support projects that benefit their local communities, or back those that will serve as good public relations or advertising vehicles for the corporation. In 1992, there were over 1,500 company-sponsored foundations, with assets of nearly $6 billion. Their total giving amounts to between 15 and 20 percent of all foundation grants. These figures, however, do not reflect corporate giving programs that are administered through advertising or public relations departments, or discretionary funds.

Corporate foundations and giving programs both operate differently from other foundations. They have different mandates and different interests. They may support only their employees or employee family members. They may operate in a very free and entrepreneurial way with outside projects, and look for special benefits for the corporation. They may prefer to support projects with in-kind or donated services. Because of the variety of corporate funders, we'll consider them separately in the next chapter.

OPERATING FOUNDATIONS

Operating foundations are a special case, not directly relevant to the grant seeker. They are set up to support a single organization or institution, like a hospital, a research institute, or a community center. At the beginning of the 1990s there were about three thousand operating foundations in existence. Of these, about half did give small grants directly related to the work of their institution, but their total grant giving amounted to less than 2 percent of all foundation grants.

PASS-THROUGH FOUNDATIONS

This is not really a separate category but a way that a private foundation may operate. Pass-through foundations do not maintain an endowed fund or hold any real assets from year to year. Instead, they receive an infusion of funds each year, often from the founder, which they immediately pass on to other nonprofit organizations (they very rarely give grants to individuals). In a way, they are like a nonprofit organization that raises a budget annually but gives the money to other nonprofits rather than supporting its own programs. An example is the Fund for Psycho-Neuroimmunology, a former client of mine. This funds scientific fellowships and research and keeps its overhead close to the bone. The director doesn't take a salary, there are no office expenses, and all the money goes to other organizations. When you find a foundation listing that shows substantial annual giving but no real assets, it may well turn out to be a pass-through foundation.

WHO'S IN CHARGE?—RULES THAT GOVERN FOUNDATIONS

The principal laws that govern foundations are the Tax Reform Act of 1969 and the Economic Recovery Act of 1981. These define the basic rules and procedures that all foundations must follow. They must file the annual 990-PF reports with the Internal Revenue Service. They are allowed to give grants to individuals for "travel, study, or similar purposes." If they give grants to individuals, the IRS must approve their selection criteria and procedures, to ensure that the selection process is objective. They must supply extensive follow-up reports to demonstrate that the money was used appropriately and accounted for. A major impact of these rules has been to discourage many foundations from giving directly to individuals.

Curiously, foundations that do give to individuals do not have to have open and publicized calls for applications and proposals. They can even give grants to individuals that they know of, without any formal application, as long as the selection process is considered objective. The most well-known example of this kind of giving is the MacArthur Foundation "genius grant," which cannot be applied for, and which is awarded without the recipient being in any way involved in the process. Many smaller foundations give grants in a similar fashion.

The 1981 law required foundations to give away a minimum percentage of their assets each year. In periods of declining interest rates, this puts some family foundations and smaller foundations under pressure—they can see their overall endowment decline. In my experience, this seems to cause them to support a smaller number of organizations or individuals that they feel more strongly committed to. They tend to make somewhat fewer grants, but larger ones.

WHO GETS THE GRANTS?—FOUNDATION GIVING PATTERNS

How does a foundation decide who it is going to fund? Each foundation has its own unique giving priorities. The governing body of the foundation—the Board of Directors or Trustees—decides each year how to allocate funds. They may have more or less freedom to choose the kinds of projects they will support. *General-purpose* foundations have broad interests and can move into new areas. They may change their priorities to respond to new social issues or problems. Any new priorities must still fit within the original philanthropic intent of doing social or common good. *Special-purpose* foundations generally stick to an original mandate.

Foundations can channel their grants into many special categories, sometimes called *giving categories*. Some may focus on certain subject areas, such as the arts or education. They may specialize even more, and support only filmmakers in Kentucky, or medical education. Some are concerned with special populations—women, minorities, Native Americans. Some may support only certain types of organizations, such as schools or research institutes. Some may give only for certain types of activities, such as research or educational projects. They may specifically rule out certain categories, such as administrative salaries, equipment purchase, or new construction.

As you know by now, some foundations support both individuals and nonprofit organizations, and some support only one or the other. Certain private foundations, like government agencies, often do consider requests for renewed funding and multiyear grants, unlike corporate funders, who usually don't. In doing your research, you will need to look carefully at a funder's giving categories to decide if they will be able to support your project. You can find some of these categories in directories, but the final word appears in guidelines and annual reports.

Foundations can range from the clearly socially responsible to the unusual. Some are particularly concerned with such cutting-edge issues as the environment, and health and welfare in developing countries. At the same time, some of the older, more established foundations are also willing to address new and urgent issues. The Rockefeller Foundation is a good example. In fact, since the larger, more established foundations have huge assets, they are able and sometimes eager to take real risks. There are quirky foundations as well, that support things like the Frisbee scholarship at the State University of New York at Purchase. No matter how unusual your project or your background, you may find a foundation to support you.

- **TIP:** For radical, activist, and New Age projects, consult the *Oryx Guide to Alternative Foundations*. Phoenix, AZ: Oryx Press, published annually.

You might also try the *Directory of New and Emerging Foundations.* 2nd edition, New York: The Foundation Center, 1994.

THINKING GLOBALLY, ACTING LOCALLY—THE GEOGRAPHICAL FACTOR

While some foundations have national or even global interests, the great majority focus their giving in one geographical region. In fact, it's quite common for foundations to restrict their giving to their own state, or even to one part of a state. Many focus on a city, county, or local community. There are a few, like the Rockefeller Foundation, that concern themselves with such global issues as world population levels, but these are the exceptions. Only about one-third of the larger foundations give on a national or even regional basis. What does this mean for you as a grant seeker? You should direct a significant part of your grant research into local and regional funds—this can be as important as subject and population group research. In fact, you can combine these approaches to zoom in on your best prospects.

GRANTS TO INDIVIDUALS

In spite of the general trend, and the extra paperwork, some foundations do make a commitment to funding individuals. Why do they? There is usually a personal passion or experience that motivates such foundations. The founder or someone on the board may have a special interest in an area, whether it be painting, filmmaking, inventing, or ecology. Or someone may have had a difficult time in their own life, or cared deeply about someone who did, and were thus motivated to support general welfare grants or medical support grants for people in similar circumstances.

The Foundation Center's *Foundation Grants to Individuals* lists approximately two thousand foundations that specifically make grants to individuals. This is only one directory, and not a complete one. You can find many other grants to individuals listed in specialized directories for subject, population, and geographical area. Further, many foundations will fund individuals through a nonprofit sponsor. No one has ever tried to compile the statistics that would show how many grants flow through sponsors to individuals, but there are many.

Foundations make grants to individuals under a variety of specialized programs, including: scholarships, student loans, fellowships, travel internships, residencies, arts and cultural projects, general welfare grants, and program-related investment grants (PRIs). There are also many broad-based and generic types of grants to individuals. These are often less specifically defined than are grants to nonprofit organizations, which is an advantage for individuals seeking a grant.

The highest proportion of grants to individuals go for educational purposes, and the two highest categories are scholarships for undergraduates and fellowships for independent projects, research, or doctoral dissertations. In fact, over half of the funders that give grants to individuals specialize in educational support. Other important categories are corporate foundation grants to company employees and community residents; grants for general welfare and medical assistance; awards, prizes, and grants through nomination; and internships and residencies.

Still other grants to individuals can address a multitude of activities and subjects. They can support, just to pick some examples, accounting, agricultural sciences, anthropology, architecture, art, art education, biological research, business, cancer research, choreography, conservation, educational studies, foreign study, graduate study, journalism, medical research, music, poetry, teaching, women's studies, and writing.

A foundation's Board of Directors can always dictate where it will allocate its funds. It might decide to grant ten scholarships and adopt ten special projects in one calendar year. Or it might decide to fund an individual who has a program that will have a positive effect on other disciplines or groups the foundation wants to support. For example, a foundation may fund a choreographer whose work will affect a specific community, such as schoolchildren, or a multicultural audience.

Many foundations making grants to individuals are small, and may have limited funds for a modest number of grants. (This is why you will probably need to apply to several foundations.) You will also want to go beyond foundation funding and explore government programs—and don't forget fiscal sponsorship as a way to expand the funding prospects for your project. When foundations give grants to nonprofit organizations, they often prefer to fund a specific project of the nonprofit, rather than general operating expenses. This really works to your advantage if you have a fiscal sponsor, because your project becomes a specific project of the nonprofit sponsor.

You should bear in mind that some hot issues of the day—education, the environment, and health concerns are current examples—may claim a foundation's primary attention. They will tend to allocate the greater proportion of their grant budget for projects dealing with these choice issues. Still, I don't think you should do what I've seen many grant seekers consider—that is, alter or change your focus to match a foundation's priorities. Stick by your convictions. There has to be a funder out there that will match your needs! At the same time, keep thinking creatively about how to relate your project to a funder's interests.

GRANTS TO ENTREPRENEURS

If you are an entrepreneur looking for financial assistance, there are several grant categories you may find useful. Grant money can support research and development, employee training or hiring, and sometimes equipment purchase or real estate purchase. Grants cannot be used for debt reduction and certainly not for investment purposes. This is not a way to make a quick buck. It *is* sometimes a way to support a business that is also doing something for the common good.

You will need to think about how best to present your ideas to make them appealing or appropriate for nonprofit funding. Start by looking closely at the foundation's mission statement. Try to incorporate some of its wording or concepts into your own statement of need. I can think of a perfect case study. I had a client several years ago who was an excellent physician, a general practitioner who came up with a fabulously clever computer system for processing insurance claims much more efficiently. He needed a quarter of a million dollars for research-and-development expenses. So we approached medical foundations with the idea of streamlining health care and health insurance for foundations themselves. He made a fortune on the project, and saved medical foundations some money, too.

In some cases—and especially if you are an inventor, are developing a new product, or are starting up a new business—you can turn to foundations for help in getting started.

One form of funding is the *program-related investment (PRI)*. This is a low-interest loan or equity investment that a foundation makes in a project that helps the foundation further its own charitable objectives. Although some foundations make PRIs available only to nonprofit organizations, others provide funding to individuals and for-profit businesses, as long as the project at hand addresses the foundation's goals.

Keep in mind when applying for PRI funding that the foundation wants to make a bona fide investment in a business or project that promises to be successful. Return on investment may not be the foundation's first concern, but they certainly don't want to throw good money away either. If you are requesting program-related investment funding, you must address the director's concerns in real business terms. You will need to establish the financial viability of the project just as you would in any business plan. You will need to demonstrate that the PRI will allow you to get started, and that the project can then become self-sustaining and possibly even profitable. A one-time event, like a festival, is not appropriate for PRI funding.

HOW TO RESEARCH FOUNDATIONS

We've already outlined the basics about researching foundations and other funding sources in Chapter 3. You learned about some of the major directories, and you know that you need to use indexes and specialized directories to focus your search according to geographical location, subject area, and any population group you may belong to. You know you can use specialized directories, like my *Free Money* books, to find grants to answer specific needs. You know that you can find some basic information in directories, but will always have to write for guidelines and annual reports in order to tell whether a funder is really right for you.

When you start to research foundations, be sure you can express your own need and mission clearly. Look carefully at the giving categories and priorities of each foundation and make sure that your need and your qualifications match these. By weeding out inappropriate funders, you can make your grant seeking immensely more efficient and successful. This process begins as soon as you open a directory.

The following is a fictional sample of a typical foundation listing. If you are using a foundation directory or scanning an information sheet that a foundation has sent you, you may see the following information:

The XYZ *Foundation*
Address
Phone number
Incorporated in year: 1952
Donor: Joe Nations, Sr.
Officers (Board of Trustees): Joe Nations, Jr., President, Shirley
 Nations, John Powell, Harry Snow, Jane Rowe
Financial data (year ended '92): Assets, $3,000,000; gifts re-
 ceived, $3,000,000; expenditures, $2,750,000, including
 133 grants (high: $250,000; low: $1,500; average: $5,000–
 25,000)
Purpose and activities: Giving largely for higher education, arts
 and culture, community service, health care, civic orga-
 nizations, and individuals, minority opportunity and
 women
Types of support: operating budgets, seed money, endowment
 funds, scholarship funds, individuals, fellowships, general
 purposes, renovation projects, special projects, etc.
Limitations: Giving primarily in the state of California, with
 emphasis on southern California
Publications: Annual report, application guidelines, program
 policy statement, financial statement
Application information: Initial-approach letter
Deadlines: March 1, September 1
Contact: Shirley Nations
Number of staff: 3 full-time professional, 2 part-time

Let's consider what this information means to you as a grant seeker.

Officers. It's the listing of officers and the donor that tells you
this is a family foundation. Apparently the founder's son and another
family member are still active in the foundation. There isn't much
else of significance to this section for you, unless you are lucky enough
to know one of the board members.

Financial Data. $3 million in assets puts XYZ into the large
foundation category, by the Foundation Center's reckoning. But it's
still small compared with some of the real biggies. The large amount
of gifts received means that this is a very active foundation, supported
by its founder and/or others.

We can see from the financial profile that in 1992 the XYZ Foundation gave 133 grants, which ranged in size from $1,500 to $250,000. This amount of giving also puts XYZ in the large foundation category, since it clearly gives more than $100,000 a year. However, the average grant range of $5,000–$25,000 is more typical of mid-sized foundations. If the total expenditures were $2,750,000, this means that XYZ probably gave out quite a few grants. (Although expenditures could also include the foundation's own operating expenses or investments.)

Purpose and Activities.   The XYZ Foundation has very broad areas of interest. Education, arts, and culture cover a lot of activities, and so does community service. This suggests that the board will be taking a very active role in deciding what the foundation will fund on a case-by-case and year-by-year basis. Projects that combine more than one of the foundation's interests might attract special consideration. These might include minority training or education or support for a women's art program. Of course, the fact that they specify higher education might rule out education for younger children, and they may support only institutions and not offer individual scholarships. A scientific research project wouldn't seem strongly supported here, though it might somehow connect with the higher education or health-care interests. You would have to go to the guidelines, annual report, or 990-PF to find out. This listing just doesn't give you all the details you need.

Types of Support.   Individuals may apply to this foundation, but you would have to read the guidelines carefully to see exactly what types of support they qualify for. The foundation supports "scholarship funds," but this doesn't necessarily mean that it grants individual scholarships. It might or might not fund individual health care. Still, the small size of some of the grants suggests that there probably are a number of grants for individuals. The mention of support for minorities and women suggests that individuals from these groups might get special attention. In addition, there are grants for operating budgets, special projects, unique cases, seed money, renovation projects, and endowment funds, which a nonprofit organization could put aside in order to earn interest. XYZ will consider many different kinds of projects, and you would have to consult their guidelines for further details.

Limitations.   The principal limitation is geographical. The founder, Joe Nations, Sr., may have lived a long and successful life in southern California. It seems he wanted to make a contribution to others in his community; therefore, grants are restricted "primarily" to the state of California, with "emphasis" on southern California. How strict are these limitations? Does someone in San Francisco still have a chance? Yes, but not a very big one. The chances of someone in Arizona or Pennsylvania? Practically nil. If they have given any grants at all outside of the region, then they would list that information here. However, the grants that are given outside their primary region will probably be initiated by the foundation itself. So if you aren't based in southern California, or your project won't benefit the population of southern California, don't waste your time by applying to this foundation.

Publications. This foundation does make the effort to communicate openly about its activities. If it looked like a potential funder for you, you would write for the guidelines and annual report.

Application Information and Contact. You are given the name of a contact person to whom you should write for guidelines and an annual report. Once you've looked over the guidelines, if you believe your project would really qualify for funding, you will write your initial approach letter. (This would be either a three- to five-page letter following the format for the "letter of request," or a short, full proposal, outlined in Chapter 9 of this book.) Since this listing specifically indicates a letter, it would be a big mistake to go over five pages, which would start to look like a full proposal. Three pages would be fine. "Initial-approach letter" means that they may ask you to send a more elaborate proposal later, if you have a large-scale project. Or, if you write a great letter of approach, they may decide to give you funding on that basis alone.

Deadlines. The two deadlines suggest that the Board of Trustees will meet twice a year to decide what grants it will give. If you miss that September deadline, you won't have a chance to get funding from XYZ for another six to eight months. And remember, it's always better to get your proposal in earlier than the deadline.

Number of Staff. Since this is a staffed foundation, there will be someone there to send you guidelines, to possibly answer a question about limitations or priorities (after you've read the guidelines), and to talk to you about your project if you have sent a proposal they are interested in.

OTHER KINDS OF LISTINGS

Community Foundations. The listing will basically look the same for community as for family foundations. The annual report and guidelines may include some discussion of the multiple sources that donate funds to the community foundation.

Inactive Foundations. Since it takes several years to put a directory together, information can be out of date, and some of the listed foundations may have become inactive. This is another reason why you must always write to a foundation for guidelines or an application before sending them any form of request.

Guidelines and Annual Reports. Foundation guidelines will tell you more specifically what they are looking for and spell out any special limitations on funding. They will give you the essential details about the application process, including any special formats or procedures.

The annual reports provide detailed information about a foundation's giving policies. They may describe the history of the foundation and the purpose for which it was founded. They will outline the principal kinds of programs and projects the foundation has funded in the past. Often they will list names of grant recipients, giving brief histories of their affiliations and the amounts of money they received. Annual reports and guidelines give you the facts you need to know before deciding whether to apply to a foundation, and they tell you exactly how to apply.

HOW TO APPROACH FOUNDATIONS

Once you have received a foundation's guidelines and you believe you may qualify for funding, be sure to note the deadlines and methods of application. The Board of Trustees may only meet once or twice a year to decide where to allocate its funds; or the board may meet quarterly, and review applications every few months. If it's not clear in the guidelines, and this is a staffed foundation, do call to verify the deadlines. *It is crucial to get your proposal or application in on time.*

The guidelines will indicate the form of approach—whether a letter of request or a full proposal. If there is an application to fill out, this makes your job easier. (Before you fill out an application or send in a letter of request, be sure to read Chapter 9 of this book, to make certain you are presenting your strongest case.)

Some foundations will tell you in their guidelines that they do not accept unsolicited proposals. This means that they only consider invited proposals. How do you get invited? This is something that is not always easy or even possible. Sometimes you can simply call up and ask what the protocol is. Usually, though, you have to know someone who will recommend you to the foundation, and then if they are interested, they will get in touch with you. If you are fortunate enough to be invited to submit a proposal, the foundation will usually want to meet with you and give you guidance and suggestions to help you prepare your proposal.

How Foundations Deal with Grant Seekers

Foundations, both large and small, are swamped with requests for money. Letters and proposals come pouring in, month after month. It's a major job just to log them in and file them. This may seem like impossible competition. But the figures are somewhat misleading. The reason is that a large percentage of those thousands of requests are totally inappropriate for the foundations they are sent to. Many of them represent mass mailings from people who have done little or no research. A great many of the foundation officers I talk to complain bitterly that they receive floods of proposals from people who have absolutely no business even requesting guidelines. They complain that many people don't even bother to look carefully at a foundation listing. Most of their applicants will take a quick glance, spot their subject area, and do no further analysis to see if they fit even the listed guidelines. They don't look to see if the foundation funds individuals, they don't look for geographic limitations, they don't look for giving categories, and they don't request guidelines, which you, dear reader, always do.

What this means is that you have an immense advantage over thousands of other applicants, simply because you are doing your re-search properly. You are approaching only a carefully screened list of potential funders, and you are contacting them in a professional way. You will have thought through your project thoroughly, and after reading Chapter 9, you will have prepared a strong, professional-looking proposal. So don't worry about those other applicants—just make your proposal shine!

What Happens After You Apply?

Whether it's a large or small foundation, someone will log in your proposal and take a quick look to see if it really does fit the foundation's guidelines. At a large foundation, a program officer will look at it, and may pass it directly to the Board of Directors or Trustees, or perhaps to a preliminary evaluation committee. The evaluation committee will then decide whether to submit it to the board. If they do, you may get a call or a letter at this point, telling you that your proposal is "under consideration" or that it is up for a grant. The program officer may ask you to submit additional information.

At a small, unstaffed foundation, the foundation director or fund administrator may be the first one to look at your proposal. They will probably scan it quickly and make an initial decision as to whether they want to keep it under consideration. Or they may put it immediately into a reject file. After considering a number of proposals, the foundation director may make some preliminary decisions, or submit specific proposals to the board. Small, unstaffed foundations are generally incapable of even responding to every request they get, so you won't know whether you are under consideration or not. If you are going to be funded, you'll be notified. Smaller foundations do not always notify grant seekers whom they decide not to fund, and you may have to contact them again after the decision period has passed.

How long does it take to be notified? It all depends on the foundation and how it is structured. Many foundations will notify you within four to eight weeks of receiving your proposal; others may take up to three or four months. The foundation's guidelines may or may not indicate a decision period. If there is an application deadline, this means that the foundation expects to consider proposals during a certain period after the deadline. If there is no deadline, the decision time may depend on how often the foundation board meets to consider proposals. As a general rule, smaller foundations will meet less frequently than more heavily staffed foundations and may take longer to make decisions.

WHO MAKES THE DECISIONS?

The final authority for making funding decisions always rests with the Board of Trustees or Board of Directors, but that authority may be delegated in different ways. At the larger foundations, there may be a program officer who does some initial screening of proposals and requests, and a committee that does a second level of screening, passing only a few proposals on to the board. No matter how active an interest board members take in the decision process, they rely very heavily on program officers and staff for advice and judgment. So at a large foundation your proposal is being reviewed and passed by a number of people, and a consensus begins to develop along the way.

An unstaffed, small foundation may have a very small board, perhaps including relatives and personal friends of the founder, who will generally support the founder's wishes and interests even after his or her death. At small foundations, the actual founder or the director will often exert a great deal of influence over grantmaking decisions, or will essentially be making the decisions and passing them by the board for approval. An attorney or accountant who manages a trust fund may be making most of the actual decisions, but the board is always there as a counterbalance.

At the larger foundations, the board will always carefully consider the directions it wants the foundation to go in and the problems and issues it wants to address. It will decide beforehand, "Let's fund this type of project this year," and will make decisions in terms of those predetermined priorities. At smaller foundations, the board or director may be a little more flexible about dealing with new kinds of projects but will generally support their existing interests.

Sometimes people imagine that grants only go to personal friends or relatives of foundation board members. Though this might have occurred before the congressional rulings went into effect, these days it is just a lingering misconception. Foundations really do distribute grants with a sense of objective purpose and fair procedure.

Can you bring any personal influence to bear on a board or program officer? Not usually. You may have more opportunity to interact with the staff of a large foundation, but you will largely be supplying information that they request. The committees and boards will form their own judgments about whether they want to support you. Smaller foundations may be more susceptible to personal influence, just because they are small and don't have the same layers of staff members and committees. The board members of a small family foundation, or the individual founder, probably do respond to some personal influence. But it's much harder to communicate with these foundations, and unless you know board members personally, you can't hope to exert any influence. Just trust that they will support good projects when they see them, whether they know you personally or not.

If you do have a genuine personal relationship with someone on a board, or with someone who knows a board member, whether it's a large or small foundation, there's certainly no harm in mentioning that you have a proposal up for consideration. It won't necessarily help you, since the board does have to maintain the integrity of its own procedures, but it can't hurt. If you don't have a personal contact, it is a breach of etiquette, and could be counterproductive, to try to contact and influence a board member. Using personal influence isn't the way to get a grant. The way to do it is to develop a solid project, to research and target the right funders, and to send them a superb proposal.

6

CORPORATE
FUNDERS

"This program was made possible by a generous grant from the Triad Corporation." You've often seen or heard this kind of acknowledgment, related to television and radio shows, printed on programs for public performances and community events, or announced from a podium. What you may not have realized is that your neighbor's children were helped through college by their mother's employer, or that a corporation in your community has been funding a drug-treatment center at the local hospital.

The fact is that many businesses and corporations play a vital role in communities throughout the United States by sponsoring events or addressing problems in numerous fields, such as health care, culture, and education. Many corporations have a sense of social responsibility to their employees and their community, and they act on this by setting up corporate foundations or by giving funds directly from their operating budgets for worthy causes. They call it "corporate citizenship."

There are several distinct kinds of corporate funding. *Corporate foundations* are much like private foundations, except that their funds come from a different source and they have different kinds of interests. *Corporate giving* means that a corporation gives grants directly from its operating budget—through a formal program, a discretionary fund, or an advertising or marketing budget. Corporate giving programs operate differently from foundations. Corporations are permitted to give a percentage of their pre-tax income to charities in the form of direct tax-deductible contributions. Only tax-exempt organizations can receive these contributions, however.

Corporations and corporate foundations have their own mandates and concerns. Some support only their employees and employee family members; others give freely to individuals and projects in their communities. They often like to support projects that will give them good advertising or public relations value. They may support projects with in-kind donations or noncash grants. As a group, corporations are probably the most entrepreneurial of all funders. They can react more quickly and individuals can approach them more easily, and for these reasons they are an important group to pursue.

Corporate foundations do operate under the same IRS and Economic Recovery Act rules as private foundations. There is no specific legislation governing corporate giving programs, though of course they must comply with the normal IRS reporting procedures, as any business has to do. Ultimately, corporations always have to answer to their stockholders, so they do need to be businesslike about their giving programs. If their stocks are widely held, they must be able to justify grant giving as somehow of benefit to the corporation.

WHY CORPORATIONS GIVE GRANTS

Although some corporations have always given charitable gifts and contributions, they didn't get into the foundation business in any significant way until the early 1950s. When they did, it was for some of the same reasons that the great boom in private foundations occurred at this time. The government was imposing high tax rates on high business profits, and both individuals and corporations found that putting some of those profits into a foundation gave them significant tax savings. This was a more cost-effective way to do charitable work than making direct contributions.

Corporations have other reasons for preferring to work through foundations. They can hire specialists to make grants and do long-range planning, instead of depending on the instincts of a marketing manager. They can contribute more money to the foundation in good years and less money in lean years. And having a foundation that bears the company's name promotes good public relations.

Of course, there are those who raise questions about corporate philanthropy. They claim that corporate giving is really a way of promoting special interests and mounting public relations campaigns. They say it supports only projects that seem useful to the company instead of addressing pressing social issues. They are skeptical of corporate support of events like the Olympics, when television commercials use the giving to advertise the company.

I know of too much corporate giving that is practically anonymous, and too many worthwhile projects supported by corporations—when government or private funders wouldn't help—to criticize them for getting good p.r. out of it. Furthermore, since company foundations are completely separate legal entities, they cannot, by law, make grants that are solely of benefit to the company that sponsors them. They do give to many projects that have no connection with the corporation's business.

CORPORATE FUNDING TODAY

In 1992, there were over one thousand five hundred company-sponsored foundations, with assets of nearly $6 billion. Their total giving has amounted to between 15 and 20 percent of all foundation grants—in 1989, it reached over $1 billion. These figures, however, do not reflect direct corporate giving programs that are administered through advertising or public relations departments, or discretionary funds. In fact, it is impossible to produce statistics on the full extent of corporate giving, for reasons we'll address later.

CORPORATE FOUNDATIONS AND DIRECT CORPORATE GIVING

Corporate foundations and direct corporate giving represent two different styles and strategies of corporate funding. Still, both are guided to some extent by the same corporate policies, and they may even share the same staff, though they keep their operations separate.

Corporate foundations are registered with the IRS and must follow the same rules and procedures as any private foundation. The foundation makes its own grant-making decisions, establishes its own giving categories and restrictions, publishes its own guidelines and annual report, and must file the 990-PF form with the IRS. Like a private foundation, it can give grants to both individuals and tax-exempt organizations. Some officers of the parent corporation will usually sit on the Board of Directors, and the parent company can thus influence which grants are made. Since the corporate foundations have their own endowed funds, they can give grants somewhat independently of the business's ups and downs.

Direct corporate giving means that a company gives funds directly out of its operating budgets and treats them as regular business expenses. A company may give funds directly through an official *direct contribution program,* or through many different departments. Companies often grant funds from their advertising, marketing, or public relations budgets. They may also give to their own employees through an official *corporate contributions program* or *community relations program.* The CEO or other executives may have their own discretionary funds. Direct corporate giving always takes place on a discretionary basis, according to the judgment, decision, or impulse of some company executive, whether the president or marketing director. Smaller companies that do not have company foundations often give funds directly, and some larger corporations have both foundations and direct giving programs.

In direct corporate giving, a company can treat gifts as a business expense—say as an advertising cost—or as a charitable contribution. This is usually an accounting decision that has to do with the company's tax profile. It doesn't directly affect you as a grant seeker, except that a company can only make charitable contributions to tax-exempt organizations. A company has to treat direct gifts to individuals as business expenses, and would have to see a real advantage for themselves in such expenditure. Ultimately, if a company president wants to give money, it can be handled in many different ways.

Corporations can be much more responsive and flexible with direct giving. They can use discretionary funds to quickly support almost any kind of project that they feel will benefit them in terms of community goodwill or public relations, or for any other reason. If the company is doing well, more funds are available. In recessions, companies generally scale back their direct giving and discretionary grants, simply because there is less to give.

FOREIGN CORPORATIONS

A number of foreign corporations have set up shop in the United States in recent years—and not only the Japanese. These corporations operate factories or distribution systems, run publishing houses, and manage entertainment and communication companies. Like American companies, and for the same reasons, many have set up their own corporate foundations and direct giving programs.

For the most part, these companies give because they want to back up their employees and the communities that support them. Of course, corporations also operate giving programs because they want to create a positive image for themselves in the communities where they operate facilities. For such reasons, foreign corporate foundations have been steadily increasing their philanthropic giving in the United States.

In 1991, Japanese corporations, for example, gave over $400 million in grants throughout the United States, seeking high visibility and a positive public image. They want to be known as generous good guys who care about their American communities. Some have set up their own company-sponsored foundations with published priorities and guidelines. These include the American Honda Foundation in California and the Toyota Foundation and Hitachi Foundation in Washington, DC. These foundations are providing important services to their communities, issuing grants to improve American educational and health-care systems, the environment, and the basic quality of life for American citizens.

Japanese and other foreign corporations do not operate any differently from American corporations in their funding, nor do they seem to have any unique interests. Although philanthropy works in different ways in different countries, the foreign companies in the United States gradually learn the American system, set up foundations according to IRS guidelines, and operate in typical U.S. fashion. There are no special tricks to researching or approaching them. Just be aware that they too are potential funders for your project.

WHO GETS THE GRANTS? — CORPORATE GIVING PATTERNS

Like independent foundations, corporate foundations establish their own giving priorities. Companies that give directly are responding on an immediate and continuous basis to what they see as community needs and opportunities. Although they are in business to make money, some corporations do feel a social responsibility to their employees and their communities. They want to be perceived as good corporate citizens. Often, they see advantages and paybacks to offering support.

For example, by supporting educational initiatives or scholarship programs, companies are really supporting their future employees and the future work force. In the past ten years, corporations have taken an increasing interest in educational issues. Companies also support areas in which they have special interests or that are closely related to their own industries. For example, an insurance company like Metropolitan Life Insurance might support grants in the health field. Banks care about their image in their communities and might support programs for general community welfare.

At the same time, companies may freely support groups and institutions that operate quite independently of the funding corporation. For example, McDonald's Corporation set up the Ronald McDonald House as an independent charity, clearly with good public relations in mind. Nevertheless, this has become the single largest research facility in the United States for cancer research for children, and is now being supported by other foundations and individual contributions. The directors of Ronald McDonald House are not employees of McDonald's, and are not supervised or directed in any way by the founding company.

What areas do corporations give to? In recent years, according to the *National Directory of Corporate Giving*, corporate funding breaks down as follows:

1. Education (primarily higher education)—about 38 percent
2. Health care—about 26 percent
3. Culture and the arts—about 11 percent (some corporations have filled in for declining government support)
4. Community issues and the environment—about 14 percent
5. Miscellaneous—11 percent

To sum up, corporations support various areas for many different reasons. Most commonly, they want to support their own community, or they see a public relations value. Perhaps top management has some personal involvement with an issue, or they may simply become involved or identified with an issue and want to establish continuity of support. For example, American Airlines has continually sponsored events to help fight cystic fibrosis. Many corporations encourage their employees to do volunteer work, and then they contribute to the organizations their employees volunteer for. Finally, companies can always make discretionary grants to meet new needs or opportunities as they arise.

GIVING TYPES

What kinds of grants do corporations give? Corporations make loans to individuals, grant fellowships, help build endowment funds, provide seed money and equipment to new businesses, and even give loans to nonprofit organizations. In general, they place fewer restrictions on how their funds are used than private foundations or the government do. They often support specific programs rather than general operating and administrative expenses. Companies want to know they are helping a particular worthy cause. Corporate foundations may get more involved in renewed or long-term support, while direct corporate giving is usually targeted to immediate, short-term projects.

Corporate funders also support projects by donating products and services. These are called *in-kind* donations, or *noncash* grants. Some estimate that perhaps as much as 20 percent of corporate giving is in the form of in-kind services or resources. These could include supplies and equipment; facilities; meeting, exhibition, or performance space; support for mailings; or computer services. Such corporations may offer the expertise of their employees in the form of free legal assistance, or help with long-term planning, public relations, or marketing. They may even help with fund raising. Noncash grants and services are generally channeled through the corporate contributions program, rather than corporate foundations.

In addition, corporations have begun to forge cooperative projects with nonprofit institutions and are getting more involved in overseeing the projects they are funding. For example, they may pick the school districts where they will support arts-in-education programs. If they are contributing to a hospital, they may get involved with choosing which drug-abuse program they would like to see affiliated with it. They may choose to offer specific tutorial programs to their employees.

Corporations may also encourage their employees to join specific volunteer groups, or offer to sponsor special events that will involve employees. They are tending to sponsor more special events, such as health fairs, sports events, and arts festivals. You increasingly see corporate banners supporting a Walkathon for AIDS, say, or a free music festival.

GIVING RESTRICTIONS

Many corporate foundations and giving programs are set up to give specifically to employees. Probably half or more give only to their current or former employees, or to their employees' immediate families. Still, many others do give beyond this immediate circle, especially to individuals with institutional affiliation. And many companies are open to unique projects from their community, to which they can apply discretionary funds.

Geography also comes into play when you are researching corporate funders. Take note of any geographical limitations, as most companies will prefer to support programs in areas where they have operating facilities or plants and where programs will benefit their employees. This can encompass a wide region. Many companies operate throughout the country, handling grant requests through their regional centers.

CORPORATE GRANTS TO INDIVIDUALS

Corporate funders tend to give more to individuals than to private foundations, simply because they award many individual grants to their own employees. They can help with educational expenses, or sometimes provide emergency funds for medical bills. If you do have a connection with a corporation as an employee or an employee's family member, you should definitely explore the possibilities. The corporation may already have a specific program set up to assist you. Sometimes even a business connection with a corporation will provide an opening.

If you are planning a larger project—such as a theater piece, a health fair, or research work—then affiliation always helps, just as it does with private foundations. If you're applying directly to a company rather than a company foundation, affiliation can give them more possible ways to grant you funds. They can easily give a charitable contribution to a tax-exempt organization you're affiliated with. To receive funds as an individual, you will have to demonstrate that helping you offers them some clear business benefit.

HOW TO FOCUS YOUR IDEA TOWARD FUNDERS

Whether you apply as an individual or through an affiliate, it's always good to think about how your project can benefit the corporation. Maybe you can provide them with good public relations by associating their name with your community project. Maybe your project will enhance the quality of life in their community, improving the business climate there. Maybe your project will reach out to their employees or their customers, or help them attract new customers.

I can think of many good examples of creative approaches to corporate funding. When tax revenues were down in the early nineties, New York State severely slashed its financial support for the Puerto Rican Traveling Theater, based in New York City. The theater's director immediately turned to the business community, and was able to raise substantial support from corporations that wanted to do business with the growing Hispanic population. Another example: a large southern California automobile dealership advertised that it would write a $100 check to a muscular dystrophy campaign for every new car it sold in a certain period of time. This offer gave them a unique advertising and promotion campaign, and at the same time contributed funds to a worthy cause. Corporations are always interested in funding projects that will benefit them and others. So think creatively about ways to attract their interest in your project.

HOW TO RESEARCH CORPORATIONS

Your first step in researching corporate giving is, of course, to go to the basic directories. As with private foundations, you will then need to contact potential funders and request published guidelines and annual reports which outline the company's giving priorities. But to explore all the possibilities, you may need to go beyond the directories and contact companies that aren't in the listings. Let's look at these steps.

RESEARCHING THE CORPORATE FUNDER DIRECTORIES

There are three principal directories that will provide you with lists of hundreds of corporate funding sources in the United States:

- *National Directory of Corporate Giving.* 3rd edition. New York: The Foundation Center, 1993.
- *Corporate 500: The Directory of Corporate Philanthropy.* 10th edition. San Francisco: Public Management Institute, 1991.
- *Corporate Giving Directory.* 1996. Rockville, MD: The Taft Group, 1995.

You should also look into regional or state directories for your area, and pinpoint corporations based in your community. (See the Appendix, page 330, for a listing of state and regional directories.)

As you look through the directories, you will find corporate funders indexed by geographic location, subject, funding priorities, type of grant, type of recipient, and so on. As with all listings, check to see if you meet all of a funder's qualifications. If your project doesn't meet the restrictions or fit into the giving categories, don't put the funder on your prospect list.

You will find many listings for corporate or company foundations, and other listings for corporate giving programs or "corporate direct contributions programs." As you look through the directories, be aware that a company can be listed under its name, such as the Exxon Corporation, or under its foundation, such as the Exxon Foundation.

INTERPRETING THE LISTINGS

Let's look at a typical, fictionalized corporate foundation listing and analyze what you can learn from it.

METROPOLITAN BANK CORPORATION
Metropolis, New York

Business Activities: Bank holding company; commercial banks.

Financial Profile for 1993: Number of employees, 20,200; assets, $34,116,000,000; Fortune 12 (commercial banking); Forbes 35 (assets).

Corporate Officers: Thomas L. Jackon, Chair; Edison Ford, President and C.E.O.; Rockwell Carnegie, Executive V.P. and Treasurer.

Subsidiaries: Bismarck Corporate Center, Bismarck, ND; Metrobanc Financial Co., Metropolis, NY; Metrobanc Mortgage Center, Weston, MD; Metrobank New Jersey, Watergap, NJ; Locality Bank, Key West, FL; Delaware Hospital Trust, Easton, DL.

Giving Statement: Giving through a company-sponsored foundation and a corporate contributions program.

METROPOLITAN BANK CORPORATE GIVING PROGRAM
c/o Public Affairs Department
P.O. Box 0000
Metropolis, NY 00000 914-123-4567

Financial Data (year ended 12/31/92): Total giving, $2,072,795, including $844,620 for grants, $403,318 for employee matching gifts, and $824,857 for in-kind gifts.

Purpose and Activities: "Since its founding in 1830, Metropolitan Bank has considered it an essential part of its role to recognize community needs and channel its resources to most productively meet them." Metropolitan Bank seeks to help meet the financial needs and enhance the health and welfare of the communities the Bank serves, to improve educational programs and opportunities for all members of these communities, to help those who require special assistance to assume a full role in society, and to participate in major public policy issues that affect the well-being of the community. Metropolitan Bank supports civic and community organizations, culture and the arts, education, including higher education, health and hospitals, social services, in-kind services, and United Way. The Bank also administers an employee matching gifts program, and in 1990 started an employee community service program. Two international business units also contribute employee time, resources, facilities, and cash; and affiliate banks in New Jersey and Florida also operate their own contributions programs.

Types of Support: In-kind gifts, operating budgets, program-related investments, capital campaigns, endowment funds.

Limitations: Giving primarily in the Greater Metropolitan region, and two other regions in NY: Upstate and Downstate; affiliate banks in New Jersey and Florida have contributions programs in their own communities. No support for religious programs. No grants to individuals, or for research projects, conferences, forums, benefits, and similar events.

Application Information:

Initial Approach: Proposal; write to nearest branch

Copies of proposal: 1

Deadline(s): 6 weeks prior to Committee meeting

Board Meeting date(s): the Corporate Contributions Committee considers requests in March, June, September, and December

Write: Eleanor Eisenhower, Manager, Corporate Contributions

METROPOLITAN BANK CORPORATION CHARITABLE FOUNDATION
c/o Metropolitan Bank
Government and Community Affairs Department
100 Bank Street
Metropolis, NY 00000   212-123-2123

Trust established in 1965.

Donor(s): Metropolitan Bank Corporation.

Financial Data (year ended 12/31/92): Assets, $12,483,323; gifts received, $4,823,986; expenditures, $4,212,914, including $4,645,289 for 352 grants. High: $100,000; low: $1,000; average: $2,500–$7,500.

Purpose and Activities: Giving limited to community organizations with programs in education, health and hospitals, social services, arts and culture, and the civic community.

Programs:

United Way: United Ways of New York; $1,066,200 for 1 award, 31 percent.

Social Services: Emphasis on human services for youth, families, and the aged. Interests, include employment and job training, food and shelter assistance, recreation programs, and multiservice organizations; $731,092, 18 percent. High: $40,000; low: $5,000; average: $2,000–$10,000.

Civic and Community Affairs: Emphasis on neighborhood revitalization efforts, low-income housing and commercial development, training for community leadership, capacity building for not-for-profit organizations, and programs to improve the environment; $600,234 for 77 awards, 16 percent. High $45,000; low: $1,000; average: $2,000–$15,000.

Higher/Other Education: Strongly committed in the Greater Metropolitan region, major contributions to ongoing programs working to improve the public schools and to school partnerships. Support for institutions of higher learning is primarily given to campaigns conducted for the institution as a whole, rather than to individual programs or departments. In addition, Metropolitan Bank assists organizations that provide services to adult learners and to those with special needs: $555,219 for 62 awards, 15 percent. High: $100,000; low: $1,000; average: $3,000–$15,000.

Culture and the Arts: Major cultural institutions, as well as smaller performing and visual arts organizations, are supported. Some emphasis is placed on arts service organizations, which increase the impact of individual groups, and community arts organizations, which help to bring arts to local communities; $499,321 for 83 awards, 14 percent. High: $35,000; low: $11,000; average: $2,000–$20,000.

Health/Hospitals: Hospital support is usually confined to capital and/or endowment campaigns. Emphasis is placed on community health centers and on organizations that help families with health care planning and treatment; $257,284, 6 percent. High: $30,000; low: $5,000; average: $2,500–$15,000.

Types of Support: Annual campaigns, building funds, general purposes, matching funds, operating budgets, special projects, continuing support, capital campaigns, endowment funds, equipment, scholarship funds, renovation projects.

Limitations: Giving primarily in New York. No support for religious or partisan causes, fund-raising events, conferences, or forums. No grants to individuals, or for research or fellowships; no loans.

Publications: Annual report, corporate giving report (including application guidelines), grants list, informational brochure.

Application Information:

Initial approach: Proposal or letter

Copies of proposal: 1

Deadline(s): At least 6 weeks before meetings

Board meeting date(s): 3rd week of March, June, September, and December

Final notification: 2 months

Write: Eleanor Eisenhower, Manager, Corporate Contributions

Trustees: Thomas L. Jackson, Edison Ford, William Withers

Number of Staff: 2 full-time professionals; 1 full-time support.

There's a lot of information to be gleaned from this type of corporate listing. First of all, it's clear that this is a "Big Daddy" type of corporate funder, with substantial assets and some far-flung operations, that really wants to be seen as a good corporate citizen, with a high profile in its community. The Metropolitan Bank operates both a corporate giving program and a corporate foundation, and clearly wants the good public relations value that it can get from philanthropic giving. This is not one of the small private or corporate foundations that want to give to special interests without great fanfare. Let's look at some specific insights we can gain from the listing.

Corporate Giving Program. This represents funds that the "Metropolitan Bank" gives directly out of its operating budget.

Financial data. Notice that the Corporate Giving Program balances its giving almost equally between cash grants and in-kind grants. Corporate funders are especially fond of in-kind grants, which are a way for them to derive secondary benefits from their buildings, salaried employees, or equipment.

Employee matching gifts are grants that a corporation gives to match a gift that an employee may make to a charitable or nonprofit cause. For example, a corporation may match an individual's private donation to a public radio station. An employee community service program means that the corporation encourages its employees to donate their time and efforts to community projects, and may grant them paid released time from their normal work duties.

Purpose and activities. Metropolitan Bank sees itself as having a long history of being a good corporate citizen, actively involved in the affairs of its community. It supports a broad range of community projects and activities. Note that you might also apply directly to subsidiaries for funding.

Types of Support. Metropolitan Bank gives to certain kinds of long-term needs, such as endowments and capital campaigns, that many funders do not. "Program-related investments" means that an educational organization that wants to set up a money-making operation, such as producing and distributing educational videotapes, could go to Metropolitan Bank for start-up funds.

Limitations. The geographical limitation is unambiguous (though there are those subsidiaries). The Metropolitan Bank clearly wants to steer away from controversial projects that would support specific religious or political agendas, or even potentially controversial research or conferences. Their focus is on projects with an obvious community benefit. They do not fund individuals directly, but if you are working with a community organization, on a community-oriented project, you could apply for funds through the organization.

Applications. Metropolitan Bank uses its branch offices as processing centers for applications, which helps its image in the local neighborhoods.

The Corporate Foundation. Metropolitan Bank may derive some tax benefits by giving through a corporate foundation, though it has to adhere to stricter government regulations for this portion of its giving. You'll notice that there are close ties between the foundation and the corporation and its giving program. The corporation is the sole donor to the foundation; the foundations's trustees include the corporation's Chairman of the Board and its C.E.O.; a single Manager of Corporate Giving administers both programs; and the Foundation Board and the Corporate Giving Committee seem to meet on the same dates and to consider grant applications simultaneously. In fact, there is no clear distinction between funding areas for the two programs. In this case, you would simply address your proposal to the Manager of Corporate Giving, and let the corporation decide whether it might wish to fund you out of corporate giving or through its foundation.

Financial Data. This listing gives you very specific information about the total funds granted, the number of grants, and the range of amounts. You can see where your request might fit into this range.

Programs. Here you get even more specific information, including the percentage of giving to each type of program and the kinds of gifts to each, as well as the dollar range. It should be easy to see whether your type of project might fit into the bank's giving patterns and to estimate the amount you might request. Though there's no clear indication of this, Metropolitan Bank may be giving its larger grants to the endowments or capital campaigns of larger, established nonprofit organizations, and the smaller grants to smaller organizations with specific or short-term projects. Or it may be the other way around. You would have to look at their corporate giving report or grants list to get a sense of this.

Types of Support. Again, we see a remarkable range of types of giving.

Limitations. Again, the same geographic limitations, avoidance of controversial or partisan or research support, and the restriction of giving to nonprofit organizations. The focus is on the community—an individual would have to be pursuing a project of clear community benefit, and apply through an organization.

Publications. Metropolitan Bank is really making an effort to get the word out about its programs, with a number of different informational publications. Write and ask for them all.

Applications. Procedures are very straightforward, identical for both corporate giving and the corporate foundation. One application will serve for both sources.

Number of Staff. If you think of it, this is a small staff for the amount of money the bank is giving away. There are only two full-time professionals, plus the Manager of Corporate Giving, and they share a single assistant. These people are working hard, and won't have a great deal of time for back-and-forth exchanges with applicants. They managed to give out 352 grants during the past year, which means about 90 grants were approved for each quarter that the Board and Committee met. And you can be sure that many more applications were received. This is a lot of sheer paperwork to keep track of, to say nothing of the careful evaluation that the staff must do for each application.

GUIDELINES AND ANNUAL REPORTS

Like family foundations, corporate foundations generally publish application guidelines and annual reports. In fact, since they are usually well staffed and well supported by the parent company, they may publish additional material, such as a corporate giving report or newsletter, a grants list, or an informational brochure. Official corporate giving programs will have guidelines, but usually not an annual report, which they leave to the corporate foundation. As you know by now, you should always request copies of these publications to help you decide whether you qualify for the funding programs. Oftentimes, companies will not provide enough information in a directory listing, because they don't want to be inundated with requests.

The annual reports provide detailed information about the corporation's giving policies. They may describe the history of the corporate foundation or contribution program, and for what purpose it was founded. They will outline the major kinds of programs and projects the company has funded. They usually list names of grant recipients, with brief histories of their affiliations and the amounts of money they received. Annual reports and guidelines will also provide information on how to apply.

You may find it much harder to get information about direct corporate giving programs. Unlike private independent foundations, which must file reports with the IRS, corporate giving programs aren't ruled by such regulations, and do not have to file any special reports or disclose any information to the public. When they make gifts from their operating budgets, they will not necessarily include these in any of their statistics.

Some of the very large corporations, like major banks that seek good community relations, will be happy to inform you about their giving programs. Smaller companies, and those without company foundations, may not wish to publicize their corporate giving. They may fear attracting an avalanche of requests, or alienating customers who might find some grants controversial. They may have no formal giving program at all and give solely on a discretionary basis, to people and projects they already know about, or to the few who seek them out.

Many giving programs will not have guidelines or annual reports, though you might find some reference to them buried in the annual report of the corporation itself. You may also find some reference to a giving program in a corporate foundation's annual report, but not necessarily. Funds may be channeled through an advertising, marketing, or public relations department and never appear in the company's financial reports as charitable giving. So how can you find out about this kind of corporate giving? You have to go beyond the listings and beyond the reports.

GOING BEYOND THE LISTINGS

When you are looking for corporate funding, it often makes sense to target companies in your community or companies that you think might respond to your particular project, and just approach them, even if they don't appear in funder listings. Small companies may not want to be listed in national directories; they may have no history of corporate funding, or simply prefer to respond to proposals on a discretionary basis.

If you have a community-based project, you might find several local companies who would be willing to support you. You might come up with an idea that would both support your project and provide a company with good public relations. Or you might look for a connection between the company's products and services and your own project. If you have a project involving children, for example, you might target a company that offers products or services for children or parents. Even when they have no traditional history of corporate giving, companies can suddenly decide to get involved. They're flexible enough to respond to immediate community needs and can come through much more quickly than private foundations and government funders.

How can you start to locate unlisted funders? The best place is in your own community. Look in the Yellow Pages, inquire at the Chamber of Commerce, and look through the newspapers, including the financial pages, to see which local companies are advertising. Check out any local business magazines or journals. You might look at some general business directories to identify local companies. Two that you might find useful are:

- *Standard & Poor's Business Directory,* which lists major companies in the United States.
- *Who's Who in Finance.* Try writing directly to some of these company officers.

When you do contact a company, inquire whether they have a foundation or a corporate contributions program, and who the appropriate contact person is. Sometimes a company will have both a foundation and a contributions department. If they are not listed in any directory and don't seem to have any official corporate contributions programs, ask for their public relations or community relations department. You can also try approaching their director of marketing or director of advertising. If it's a very small company, try to get through to the president. At any company you approach, remember to ask about noncash grants and in-kind donations as well. Be creative in thinking of corporations that might help you with goods and services.

One word of warning: it's essential to be as careful about judging an unlisted company's potential interest in your project as you are when you look at directory guidelines, funding limitations, and qualifications. Perhaps even more so. Try to decide if there really is some logical reason why a company would be interested in funding you. Rule out companies for whom this seems unlikely. You not only want to concentrate your efforts where they'll do the most good, you want to avoid harassing companies with inappropriate requests.

Carefully research the companies you're interested in approaching. Ask for any public relations literature about them, find out who their officers are, and what their major corporate divisions are. Do some research in your public library, or at the local Chamber of Commerce. Never, never send out mass mailings headed "To Whom It May Concern." Nothing could be more destructive to your fund-raising campaign. When you approach a local corporation, you want to show that you are a thoughtful, careful person, worthy of serious consideration for funding.

HOW TO APPROACH CORPORATE FUNDERS

After you have thoroughly researched corporate sources, you should have an idea of their giving priorities and restrictions. How you approach the corporation depends not only on your own project, but also on the way they set up their corporate giving. If they have a foundation, and you meet its qualifications, then you will apply to it just as you would to any other private foundation (see Chapter 5). If they have an official corporate contributions program, and you've researched guidelines and applications procedures for the program, then you simply follow the published procedures. If you are requesting in-kind services, such as the donation of computer equipment, office space, etc., then you will generally apply through a direct giving program.

If a company has a foundation but you don't qualify for its funding or you are interested in noncash donations, you may want to see if there is a corporate contributions program that you might qualify for.

You can write the foundation, or call if you know it's well staffed, to ask if there is such a program administered directly by the company.

It may be that you will need to approach a corporation that you haven't discovered in any listing and that doesn't publicize guidelines or information about its programs. In this case, it is okay to make an initial telephone call, since you need to identify the individual you should approach. If it's a large company, start with a community relations, public affairs, or public relations office, and ask whether the company has a corporate foundation or a corporate contributions program. If they do, ask for any published guidelines or information about the program that's available. If there are no published guidelines, ask for the name of an officer to whom you could write a letter about a project they might be interested in. Try to find out who handles the corporate contributions program. If there is no official program, find out the name of the director of advertising or public relations. If it's a small company, you may be told to write directly to the president.

You will need to approach a corporate giving program differently from the way you'd approach a corporate foundation. A corporate foundation is like a private foundation, and you will be submitting a proposal or application. When you approach a corporate giving program, especially if there are no guidelines, the best way to make contact is to write a simple letter of request to the officer whose name you've been given. (See Chapter 9 of this book for help with writing this letter.)

When you're dealing with corporate giving programs, as opposed to corporate foundations, you may want to go ahead and make brief telephone contact with the contributions officer. Ask if you can send a letter of request, or whether they might consider your type of project. You don't have to be as strict about sticking to written correspondence as you do with foundations. By making a call, you save yourself the trouble of writing a letter of request if they are out of funds at the moment, or if they do not fund in your area. If they don't have funds available, you might find out if there is another way they could support you, such as through in-kind services.

However, you want to be careful not to bother these very busy people. Corporate funders are constantly bombarded with requests, many of them inappropriate, just as the private funders are. If you do call, be sure you've done some research and careful thinking, so that you can quickly explain why you think your project might be of interest to this particular corporation. Let the program officer take the lead.

If you're lucky, you may develop a rapport with a program officer that can lead to valuable support. But never, never just launch into a long speech about yourself and your project without letting the officer get a word in edgewise. Summarize your project in two or three sentences, and ask if you could send them a letter describing it in detail. If they want to know more, they'll ask. Otherwise just thank them and get off the phone.

If you are contacting a large national corporation, try to make telephone contact with a corporate program officer at the regional office nearest you. Some corporations have locations and subsidiaries throughout the country, and there are usually program officers at these regional locations. Your local office will probably review your application, so it will help you to have a clear sense of the particular interests of the regional office.

You should never send a letter or proposal to several people at the same corporation. Never write separately to the advertising director *and* the director of public affairs. Pick one person for your initial contact, and go through them. If they don't think your proposal is likely, ask if there's someone else at the company you might contact. If they feel they should pass you along to someone else, let them make this decision. *Never approach two people at the same time.* It will look as if you are playing games and trying to manipulate people. This will only create a bad reputation for you at the company.

THE APPLICATION PROCESS

If you've received application guidelines for a corporate foundation or corporate contribution program, just follow the instructions. There's no one typical type of application. They may have an application form, or they may request anything from a simple letter to a full-blown proposal. If there are no published guidelines and you do talk to a corporate contributions officer, ask if there's any particular format they would like you to follow. Otherwise just use the "simple letter of request" described in Chapter 9.

If they are interested in you, they may contact you to arrange for a meeting. Generally, you will have a meeting with the corporate foundation or contributions staff only if they are seriously considering you for funding. They may also want to visit your facility or project, if you have one in operation.

Always be sure to verify deadlines, which are strictly adhered to because of budget allocations. If the contributions committee is meeting in December, that is when they will be allocating a specific amount of funds. This is similar to a meeting of the Board of Trustees at a private foundation.

How Corporations Respond

Corporate funders get swamped with requests, many of them inappropriate, just as the family foundations do. They too have to wade through hundreds of completely inappropriate requests from people who haven't bothered to read their guidelines. Even if you have carefully targeted a corporate funder and believe you fit within their guidelines, you will have to give them time to weed out the proposals that don't.

Corporate foundations generally have staffs, and the larger the corporation the larger the staff. This means that you will generally find it easier to get information from them than from other foundations. They will usually be able to track your proposal and give you a response. Established corporate contributions programs are also staffed. But if you are seeking discretionary funds from a company that doesn't have an established contributions program, you will have to be patient and especially considerate. People who have other full-time duties at the company may be looking at proposals on a volunteer basis. To deal with your proposal, they may have to shift their time and attention away from important corporate activities and enlist support from other corporate officers. Take this into account when you are contacting them or waiting for a response.

When you send a proposal to a corporate foundation, follow the same rules that you would with any foundation: read the guidelines about response time and wait for them to respond. If you are applying to a corporate contributions program or to another corporate department, it's okay to follow up your letter or proposal with a short phone call to the contributions office to make sure it has arrived. You can ask for an estimated response time if you can't find one in any published guidelines.

Corporate foundations generally operate the same way as private foundations in terms of response time and notifying applicants. Some corporate giving programs may have a somewhat quicker turnaround time and may want to have more personal contact with you, but it all depends on the particular company.

WHAT HAPPENS AFTER YOU APPLY?

Corporate funders process proposals in much the same way that private funders do. At corporate foundations, the process is the same: review by a program officer, review by a contributions committee, and final decision by the Board of Trustees. With corporate giving programs, a program officer will initially review your proposal, then recommend it to a contributions committee, which will vote on whether to fund it or not. It may or may not go to any higher level. If you submit a request where there is no formal contributions committee, a marketing director—or even the president, if it's a small company—may make the decision.

At a corporate giving program, it's often an individual who decides on your proposal, though it may go to a contributions committee or need to be approved by top management. Many times, corporate foundations and giving programs have different people making the decisions. And they do deal differently with decision making: the foundations will stick more closely to their mandate and mission, while the giving programs may respond to a wider range of projects.

With some of the larger national corporations, you will very often apply to a local or regional office, and that office may decide on your proposal. AT&T, for example, likes to work through its regional offices. The company feels that the regional office is simply better qualified than the national office to assess and react to the needs in a particular community.

You may have to research corporate funders a little differently than others. You will also have to think about how your project will benefit a corporation, directly or indirectly, and you may have the opportunity for a little more personal contact than with private foundations. In the end, though, any funds you raise from corporate sponsors will be one more important portion of your total funding.

7

GOVERNMENT
FUNDERS

Budgets go up and budgets go down, but everyone knows that governments have deep pockets. Every year your local, state, and federal government together contribute billions of dollars to fund thousands of programs for individuals and organizations. Governments don't just repair roads and build bombers—they contribute money for scholarships, loans, community service programs, artists grants, research, and start-up costs for new business ventures. In fact, there is scarcely a region, a population group, or an aspect of contemporary life in which some governmental agency is not trying to make a positive difference.

Many different kinds of government agencies give grants. Indeed, so many do that it can be a little confusing to sort out the various levels of bureaucracy and the special programs. Let's just look at the federal programs, for instance. On one level, you have the major government departments like the Department of Energy and the Department of Health and Human Services. Within each of those departments, there are a number of separate agencies or "administrations," and sometimes offices within agencies. These lower-level agencies administer *federal programs,* which are authorized by acts of Congress. It's the federal programs that actually distribute grant money, and goods and technical assistance. They have names like "Promotion of the Humanities," "Travel to Collections," and "Minority Business Development."

In addition, there are free-standing, independent government operations that are not part of federal departments and agencies but that do give grants. These include institutions like the Library of Congress, the National Gallery of Art, and the National Institutes of Health; commissions like the Appalachian Regional Commission and the Commission on Civil Rights; and other entities like the Corporation for Public Broadcasting. All federal programs, no matter what agency or office administers them, have an individual federal program number, and all have been authorized either directly by Congress or indirectly by department policy. Some, like the Corporation for Public Broadcasting, disburse funds that are considered actual payments for product supplied rather than grants. These are not federal programs and do not appear in lists of grants with program numbers.

Though it may be the biggest in terms of sheer dollars, the federal government is only one part of the government funding picture. Myriad grant programs operate at the state, county, and municipality levels throughout the country. Many are official programs, like state arts councils. Others operate on an almost discretionary basis, especially through city and county governments. Cities and counties fund all kinds of special projects and events through offices like the parks and cultural affairs departments.

On the federal level, grant programs are authorized by Congress and must adhere to strict rules, procedures, and limitations. On the very local level, a mayor's office may have a good deal of discretion in supporting small projects.

A LITTLE HISTORY

Since President Roosevelt's New Deal in the 1930s, government funding has helped individuals buy homes, lease equipment, finance their education, hone their skills, and start businesses. Government funding has supported development of inventions, including the fax machine and other consumer products.

Broad-based government funding really flowered during the 1960s and 1970s, fueled by the social consciousness and economic surplus of the Kennedy and Johnson years. In those decades, lawmakers proposed that the federal government should take responsibility for basic societal needs—feeding the hungry, building low-income housing, underwriting the arts—and a great many programs were set up to fund both individuals and nonprofit organizations.

Under President Reagan, the 1981 Budget Reconciliation Act dramatically reversed this trend. In one fell swoop, this piece of legislation severely cut the overall amount of federal monies available and effectively killed the broad spectrum of federal funding programs established by the previous administrations.

However, the consensus of support for this funding shift soon crumbled, and the public called for the reinstatement of a broad base of socially responsive federal funding programs. During recent years, lawmakers have responded to the perceived needs of their constituencies, and have continued government support of the general welfare and specific initiatives through grant programs. Each year, of course, and at every level of government, the shifting political climate influences the level of support available for specific programs. Support levels are affected by which political party is in power, the popularity of certain causes with the public or the media, demographic shifts, and the strengths of competing social needs. All of these factors influence the amount of money available for things like environmental cleanup, AIDS research, support for the homeless, and support for the arts. While funding for some programs has dried up, other programs have sprung up to replace them. Budgets rise and fall, programs come and go, but government funding remains an important potential source for the grant seeker.

GOVERNMENT FUNDING TODAY

According to the *Catalog of Federal Domestic Assistance*, in 1995 the federal government made available more than $875 million in grants, through nearly 1,390 federal assistance programs, administered by fifty-three federal agencies. Approximately 55 percent of these programs offer grants to individuals and nonprofit organizations through direct payments, direct loans, project grants, and other means. (Some of the government programs only fund state and local government projects.) State and local governments add their own contributions to this picture.

THE GOVERNMENT FUNDING MAZE

Private foundations all function pretty much alike, and are easy to identify. This is not true for government funders. Government funding is administered by a huge variety of departments, agencies, offices, commissions, and institutes; there can be agencies nested within other agencies, and multiple programs within departments, each with its own separate administrative structure. Similar programs can be administered by different agencies, which may or may not know about their counterparts. States have their own departments and agencies, which sometimes parallel the federal ones, but many have different names or missions. Counties and municipalities may have some similar offices, like parks departments, but can vary widely in their individual programs. Often the federal government will allocate monies to state or local governments, which will then administer programs locally.

This incredible variety of programs has its good and bad sides. On the positive side, there are a vast number of programs out there that can offer support to grant seekers and to projects of almost every imaginable description. On the other hand, it can be frustrating and difficult to thread your way through the maze of offices and agencies to find the specific programs that can help you. Just researching government programs can be difficult—the standard directory for federal programs has over 1500 pages, while state and local governments do not even publish such references.

Once you find a program that might help you, you may run into further difficulties. Though many procedures are standard from program to program, each agency or office will have its own peculiarities. Some are very good at dealing with the public, while at others you may find it difficult to get anyone on the phone or to get a response to a letter. Some program guidelines will be very clear, while others may use bureaucratic jargon and refer you to obscure government regulations and pamphlets. It can be difficult to get help in deciphering these guidelines. You will apply to some programs through a national office, but for others you will have to locate a regional office to process your application. Government application forms can be extremely detailed. You may have to break down your project and budget information differently for different programs. And government staff will go over them in detail, sometimes rejecting applications that don't follow instructions to the letter.

This is not to scare you off, because the government is a very important funding source for both individuals and organizations. There is a lot of money available, and government grants, unlike many private ones, can be large enough to single-handedly fund entire projects. Government grants can be renewed and can be extended to cover multiyear projects. But you will need to take extra time, and call on all your patience and perseverance, to pursue government funding. If you know what to expect going in, it is easier to adjust to the process of seeking government grants.

WHAT KINDS OF GRANTS DO THEY GIVE?

Government agencies help citizens meet their goals through a huge variety of different kinds of support. Besides outright project grants, these include loans, technical assistance, training grants, research or scholarship money, and planning grants for specific projects. The type of funding varies from agency to agency. Many programs offer technical assistance, which means they will help you manage or operate your project activities. They can help you raise funds, or budget and plan your project. They can give you legal or marketing advice and help with other aspects of project management. They don't only help with nonprofit activities—many programs assist small businesses.

As with private foundations, the largest number of individual federal grants are given for scholarships. Then comes money for fellowships, for independent projects or research, and for doctoral dissertations.

Government agencies, more so than private funders, do react well to requests for renewed funding and long-term support. Local governments sometimes help to fund special events, often in coordination with local businesses and private foundations.

GIVING LIMITATIONS

Geographical limitations clearly come into play for state and local governments. Federal grants are usually focused on subjects or issues and are available nationwide. Often, though, federal funds will be allocated on a regional basis to federal offices or local governments, and you will apply for funds through the regional office of an agency.

Even state governments may channel funding through regional or local offices.

Many government programs are available to the general public, but many others limit their giving to certain populations or industries, such as minorities, farmers, Native Americans, and the economically disadvantaged. If you meet the very specific requirements and criteria, you have a good chance of getting funding.

GRANTS FOR INDIVIDUALS

The federal government has a history of granting awards to individuals, and many departments and agencies do so. Grants go to individual artists, scholars, researchers, scientists, business people, and veterans. In comparison with private foundations, government agencies are remarkably willing to fund individuals. Of course, some programs will restrict their funding to organizations, but even here the range is very wide. Government grants go to both profit and nonprofit organizations and institutions, to public and private agencies, to businesses, partnerships, and joint ventures. So if a program you are interested in doesn't fund individuals directly, there are many institutions you can affiliate with to receive flow-through funding.

WHAT AREAS DO GOVERNMENT FUNDERS SUPPORT?

Government programs fund a great variety of activities, subjects, and social issues. These programs support the arts and literature, historical studies, business development, education, the environment, health care, medical research, and scientific research, among other things.

Government grants are a significant source of funding for nonprofit organizations in several key areas. In 1990, they provided about 40 percent of the budgets for social services agencies and about 35 percent of health organizations' budgets. They provided between 10 and 20 percent of the budgets for organizations working in the areas of education and research, and arts and culture.

As you begin your research, you will start to get a better feel for the multitude of government departments, administrations, agencies, and programs. But let's look at some examples.

Agriculture. The Department of Agriculture funds many different programs. Just a few examples: they offer housing and business loans to farmers who have suffered from a natural disaster; the Animal and Plant Health Protection Service protects U.S. agriculture from plant and animal diseases and offers project grants; the Distant Learning and Medical Link Grants (under the Rural Electrification Administration) provide funds to set up telecommunications and computer networks to provide medical and education benefits to people living in rural areas.

The Arts and Culture. The National Endowment for the Arts (NEA), which has persevered despite much controversy, fosters American art and new talent through the funding of choreographers, filmmakers, writers, performers, artists, opera singers, etc. The NEA operates many programs, and one must apply to the individual program—whether the Opera/Musical Theater Program, the Dance Program, or whatever. The NEA funds both organizations and individuals and supports arts education and special events as well as the creation of original work.

The National Endowment for the Humanities (NEH) operates a number of programs that fund projects in literature, history, languages, and the like. They support everything from original research to projects like Ken Burns's major television series, *The Civil War*.

Both the NEA and the NEH give funds to state arts agencies, historical societies, and nonprofit citizen councils, to support the arts and humanities on the state and local level.

Commerce. The Department of Commerce administers many different grant programs through its agencies. For example, the National Oceanic and Atmospheric Administration, which is part of the Department of Commerce, operates a program that helps compensate people in the fishing industry for damage or loss of their vessels caused by foreign fishing vessels.

Education. For students, the federal government offers five financial aid programs for higher education through the Department of Education. These are the Pell Grant Program, the Supplemental Education Opportunity Grants (SEOG), the Perkins Loan Program, the Guaranteed Student Loan, and the College Work-Study Program. All of these grants and loans are based on a student's financial need. The central Office of Student Financial Assistance in Washington, D.C., works closely with colleges and universities to administer these programs.

Departments and agencies besides the Department of Education offer scholarships for specific areas. These include the Department of Health and Human Services, the Department of Energy, the Department of Housing and Urban Development, the Department of Justice, the Bureau of Indian Affairs, and the National Emergency Training Center. For example, the Department of Health and Human Services offers grants to repay educational loans of doctors and scientists who agree to do AIDS research.

Health. The Department of Health and Human Services administers many different grant programs that support health and medical projects. For example, it administers programs that research and address alcohol and drug abuse, such as the Demonstration Grants for the Prevention of Alcohol and Other Drug Abuse Among High Risk Youth. The National Institutes of Health also supports medical research and health projects.

Housing. The Department of Housing and Urban Development, better known as HUD, administers programs like the Home Equity Conversion Mortgages, which help elderly people convert their home equity into retirement funds, and the Home Ownership and Opportunity for People Everywhere program, which helps low-income people become homeowners.

Science. Departments and agencies that fund science projects include the National Science Foundation, the Department of Defense, the Department of the Navy, the Department of Energy, and others. For example, the Department of Commerce, through the National Oceanic and Atmospheric Administration, sponsors basic and applied research in clouds and precipitation, to help scientists who are trying to discover ways to induce rainfall. The same administration also supports research into both long- and short-term climate forecasting.

Another example: the Department of Health and Human Services provides research grants to small businesses to develop scientific information about potentially toxic or hazardous chemicals.

Veterans. The Department of Labor sponsors many programs to assist veterans, such as the Veterans Employment Program and regional programs to assist disabled veterans with jobs and job training. There is even an Assistant Secretary of the Department of Labor for Veterans Employment Training. The Small Business Administration (SBA) offers a program called Entrepreneurial Training for U.S. Veterans.

This is just a small sampling, but you get the picture: almost every government department or agency offers a range of grants to support individuals and groups, either directly or through research and projects that further the goals of the agency.

FUNDING FOR SMALL BUSINESSES AND ENTREPRENEURS

The federal government has a special interest in supporting American businesses, particularly small businesses. Many different agencies support small business ventures—through grants, loans, contracts, and technical services. Federal assistance helps small and new businesses provide new jobs in local communities and opportunities for people to better their lives. Federal grants help minorities and the disadvantaged by assisting them to start and run profit-making businesses that will contribute to the economic health of the community. The U.S. Government also gives selective research grants to businesses in order to further scientific and social aims.

State and local governments also understand the benefits of encouraging small businesses, and they assist with contracts, grants, and services. Some state programs even help entrepreneurs obtain venture capital—in other words, they lend a business money and become its partner. (Contact the Department of Commerce or Office of Business Development in your state to explore this type of funding.)

Many federal departments and agencies give grants and other direct support to small businesses in order to further their own particular goals. The National Institute of Mental Health, the Appalachian Regional Commission, the National Institutes of Health, the Department of Agriculture, the Department of Commerce, the Department of Transportation, the Department of Labor—all of these, and others, give grants to small businesses.

There is also a free-standing agency devoted entirely to the support of small businesses: the Small Business Administration (SBA), which has field offices throughout the country. The SBA administers special programs to support businesses owned by women, minorities, and the disadvantaged, as well as a wide range of general business development programs. It gives grants to assist research into business development and to provide services to business. It offers technical and management assistance through several programs.

The Small Business Administration also offers various kinds of nongrant support, including loans for special needs and circumstances. The Direct Loan Program, for example, offers low-interest business loans to creditworthy, low-income individuals and to privately held businesses located in areas of high unemployment, which have had trouble securing loans from commercial lenders. Direct SBA loans of up to $150,000 are available (the average loan is $68,000), and loan repayment can be structured over a long time period. (There are some restrictions on the types of businesses that can apply.) The SBA wants to help small-business owners get started, but it also wants to make sure it gets its money back.

- **TIP:** For literature on federal business loans, write or call
  The Director, Loan Policy and Procedures Branch
  Small Business Administration
  409 Third Street, S.W.
  Washington, DC 20416
  202-205-6490

Other government agencies offer grants and quasi-grants to support specific kinds of business projects. For example, the Corporation for Public Broadcasting, the Public Broadcasting Service, and the Independent Television Service all offer money to fund television programs and series. They may call for producers to address a specific subject or to come up with an original idea. These aren't strictly free grants, since they involve a contractual agreement to provide specified programming for broadcast on specified dates. There may be other restrictions on how the producer can show or distribute the work, and producers may have to come up with some of the money from other sources. But they generally do extend some rights of ownership to the producer, once the original broadcast schedule has been met.

How to Steer Your Idea Toward Government Funders

Seeking government grants doesn't require creative thinking so much as very careful research to find the programs that are right for you. The process can be frustrating, but if you are patient and persevere, the rewards can be great. Many government funder programs are so narrowly focused that if you meet the application requirements, you may almost automatically receive a grant. Other programs are very competitive, with committees that make judgment calls on the proposals they receive, just as they do at private foundations. But you can win some grants just by going through those listings with a fine-tooth comb.

When you are seeking funding on a local, county, or municipal level, things may be a little bit looser. If you are seeking funding for a community-oriented project, it may be important to make some personal contact with local officials, have a meeting, or get them to visit a facility you are operating. You will need to show that your project is going to make a real contribution to the life of a neighborhood, community, or population group. It may be helpful to indicate that there is already strong community support or interest in your project. Local officials will often respond for purely political reasons when they see active community interest.

HOW TO RESEARCH GOVERNMENT GRANTS

It's almost mind-boggling to consider how many different departments, administrations, agencies, and programs in existence can provide you with funds. This adds to the amount of paperwork you'll have to wade through, and the number of people you'll need to contact for information. However, the best place to start, as always, is with directories and listings.

You can turn to various kinds of sources: (1) independent guides and directories to government funding; (2) directories for specific subjects, geographic areas, and population groups, which list federal and local government programs along with private funders; and (3) the master guide for federal programs, the *Catalog of Federal Domestic Assistance.*

For some useful general guides to government funding, you can refer to the following:

- *Financing a College Education: The Essential Guide for the 90s,* by Judith B. Margolin. New York: Plenum Press, 1989.
- *The Federal Educational and Scholarship Funding Guide.* West Warwick, RI: Grayco, 1989.
- *The United States Government Manual* (Washington, DC: Office of the Federal Register). This describes the broad responsibilities of all the major federal government departments and agencies. It doesn't list grant programs specifically, but it does list various publications that are offered by each agency. If you know that an agency gives grants—and many do—you can find useful information about them in some of these publications. You can contact the relevant agencies to have your name put on their mailing lists for program information.
- The U.S. Department of Education's *The Student Guide: Five Federal Financial Aid Programs* (Washington, DC: Government Printing Office). This describes federal assistance through Pell

Grants, college work-study programs, student loans, and other grants.

- *Free Money®* *from the Federal Government,* by Laurie Blum. New York: John Wiley & Sons, 1996.

- **TIP:** To get a free copy of *The Student Guide,* the official "bible" of the federal government's financial assistance programs, write to:

Federal Student Aid Program, Dept. J-8
Pueblo, CO 81009.

Or telephone the Federal Student Aid Information Center, Rockville, MD, at 301-984-4070.

For state and local funding, you'll need to dig a little deeper. Many state and local governments publish some kind of guide to their departments and agencies, similar to the *U.S. Government Manual.* These will have descriptions of program responsibilities and office addresses. You can also ask your local librarian to direct you to any reference materials about regional funding. You may even be able to get research help from the office of a state senator or representative.

Most guides that are not published by the federal government are fairly easy to use, and they will resemble the foundation directories you may already be familiar with. The biggest and most complete guide, however, is published by the federal government itself, and it's *not* so easy to use.

CATALOG OF FEDERAL DOMESTIC ASSISTANCE

The *Catalog of Federal Domestic Assistance* is the bible for federal funding. It lists every single federal grant program, and identifies the many departments and agencies that administer federal grants. (It's worth noting, though, that the *Catalog* does not list some sources of federal funds, such as the Corporation for Public Broadcasting and the National Institutes of Health. These do fund projects, but through their own procedures, not through official federal programs established by Congress.)

The *Catalog* is a massive resource. You can't even call it a book, since it is so big—about 1,500 pages—that the government doesn't bind it. Instead, they offer it in looseleaf form, for purchasers to put into their own binders. It's revised every six months, so more pages keep coming. You can find it at well-stocked libraries, and it is also available from U.S. Government bookstores. Considering its size, the price is surprisingly reasonable: $46. Given the heft of this monster, though, you'll probably be grateful to your library for housing it. (If you do decide to purchase one, see the Appendix, page 324, for the phone number for the U.S. Government bookstores.)

The *Catalog* can be both a rewarding and an infuriating resource. The physical form is daunting, and not only because of its sheer size. It's printed on very thin paper, with two text columns per page, in very small type. There are no tabs, color coding, or anything to help you find your way through the sections. It's written in bureaucratic language, which is sometimes difficult to decipher. It does have some useful indexes, and others that may seem impenetrable or irrelevant. There is so much information, compared with other kinds of directories and listings, that it's difficult to wade through, and it can take time to digest what you find.

Still, you can find programs and resources here that you may find nowhere else. If you approach the *Catalog* with the right attitude, you will find it useful. The first step is to prepare yourself mentally and otherwise. You are going to have to spend a lot more time with this than with other directories, including some time just getting familiar with it. Use reading glasses, or a good reader's magnifying glass, to help with the fine print. If you have decided to buy your own copy of the *Catalog,* try to make it physically easier to use: get several large ring binders to hold the different sections, and use looseleaf dividers with tabs to mark off sections. Don't expect to find everything you are looking for in the first section or two. But rest assured—it gets easier as you get more familiar with it.

To help get you started, let's look at some specific sections of the *Catalog* that you will find useful.

The Indexes. These are at the beginning of the *Catalog*, instead of the end. Some are useful, others not. The first index lists government departments, subdivided by agency, followed by all the free-standing entities, like the Library of Congress. If you browse through this, you'll get a feel for the great variety of administrations and agencies, and may run across an agency that you want to look into. It's only useful as an index if you already know that an agency gives a grant that would apply to you but you don't know the program name. If you know the name of a specific program that an agency administers, you can find it in the second index, which lists programs by name. The third index, called the Applicant Index, lists departments and agencies again, with columns and checks to indicate types of grant recipients. You can scan these pages quickly to see which agencies give grants to individuals, for example. There is also a deadline index, which is not very useful, and an index that gives the functions of all departments and agencies, which you can refer to if you're interested in a particular one. Probably the most useful index is the last one, which lists specific program numbers by subject area.

As you browse through the first index—the Agency Index—you'll see that under each department heading, there are subcategories for agencies and programs. For example, under the Department of Agriculture, there are programs and grants in soil conservation, forestry, etc. There are also other agencies, such as the Forest Service and the Farmers Home Administration, which might fund similar projects. Carefully consider more than one agency for funding, since the giving interests of some agencies can overlap.

The Listings. These make up the bulk of the *Catalog.* They're in two columns per page, in very fine print. Though they're hard to read, and you have to decipher the government-speak, they do offer a wealth of information about each program. These listings are much more thorough than typical foundation listings or third-party listings— they give you nearly all the information that you would find in a set of guidelines and an annual report from a private foundation. But you really have to concentrate to absorb all this information and decide if your project fits the guidelines. It's all there for you, but it takes time to pore over the details.

At the back of the *Catalog* you'll find several appendices, some of which are useful.

Appendix 4, Agency Regional and Local Office Addresses. The program listing may not give a contact address, but instead refer you to your local or regional agency office. This is where you find it.

Appendix 5, Additional Sources of Information. This section describes the Federal Information Center Program, with offices in seventy-two metropolitan areas, and a midwestern regional area, which you can call for general information about government programs.

Appendix 6, How to Develop and Write Grant Proposals. This is a useful section, in larger type than the listings, that discusses the specific requirements of proposals for federal grants.

Connected with the *Catalog* is a computer database, called the Federal Assistance Programs Retrieval System (FAPRS), which allows grant seekers to search for the same program information by computer.

There are designated access points in each state where you can ask for a computer search of the database. You can also access the database through some commercial computer network companies. For more information, contact:

- Federal Domestic Assistance Catalog Staff
  General Services Administration
  Reporters Building, Room 101
  300 7th Street, S.W.
  Washington, DC 20407
  800-669-8331; 202-708-5126

Let's look at an actual listing from the *Catalog*. This program does not have the complications that some listings do, but it does use terminology that you'll see in other listings. Since it is an actual listing, I must beg you, please, to note very carefully the specific restrictions that apply to this program. This is the kind of program that is focused so specifically that any applicant who meets the requirements is likely to get funded. It is also so specific that perhaps not more than one or two of the thousands of readers of this book would come close to qualifying. Please do not hinder this agency from going about its valuable work, and *do not* contact the agency unless you really are the one in a thousand readers who has all the specific credentials to apply.

15.114 INDIAN EDUCATION—HIGHER EDUCATION GRANT PROGRAM
(Higher Education)

Federal Agency: BUREAU OF INDIAN AFFAIRS, DEPARTMENT OF THE INTERIOR.

Authorization: Snyder Act of 1921, Public Law 67-85, 42 Stat. 208, 25 U.S.C. 13.

Objectives: To provide financial aid to eligible Indian students to enable them to attend accredited institutions of higher education.

Types of Assistance: Project Grants.

Uses and Use Restrictions: Grant funds are to supplement the total financial aid package prepared by the college financial aid officer. Funds are intended to assist students in pursuing regular accredited college courses necessary for achievement of a college degree.

Eligibility Requirements:

Applicant Eligibility: Must be a member of an Indian tribe or Alaska Native Village being served by the Bureau, be enrolled or accepted for enrollment in an accredited college, have financial need as determined by the institution's financial aid office.

Credentials/Documentation: Certificate of Indian blood; college financial aid package; statement of acceptance by college, Bureau of Indian Affairs grant application; high school transcripts and grades for each term.

Application and Award Process:

Preapplication Coordination: Acceptance at a college or university and application for financial aid from the college using their approved needs analysis system.

Application Procedure: Students must be accepted by a college or university. Application forms are completed by applicant in accordance with instructions available upon request from the area office, agency or tribal contractor administering the program for the applicant's tribal group. Completed forms are submitted to the student's higher education program office at the agency, area, or tribal contract office of higher education.

Award Procedure: When an award is granted, student is notified and funds are sent to the applicant in care of college or university financial aid office.

Deadlines: March 15 for next regular academic term. Students should also meet college financial aid office deadlines. This is usually March 15.

Range of Approval/Disapproval Time: 6 to 10 weeks when all required documents are submitted.

Appeals: From the administering office to agency/Area Education Program Administrator, to Director, Office of Indian Education Programs, to Assistant Secretary—Indian Affairs to Secretary of the Interior or through tribal appeal process for tribal contract programs.

Renewals: Grants may be continued through undergraduate or graduate levels if student maintains acceptable progress and academic standing. Renewal applications must be submitted yearly by March 15 with updated grades or transcript.

Assistance Considerations:

Formula and Matching Requirements: Students are expected

to take advantage of the campus-based financial aid programs offered to all students, and any other scholarships which may be available to them.

Length and Time Phasing of Assistance: Grants are generally made for the academic year on a quarter or semester basis. There is an 8 semester limit for undergraduate degree programs unless an exception is requested for a program that takes 10 semesters to complete.

Post Assistance Requirements: of academic progress, change of courses, dropout intentions, and graduation (degree received and date of graduation).

Reports: Grade reports of students applying for continuation of grants are to be submitted at the end of each semester or quarter.

Audits: None.

Records: None.

Financial Information:

Account Identification: 14-2100-0-1-501.

Obligations: (Total program funds including grants) FY 91 $27,635,000; FY 92 est $26,960,000; and FY 93 est $0 [figure not yet available].

Range and Average of Financial Assistance: Average for fiscal year 1990 $1,800; 1991 $1,402; Range $200 to $7,000.

Program Accomplishments: In fiscal years 1991 and 1992 it is estimated that 14,800 students will be assisted.

Regulations, Guidelines, and Literature: 25 CFR 40; Bureau of Indian Affairs Manual, 62, IAM 5.

Information Contacts:

Regional or Local Office: See area offices or agencies in Catalog Address Appendix IV.

Headquarters Office: Office of Indian Education Programs, Code 522, Room MS 3516, 1849 C Street, NW, Washington, DC 20245.

Related Programs: 15.108, Indian Employment Assistance.

Examples of Funded Projects: Undergraduate applicant (typical): Student, single, freshman; 41/64 Oglala Sioux; Black Hills State College, South Dakota; major/minor, Undecided; degree objective: BS; total budget $5740. Student Contribution $700, Pell $2200; BIA $2800. Married or advanced degree applicant (typical): Student, married with three family members, 1/2 Sioux Tribe; University of North Dakota; major-medicine/minor-Biology; degree objective: MD; total budget $12,245; Pell $1625, CWS $1200, NDSL $1200, SEOG $400, Student Contribution $700, BIA $5,900.

Criteria for Selecting Proposals: A member of an Indian, Eskimo or Aleut tribe served by BIA. Enrolled in an accredited institution in pursuit of a regular or advanced degree. Must have a demonstrated financial need as determined by the institution's financial aid office.

INTERPRETING A LISTING

As you can see, the catalogue listing offers a great deal of information. The listing format is the same for each program, and once you get familiar with it, you'll find it easier to interpret new listings. As in the listing above, program information is sometimes spelled out in several ways in different sections, so you should have no trouble determining if the program is right for you. Let's look more closely at some of the sections and subsections.

Program Title, Federal Agency, Authorization, Objectives. The program Title begins with the federal program number, which is used for referencing and cross referencing in the catalogue. You are told which federal agency and department administers the program, and which acts of Congress authorized it. There is a clear statement of the objectives of the program.

Types of Assistance. These include direct project grants, as above, grants through state or local agencies, direct payments of expenses, direct loans, technical assistance, or other types of assistance or services.

Eligibility Requirements. These are usually spelled out in great detail, as in the example above. Note that the applicant may be different from the beneficiary of the grant, although in this example they are the same. (A state government might apply for assistance to disabled toddlers, for example.) This section, including the Credentials/Documentation requirements, should make it clear whether the program is right for you. In this example, you must not only be a member of an Indian tribe served by the Bureau of Indian Affairs but must provide a certificate of Indian blood.

Application and Award Process. The whole process will be spelled out in detail, including deadlines, approval time, the appeals process, and the renewal option, if it exists.

Assistance Considerations.　This spells out more details about the program and additional requirements.

Post-assistance Requirements.　This details the sort of information and reports that you must supply to the granting agency if you do receive a grant. Note that for certain programs, you may have to supply financial records and submit to an audit.

Financial Information, Program Accomplishments.　The financial information includes the total budget for the program, both actual and estimated for future fiscal years (FY's). (In the example, the budget was estimated only one year in advance.) The Program Accomplishments may tell you (in actual or estimated figures) just how many projects, programs, or individuals are served, what services are provided, or what percentage of eligible applicants are funded.

Regulations, Guidelines, Literature; Information Contacts.　These sections tell you how to find out more about the program. You don't have to locate or decipher all the printed government regulations about a program; just contact the appropriate office and ask for any printed information or guidelines they may have. The example above refers you to local offices and agencies that are listed in one of the catalogue appendixes; you may also be able to contact a national office directly.

Related Programs.　This will refer you to other federal programs that may offer support for similar needs or projects.

Examples of Funded Projects.　As you can see from the example, this may spell out in some detail the kinds of projects that have been funded and the dollar amounts of funding. (This program's grants are identified by "BIA," Bureau of Indian Affairs. Unfortunately, not all agencies will offer such helpful details, or any examples at all.)

Criteria for Selecting Proposals.　As in the example, this may repeat information offered elsewhere, may list specific criteria, or may simply indicate that all eligible applicants will be funded. Or the agency may offer no further information about criteria.

CONTACT THE AGENCY

Once you have pinpointed one or more programs that are suitable for you, you will need to contact the agencies that operate them for more information. You can also try to glean information about other programs offered by the agencies you contact, and there may be other agencies that offer matching funds or similar programs. This is where you begin to negotiate the maze of government bureaucracy. Be patient, and remember that the money is there. You just need to locate the programs that will disburse it to you.

When you contact each agency and confirm that you are eligible for the program, ask them to send you their most recent guidelines and application forms. Also ask if there are any special publications with program announcements. Remember that deadlines, programs, or policies may have changed since the listing you read was published.

If you have trouble with some of the jargon in a listing or guideline, try to get someone at the agency to explain it to you.

Getting More Information by Telephone

With federal programs you will often need to confirm that you are contacting the correct agency or department, so your procedure will differ a bit from the way you approach other funding sources. Some agencies, like the NEA and the NEH, have good, clear procedures for dealing with the public, and you may be able to pursue a grant entirely through written correspondence. With many government sources, however, you will need to use the telephone for some of your follow-up investigation. You'll need to get on the phone with Washington, or a regional agency office, or with your state or local government, to get guidelines and details about your eligibility for specific grant programs.

If you are working from a listing, start with the contact person mentioned in the reference directory. If it's a small or local program, this may be the program director. If it's a larger agency, you may talk to a program officer for a particular region or subject area. For example, if you're a writer, you'd talk to someone in the Literature Program at the NEA. Some federal programs may refer you to a regional office. Be patient but persistent in trying to get through to speak with someone.

When you do reach someone, you can be more open about your project than I've advised for private foundations. Ask for any information you still need, such as whether you meet their funding criteria. It's okay to offer a brief summary of your project or need. If the program officer does not think you should apply for funds from the agency, ask if they can refer you to another agency (though they won't always be able to).

Do not become flustered if you are put on hold, transferred to someone else, or asked to call back. Just keep asking, "Who can help me?" until you get through to someone with answers. You may run into dead ends, you may get shifted from department to department, or you may be told that everyone is on vacation this week. Be patient, and always be polite. Don't get annoyed and make speeches about your rights as a taxpayer. If you run into a dead end, call back the switchboard and ask if there is a different person you can talk to. As in most organizations, you'll reach some people who don't want to be bothered, and others who will take the time to talk to you and be helpful; if you are polite and persistent, you'll eventually get through to the helpful ones.

OTHER RESEARCH TIPS

- **Ask about previous grant recipients.** You may want to ask the agency you have contacted if they can send you a list of people or projects they have given grants to in the past year or so. This will give you a better idea of their funding priorities and the kinds of projects they like. As a general rule, most agencies are forthright about disclosing who they've funded in the past. Some, however, like the Small Business Administration, are just too large to do this easily. While it's true that agencies must legally disclose such information, it may be more trouble for you trying to get it than it's really worth. Just ask politely if they have such a list or have funded any projects like yours, and leave it at that. This is not something to make a big deal out of.

- **Agencies and programs can change.** Do keep in mind that government agencies and policies often change, and government programs can be canceled at any time. They are much more volatile than corporate or private foundations, which are solid entities with established giving priorities. You may find that when you call a government agency, the program you are interested in has been eliminated or its funding has been curtailed. Or the agency may have shifted its focus to another giving area.

    Do not stop when you hear this. Ask whether a different program has replaced this one or if there are funds from another agency that now support this area of interest. Very often, money for a given area can come from more than one department and be channeled through various agencies. This part of the bureaucracy can actually work for you. You may find several programs that will contribute to your project.

- **Explore other resources.** One last resource from which you can seek information is the Federal Information Center located in your state. Check your telephone directory, or ask your local librarian if there is an office providing information on federal programs in your state; most states have such information centers. You can also look up these centers in Appendix 5 of the *Catalog of Federal Domestic Assistance.* Or contact the main Federal Information Center office, listed below, to find the center nearest you:

    Federal Information Center
    P.O. Box 600
    Cumberland, MD 21501
    301-722-9000

- **Don't be discouraged.** Do not get discouraged by all of this detective work. Do not let regulations, policies, and application forms prevent you from applying for a government grant. The government does not always make it easy, and you may have to wade through paperwork, cope with policy procedures, and cut through red tape. But if you persist, you may well find the free money there waiting for you.

How to Approach Government Funders

Just as there are many different sources of government funds, there are many different ways to approach them. With some, you simply have to show that you meet their criteria. With others, you will have to prove that you are a good investment, since they have to be able to demonstrate that they are spending taxpayers' money responsibly and wisely. And with still others, you will face stiff competition, and your qualifications and project will have to compare well with those of other applicants.

With some agencies, you'll simply fill out the appropriate applications and wait for their response. With others, particularly at the county and municipal level, it may be important to make personal contact with someone at an agency.

Before you apply to any agency or program, ask yourself two key questions:

- Do you really meet all the requirements and fit within the limitations and restrictions of the program?
- Have you checked to see if there are other agencies or programs that offer similar support?

If you are eligible for several programs, do make multiple applications. This can only increase your chances.

Once you have researched your sources and contacted the appropriate agencies, and you know you meet their requirements, you are ready to submit an application or formal proposal. Government applications and proposals can be complicated, and may look different from those you send to private foundations. You'll find a special section on them in Chapter 9.

You'll need patience to fill out the detailed application forms and to prepare the requested credentials and supporting materials. In fact, it will help to be a little obsessive about this. You *must* follow directions to the letter. You may have to file applications in triplicate, put pages in a certain order, provide very specific credentials, and so on. Program staff will expect every "i" to be dotted and will put your application or proposal through a very thorough evaluation and review. So make sure your application follows all the rules.

When you are applying for a government grant, you may be competing for funding with many other individuals, businesses, or organizations. Your application must not only be perfect, but must also stand out from the rest. Don't give any staff member an excuse to put it in an "incomplete application" file. If you provide the agency with all necessary forms and materials, they will review your application and you will have a chance for approval.

How Agencies Respond

While some little-known programs get relatively few applications, many are flooded. The well-known agencies, like the National Endowment for the Arts and the Small Business Administration, process thousands of applications each year. And just like private funders, they get many applications that don't fit their guidelines and don't follow their instructions. This is why they are so quick to reject incomplete or inappropriate applications.

In general, government agencies have a longer, more thorough review process than private funders. It can take up to six months for an agency to notify you. Program guidelines usually clearly state waiting or notification times. Part of the reason for the extended waiting period is that many people will be looking at your proposal. Since these are public funds, agencies want to make sure that taxpayer money is allocated in a very even-handed and careful way. Your application or proposal will first be reviewed by a staff, to make sure it is complete and meets all the requirements. The staff may then split off sections of your proposal, and have specialists look at the different sections—a budget specialist may look at the budget, for example. This careful scrutiny means you should be very detailed and thorough in preparing your proposal.

After the initial staff review, your application or proposal goes to a committee or panel that will make the initial funding decision. The agency may use an internal committee, made up of government employees, or may call in an outside advisory panel of your peers or of experts in the field. The initial decision must still be confirmed by the chairperson or director of the agency, who may disapprove certain grants for political or policy reasons.

Established government programs must follow their basic requirements and mandates. Within their mandates, however, they can apply a great deal of discretion. They can judge individual applications according to many different criteria; they will look at your qualifications, the strength of your application, and the care and preparation that went into it. A committee or panel can have its own biases and interests and may be influenced by the general political climate. It's even possible for a panel to have interests and concerns that conflict with those of the agency or its director. In such cases, the director will always have the last say. A panel that chooses its own successors may perpetuate a particular viewpoint from year to year. A panel can also change quite radically if joined by one or two outspoken new members.

You cannot do anything about these factors—just remember that there is always turnover in government and that advisory panels change every year. You are, in a sense, stuck with the luck of the draw and the state of the agency at the moment you submit an application. Still, political factors change, and do not directly affect every program and agency. The majority of government programs will simply respond to your qualifications, the quality of your proposal, and the nature of your project—all factors that are under your control.

8

INDIVIDUAL
DONORS

Surprisingly, individual donors, rather than foundations, give away by far the largest amount of money in the private sector. In 1989, for example, gifts from individual donors amounted to 84 percent of all private giving in the United States. At the same time, individual donors are probably the least likely prospect for you as an individual grant seeker, even if you are affiliated with a nonprofit organization. Let's examine this seeming paradox.

You may be an individual donor yourself—if you've ever put a dollar in a collection plate, made a contribution to United Way, responded to a telethon, paid a voluntary admissions fee to a museum, or written a check to a public radio or television station during a membership drive. More than half of all individual donations go to churches and religious organizations and are tax-deductible. Most of the rest go to other kinds of nonprofit organizations, from the American Cancer Society to the National Wildlife Federation—and these contributions are also tax-deductible. In fact, tax deductibility is a key factor in attracting donations, especially substantial ones. As an individual, you can't offer this benefit to potential donors.

There's another reason why individual donors are not a useful source of funds for most individual grant seekers, or even for many nonprofit organizations. It's just too difficult to identify and track down likely prospects and then get them to donate any meaningful amount of money. The wealthy individuals who do give substantial funds to worthy causes and projects are not easy to find. You can look up the names of thousands of foundations in directories, but there are few directories of wealthy donors. Even if you identify some prospects, it's not easy to make contact or arouse interest. Development officers at established institutions like colleges and museums sometimes devote years to cultivating a wealthy donor in order to get a substantial gift.

Even when an organization seeks smaller individual donations, the process is cumbersome and the rewards may be slim. It takes time to compile mailing lists, it's expensive to print up brochures and do mailings, and the return is often quite limited. Organizations may decide to do this anyway, as part of their general outreach effort, but it rarely makes sense for individuals.

Still, there are cases where individual donors may help your cause. In this chapter we'll look at some different ways to find and approach individual donors and to enlist their support, as well as some of the pitfalls to avoid. You will then be able to make the decision yourself as to whether this is an option worth pursuing, though I'll say again that in most cases it isn't.

There are three general types of individual donors, and three ways of approaching them. First, you can try to raise funds from multiple individual donors, asking each for a limited contribution or for whatever they wish to give. Many nonprofit organizations pursue this option. Second, you can try to identify and solicit a wealthy individual to act as a patron or principal contributor. Organizations often try to do this, and on rare occasions, a few individuals do succeed in finding a patron. Finally, you can try to identify bequests that are directed to give funds to individuals with your specific type of interest. Someone might decide to leave all or part of their estate in trust to support individuals from their own town who want to study medicine, for example, or the arts.

Since these three different types—multiple individual donors, patrons, and bequests—require different approaches, let's look at each of them separately.

MULTIPLE DONORS

Nonprofit organizations often seek to raise funds by approaching multiple individual donors. They may send out mass mailings or stage benefits to solicit contributions from many individuals. For example, a theater company I know of in New York City was facing a budget crunch. Its director sent out an appeal to 35,000 current and past ticket buyers whose names they had collected over the years. They got their largest check from the mayor, for $1,000; the rest of the response came in as a trickle of donations, ranging from $10 to $150 each. In the end, they received $8,000 in response to 35,000 letters of request. Although they raised only a small portion of their budget, they felt it was well worth the effort.

Approaching multiple donors does not make much sense for individuals. It takes time and work to develop mailing lists (and money, if you buy them), and it's easy to spend hundreds of dollars on postage. The usual rate of response to mass mailings is only about 1 to 3 percent. You will find it much more rewarding to put your time into grant research and proposal writing. Still, every once in a while you hear of an individual who decides to do a mailing like this and gets results. I recall the case of a young woman who wanted to raise money to pay for her university tuition and living expenses. She wrote a personal letter to absolutely everybody under the sun that she could think of, including perfect strangers as well as people she and her family knew. Believe it or not, she was very successful.

HOW TO RESEARCH POTENTIAL DONORS

A good starting point is the reference section in your library. You can refer to *Who's Who*, social registers, and other biographical and professional directories to get names of potential donors.

Start to build your own mailing list. Build on your address book, and add all the people you've already contacted about your project. Ask your friends for names and get mailing lists from groups whose members might be interested. If you ask a group for their list, you will either have to get their approval for your use of it or pay for it, or both. If you have access to a personal computer, use a database program to enter the names, so you can sort them and "merge" them with a letter of request. When nonprofits do direct-mail campaigns, they either use names from their own constituency base or they buy very targeted lists.

HOW TO APPROACH POTENTIAL DONORS

The standard method is a mass mailing, but this is a better tool for nonprofits. It doesn't usually make sense for individuals—the costs are too high, the returns too low. And an individual cannot offer the charitable tax deduction to contributors. However, if you are doing a community-focused project, a mailing might increase community awareness of your work. If you are affiliated with an organization, or can get this kind of support from one, see if they will assist you in doing a mailing or let you use their facilities. You might get the organization to accept contributions in its name, making them tax-deductible, and extend you support or services in exchange. Perhaps you can get a corporation to underwrite the cost of a mass mailing, which can run into hundreds or thousands of dollars, depending on the size of your mailing list.

There is another way to get individuals to give money to your cause—through benefits and special events. Again, nonprofit organizations do this all the time, staging benefit performances, demonstrations, and dinners. I am a big fan of benefits—as long as I don't have to do them. They take an enormous amount of work, but they can raise substantial funds and inspire a lot of goodwill. If this seems like a good way to raise money, you must ask yourself the all-important question: Will the benefit pay for itself? Halls cost money to rent, drinks and refreshment expenses add up. When organizations do benefits, they usually only raise money if somebody is making a contribution to the benefit itself—providing free space and refreshments, printing the invitations, etc.

For individuals, benefits or dinners are generally too much sheer work, and the fact that contributions aren't tax-deductible limits the amount that people will want to give. Still, you might consider throwing some kind of small-scale benefit or reception, or getting a friend to sponsor one in your honor. Or you might hold a private performance or presentation of your work: read from your poetry or novel-in-progress, show slides of your photographs, perform your music. Ask for voluntary donations, or charge something for admission. If you are not working through a nonprofit organization, make sure the guests know that their donations are not tax-deductible. Most people don't mind paying a modest amount for a reading or a performance even if they know they can't write it off.

In fact, you might think about ways of making your work partly self-sustaining. You could regularly sell tickets to your readings/performances or sell examples of your work, such as paintings, sketches, jewelry, quilts, and crafts. In many cases, this is your ultimate goal, anyway. A benefit or some other form of introductory event might help get you started.

If you do get contributions from individual donors, always recognize their generosity by sending them thank-you notes. Notes can be time-consuming, but it is very important to show your appreciation, and they can lead to an ongoing commitment.

INDIVIDUAL PATRONS AND MAJOR CONTRIBUTORS

Patrons are wealthy individuals who use their money and influence to support other individuals, usually (historically) artists, dancers, theater people, and the like. In most cases, a patron provides financial support to the artist by commissioning or purchasing his or her work. (In rare cases the patron supports the artist without claim to the work, but even that relationship is not without expectations.) Wealthy individuals can also take an interest in community projects and nonprofit organizations and offer major, sustaining support.

Patronage is a concept that has long been familiar to artists and creative people. Mozart had patrons; Beethoven had patrons; Fabergé had patrons. Even this century's great fashion designers—Chanel, Dior, Halston, Saint Laurent, and Givenchy—had patrons. In the twenties, Peggy Guggenheim supported some of the most talented Surrealist painters; in the seventies, Ralph and Ethel Skull supported Andy Warhol and other Pop Art painters. Raphael and Michelangelo had perhaps the wealthiest and most powerful patron of all—the Pope. In each case, whether the patron's clout was political, royal, social, or religious, you can be sure it was backed up with money. Individual patrons are best known in the arts, but they do support other areas, such as science and inventions.

How They Can Help

There are still patrons who support individual artists or make major contributions to nonprofit organizations. Some support individuals by commissioning work—from outdoor sculpture to personal and family portraits to architecture. A wealthy individual who purchases someone's work on a regular basis, or buys several pieces at once, is acting as a patron (just as a customer who "patronizes" your store regularly spends money there). Some patrons will even make outright gifts of money to support an individual.

Patrons can support an individual or organization in nonmonetary ways as well. These are not to be discounted, as they may have real practical value. Patrons can champion your cause by introducing you to other individuals who may make financial contributions. They can use media contacts to generate positive publicity for you and your work. They can offer you the use of an office, studio, or laboratory.

It is true that one wealthy individual could easily provide you with the funding you need to complete a project or to survive during a period of high creativity and low income. A patron could purchase your completed work, commission new work, provide you with a place to work, introduce you to other wealthy individuals, draw you into the media spotlight, or offer you outright financial support.

Why, then, are we discussing this funding approach so late in the book?

Because patrons are hard to come by. If you look at a list of the wealthiest men and women in America, it may seem that any one of them could cover your needs without missing what amounts to their spare change. But there are thousands of other people drawing the same conclusion, which is why the wealthy are often well insulated from unsolicited requests. You probably haven't run into too many people who are eager to support your ideas with money. What's more, why should they bother? Why should they take responsibility for your needs?

The Tax Question

Here is the crux of the problem: wealthy individuals have very little motivation to give money to other individuals, since gifts to individuals do not qualify for tax deductions. And tax deductions are the biggest incentive for charitable giving in the United States, no matter what socially conscious and idealistic reasons donors claim. If Madonna is going to give money away, don't you think she wants some tax credit for it? Her accountant certainly does.

This means that nonprofit organizations will always get more funds from wealthy donors than individuals will, though it's not easy even for them. There usually needs to be some kind of personal connection or interest; after all, there are thousands of nonprofit organizations out there looking for funding, just as there are thousands of individuals.

There are ways around the deductibility issue. If you do have a potential patron or major contributor in sight, you could always try to affiliate with a sponsor, or even set up your own nonprofit organization. I know of one performance artist who has been supported for years by a patron—the funds are channeled through the artist's own nonprofit organization. Of course, it certainly wouldn't be worth going through the trouble of setting up a nonprofit organization without already having interest from a likely prospect.

Wealthy individuals can themselves initiate something like a patronage relationship while retaining the tax deduction. They can set up their own private foundations, which are so closely controlled that they pick and choose the artists or recipients they want to support. This is done much more frequently than is generally known and really amounts to patronage. A wealthy business person could operate a corporate foundation in the same way. This is why many small foundations shy away from publicity; they want to be free to fund individuals or projects that the founder or founder's family has an interest in. There's nothing wrong with this—in our free society, everyone has the right to spend their money as they see fit. But it does explain why it's much easier to pursue foundations that publicly list their giving patterns and interests than to seek out individual donors.

WHAT MOTIVATES INDIVIDUAL FUNDERS?

Without the lure of tax incentives, what factors do motivate the wealthy to fund the work of others? They may be personally interested in your work, or they may want to link their name to your work in order to improve their public image. They may be looking for positive publicity. They may identify with your goals and, while lacking the talent, motivation, or ability to pursue such work, may want to somehow be involved with it. If they are contributing to your organization or community project, some of the same motivations may apply, or they may want to do some real social good. What might patrons expect of you, in return for their financial generosity? They may want your genuine and public gratitude, or they may insist on anonymity. They may want your allegiance in matters beyond the scope of your work. They may want to use their support of you to demonstrate that they belong to the cultural elite. They may want to claim you as a "discovery" or protégé.

These things seem harmless enough. But some patrons may want to induce an overwhelming sense of indebtedness (which makes them feel powerful). Or they may want to influence your work to such a degree that your integrity is compromised. Beware of such "generous" patrons.

In any situation with a patron or major contributor, you must try to anticipate your patron's expectations and decide whether or not they are acceptable to you—before you take the money. This can be difficult because patronage is usually an informal arrangement. There is nothing spelled out on paper. You've got to go on instinct. So try to get a sense of the patron's motivations.

In an ideal arrangement, a patron or major contributor can relieve you of financial concerns and allow you to devote all of your energies and attention to your project—or even to a series of projects, if the patron takes a long-term interest in your work.

HOW TO FIND PATRONS AND MAJOR CONTRIBUTORS

How do you find a patron? The wealthy are out there, but it can be difficult to contact them and even more difficult to get them interested in your work. The truth is, it often boils down to good timing and personal connections.

Begin by exploring your own network of friends and acquaintances. Do you already know anyone—or do they know anyone—who has the financial resources to support your work? If you know any lawyers or agents, they can be a good source of possible contacts. You may come up with one name or a list of names of potential patrons or contributors.

You can also use the reference books in your local library for information on potential donors. Look at the biographical compilations, professional directories, and social registers. Concentrate on your geographical area, but also seek out individuals you know to be interested in your field. Read the society pages and community pages of your local newspapers, noting who attends the benefits, who is supporting what kind of community efforts. Look in the periodical indexes for articles on prominent individuals. And study the following references to get ideas about the kinds of individuals you are looking for:

- *Biographical Dictionaries Master Index.* This gives information on different publications of biographical references to living individuals.
- *Current Biography.* New York: Wilson Company, monthly and annual.
- *Martindale-Hubbel Law Directory.*
- *Medical Specialists Directory.*
- *The Social Register 1996.* New York: Social Register Association, 1996 (annually). Lists prominent families, with names and addresses; also clubs, organizations, and affiliations.
- *Standard & Poor's Register* for corporate executives.
- *Trustees of Wealth.* Washington, DC: Taft Corporation.
- *Who's Who.* Various volumes, by profession, population, and region. Consider which volumes might best lead you to potential donors.

It can be interesting to look through these lists, and you may find names that seem like likely prospects. But remember: ultimately, you will have to develop a personal contact. It's very easy to go off on flights of fancy and imagine that this person or that could support your project or need. But this is not the same as looking at lists of foundations, which have been set up for the express purpose of giving away money. You can spend a lot of time and effort writing to individuals or trying to make personal contact and never come up with anyone who really wants to contribute directly to an individual. So your first line of approach should always be to research the foundations and government programs. It's only worth trying to approach individual donors in those rare cases when you have some special kind of access, your work is known, or your project would be of particular interest to someone. Be realistic—don't waste your time dreaming about patrons if you can get real money through conventional grant programs.

How to Approach Potential Donors

If you are referred to a potential patron or contributor, plan to approach them with tact and restraint. It's certainly best to go through a personal contact or recommendation, and you should try to do it this way, even if it means going through a friend of a friend. Still, you can sometimes get through to people by writing them cold. Be aware that many wealthy individuals are shielded by their personal or business staffs, private secretaries, or agents. Though you may think you'll have better luck if you can find a clever way to bypass these intermediaries, this can backfire. These people are performing a valuable service for their employers, protecting their privacy and shielding them from all kinds of demands. Even if you can get a personal recommendation or introduction on a social basis, you still may need to deal with secretaries or staff, so do so graciously. You may get a trusted employee on your side, which can only strengthen your case.

Find out what you can about prospective donors before you write to them or meet with them: What are their fields of business? What are their personal interests and hobbies? Are they familiar with you or your work? Based on the answers to these questions, is your project likely to be of interest to them? Do they have a history of supporting individual efforts?

If you can't arrange a personal introduction, you can always try writing a letter. This should touch on many of the points in the basic letter of request outlined in Chapter 9, though the format could be slightly less formal (but no less businesslike). You do want to explain your mission and supply some background about yourself and your project.

If you are lucky enough to get a personal introduction or recommendation, your chances are better. You might then be asked to send a letter or some background information, or a meeting might be set up. The first meeting could take place either socially or in a more formal context. You'll have to tailor your discussion to the nature of the meeting.

If you meet in an informal setting, don't make a heavy sales pitch unless you think it's expected, or you are asked. If you are an artist, you might arrange to meet someone at your studio or at a gallery where your work is being displayed. If you are a scientist, inventor, or community activist, think about creative ways to expose potential patrons to your work. Give a tour of your laboratory or facility, or invite them to a reading or performance. You'll do well with this informal approach to fund raising if you can carry on a conversation easily, think on your feet, and feel comfortable interacting with different kinds of people. At the same time, be yourself. Don't feel like you have to put on an act. You and the potential patron are sizing each other up. You want to make a good impression, but you also want to get a sense of what the patron's expectations are.

Talk about your work and your needs informally in the course of conversation. Potential donors will make their decisions based on the way you describe your work and your plans, their knowledge of your professional reputation, and their reaction to your work. If you can do so casually, remind them about any positive publicity you've received and your accomplishments or awards.

Remember, patronage can be an informal arrangement. Patrons or major contributors may simply hand you a check and wave you away, or they may buy several pieces of your work and give you no idea whether they have any interest in future support. On the other hand, they can behave as if they're buying a company and feel entitled to criticize or even make suggestions about the future direction of your work. Once you've got their money in your bank account, you may never see them again, or they may call you every day. If you're working on a theater production or a community project, they may want to get closely involved. Depending on the person and the kind of involvement, this could be extremely helpful or totally disruptive. Size up any potential patron or contributor according to your own good judgment. If your gut instinct tells you not to get involved with someone, steer clear. If you find someone who seems willing to help you with a minimum of interference, take advantage of your good fortune.

BEQUESTS

Individual donors can continue to extend their generosity even after they've gone. Aside from establishing large endowments for continuing fellowships and prize programs, wealthy individuals sometimes bequeath money for specific purposes or populations. These funds may not be well known, and are usually tied to very specific kinds of qualification, often supporting members of a local community. A wealthy individual with a passion for landscape design, for example, may bequeath money to encourage other people from his hometown to study horticulture after his death.

How can you seek out and connect with bequests? You really do have to poke around, and get lucky. Keep up with the local newspapers, chat with any bankers or lawyers you know. If you do identify a bequest, you may find that it is administered by an accountant, a bank trust department, or a lawyer. Usually a single trustee makes all the funding decisions, without going to a committee or board of directors. They handle requests in a similar way to small family foundations. You can ask about any special application procedures, but normally you will submit a letter of request, using the three-page format described in Chapter 9.

If there's a positive response, the trustee or administrator may want to interview you, but in general follow the same procedures and etiquette as you would with a foundation.

9

THE
PROPOSAL

Your proposal is just one part of the fund-raising process, but it comes at the exciting moment when you are ready to "sell" your project to funders. Whether it's a simple letter, an application form, or a many-page proposal, all funders will want something in writing that tells them about you, your project, your mission, and what need you hope to satisfy or what you hope to achieve. You will use your proposal to convince a funder that you deserve a grant and that you merit funding over other viable candidates. A well-written proposal will communicate your goal and your plan for achieving it. If you can do this clearly, and show that you've thought things through, your proposal will attract attention and you will have a good chance to get funding.

Writing a proposal takes some thought and care, but there are no secret formulas or code words to use. However, there are some general rules and guidelines that fund raisers follow, that funders expect, and that will help sell your project. In this chapter, I'll show you how to construct an effective proposal from the ground up, and how to make it the best possible representation of your project. Bear in mind, preparing a proposal does require thought, effort, and time. But if you're serious about your project, this is where you begin to make your vision real.

Since proposal writing is not done by formula, what works for one person, or for one funder, will not work for all. Every project is unique, and funders recognize this. However, the guidelines in this chapter will help you effectively apply for most government, foundation, or corporate grants. It is worth noting that writing a proposal for a government grant is very different from writing one for a private or corporate foundation grant. Government programs often require you to fill out elaborate forms and package your information in specialized ways. That's why I've included a section in this chapter specifically to help you with proposals for government grants.

Doing a proposal is really not that daunting a task. It should flow naturally out of the planning you've been doing and the project outline that you've already prepared (back in Chapter 1). But it does take time. It's a little like doing a jigsaw puzzle—there are a number of components you have to piece together. As long as you have a clear vision and have thought through your project, you won't have a problem. As you start putting together a proposal, though, you may find that there are some things you haven't really thought through, some additional research you need to do. That's fine, and all part of the process; but it's also one reason why you need to leave plenty of time to work up your proposal. Don't push the deadlines.

HOW TO KNOW WHEN YOU'RE READY TO START

Before you sit down to write your proposal, make sure you've done all the necessary preparation. Here are some points that will help you decide when you are ready. Some have to do with your project development, some with your funding research.

PROJECT DEVELOPMENT

1. *You have a clear mission statement and outline for your project.*
   Remember, a good proposal starts with a good idea. You

need to have a clear understanding of how your idea will solve a problem or satisfy a need.

2. *You've developed your idea in outline form.*

If you haven't looked at your project outline (see Chapter 1) in a while, or if you have new details to add, go back and bring it up to date. Be sure you have thought through the exact locations where your project will take place, each step you'll have to complete, and a timeline or schedule you'll follow.

3. *You've done your basic budget research.*

You need to have looked up the basic costs of the materials, services, or salaries that you need the grant money to pay for. You may have collected some price lists and have them on hand, or you've called vendors for price quotes.

4. *You've thought about and contacted any essential personnel besides yourself who will be involved in the project.*

If other people will be involved, you have contacted them and received a commitment or at least an expression of interest. If you do have commitments from some key people, you've asked for copies of their résumés. If you're going to have to hire staff or pay for contracted services, you've researched what the salaries or fees will be.

In fact, one of the best things you can have going for you as you ask for funding is a commitment from a few key people who have good professional credibility. This makes it look like you have a solid project that is really taking shape. So do try to get some commitments lined up. Of course, these will be tentative, because you can't really have anybody clear their schedule or start work until you have the funding. But funders understand this, and will appreciate any efforts in this direction.

5. *You've collected the endorsements or supporting materials that you want to attach to your proposal.*

You don't want a massive amount of material, but if you have collected one or two key endorsements or articles, this is all on file.

FUNDING RESEARCH

1. *You've researched and refined your prospect list.*

    Before you even start to write a proposal, you need to know that your project does truly match the giving interests of your potential funders. Be sure that you've thoroughly researched each prospective funder still on your list and that you know their objectives, areas of support, and any limitations on giving. If prospective funders see that your project and proposal are closely attuned to their interests and practices, they will know that you have taken the trouble to find out about them, and they will consider your proposal and idea much more seriously.

2. *You've requested guidelines and an annual report.*

    Never consider sending out blind proposals to multiple funding sources without contacting them first. This is a surefire way to give your project a bad name in the nonprofit world. Only after looking at guidelines and an annual report will you be able to make a final decision about whether your project is right for a specific funder.

    Remember, when you write for guidelines and an annual report, do just that. If you start to say anything about your project, your letter may be treated as an informal proposal and rejected out of hand.

    What if you write to one of the very small private foundations and ask for guidelines and an annual report, and they simply don't respond? This is not so unusual. You may write to thirty-two foundations and get only twelve responses. Some of these small foundations are swamped with inappropriate requests, so if you haven't heard anything after six or eight weeks, you may want to drop them a polite two-line request for guidelines and a grant application. If you still don't get a response, cross them off your list and go on to the next prospect. It never pays to send in a proposal without some preliminary contact.

    Not every funder will have an annual report to send out. They will usually send you some sort of guidelines, even if it's a few lines in a form letter. If they have no guidelines, just send them the generic proposal (described later in this chapter).

3. *You have the name of the contact person for each funder you want to send a proposal to.*

I go nuts when people write me letters addressed to "Dear Sir" or "To Whom It May Concern," and so do program officers. Always, and I mean always, find out the name of the appropriate program officer to send your proposal to. Some funders will indicate one person that all proposals should go to. If you're targeting a large foundation, you'll need to find the officer who deals with your subject area or your type of funding. There may be one program officer for the social sciences, one for the medical sciences, and another for the arts.

You'll often find an appropriate contact person named in directories, but you should use the name listed in any guidelines you receive, since it will be more up to date. Always call to double-check on the name. Nonprofit people move around a lot, and the contact person may well have changed in the time since a particular directory was compiled. If you can't find a contact person's name, call and ask who is the appropriate person to send a proposal to. Don't talk about your project, just say that you want to send a proposal and ask who you should address it to. If you still can't find this out, don't send in a proposal. You just don't have enough information to approach this funder effectively.

4. *You've researched the average size of the grants that a funder gives, either through listings, annual reports, or the IRS 990-PF forms.*

You can't write a proposal without knowing how much you will request from each potential funder. If you ask for too much, you can turn off a funder—they won't take you seriously. If you ask for too little, you simply haven't maximized the return from all your efforts. You can't just make a guess as to how much a funder might offer. For most projects, you will have to put together funding from several different sources and usually cannot ask one funder to cover the total cost of your project. And you can't just divide the cost of your project by ten and apply to ten different funders. If you have a $50,000 project, you will probably end up piecing together the funding from different sources: $5,000 from this foundation, $7,500 from that one, $15,000 from another. How will you know what to request from each one?

You should base your request on the giving patterns of the funder. The key to knowing how much you can request is research. You have to tailor your request to what you have learned about the funder. Go back to your notes from the listings, go back to your notes from the 990-PF IRS forms. Look again at the range of grants given, and the average grant. If you don't have this information, you need to go back and dig it up.

How do you use the information? If you have a project with a relatively small cost, ask for an amount at the low end of the range. If you have an expensive project, ask for something at the medium point or just slightly above. Don't get greedy and request an amount equal to the highest grant given. Those grants are going to organizations, and very often to ones that have developed a relationship with the funder and have a track record. It is much better for you to get a modest grant in hand and go on seeking other funding than to get turned down because your request seemed arrogant or out of line. Remember, having one or two modest grants in hand makes your requests to other funders that much stronger; it's evidence that someone has confidence in you and your idea.

What if you just can't dig up the information about a funder's giving patterns? Go ahead and apply, but request a modest amount. For an individual project, ask for somewhere between $2,500 and $7,500. For a big-budget project, sponsored by an organization, ask for $5,000 to $15,000. Again, a smaller request will cause a lot less soul searching on the part of the board. You don't necessarily want board members balancing your larger request against all the other interests and commitments they may have. Let someone say instead, "It's an interesting project, and they're not asking for much money. Let's give it to them." Make it easy for a funder to give you the grant.

WHAT MAKES A GOOD PROPOSAL?

There are three things that a good proposal must do. First, it should convey all the vital facts about your project clearly and concisely. Second, it should make clear the importance of, or the need for, your project. And finally, it must sell you, succinctly and convincingly communicating your strengths to the reader.

It is essential to provide all the necessary information. If funders are going to consider your proposal seriously, they have to understand exactly what you are proposing. They will want to know why the project is needed, how you will meet that need, exactly how your project will be carried out, where it will take place, and how long it will take to see it through. They need to know who is applying for the grant, who will receive the funds and manage the project, and who will benefit from the grant ultimately. They need to know how much your project will cost, and how much you are asking them to contribute.

But facts alone are not enough. You also need to show them what makes your project exciting and unique and, ideally, to cause them to feel something of your own enthusiasm for it. Why is the need for your project pressing, what makes your solution especially creative or effective?

Finally, you must convince the reader that *you* are especially deserving of the funder's money. Foundations and corporations are bombarded with thousands of requests for funds. You need to show that *you* are in some way uniquely worthy of their financial support.

You'll find that if you have written a good mission statement, as described in Chapter 1, and you've outlined your project, a good proposal will follow naturally. Without the research and planning, there will be no proposal. You start with an idea, make a skeleton outline, and gradually flesh it out. If you approach the task seriously and meticulously, following the guidelines in this chapter, you will come up with a proposal that funders will consider seriously.

Is it essential to have an effective proposal? Yes. I've seen too many really good projects turned down because the proposals weren't clear, concise, or sufficiently developed. I have known the rare case, with a proposal submitted by a nonprofit organization, when a program officer so admired the project itself that he or she helped to redo the proposal. But this is something that they will seldom do for individuals. Your proposal is the first (and sometimes the only) sample of your work and evidence of your abilities that a funder will see. If you submit a good proposal, the funder will be predisposed to believe that you can follow through with a good project.

THE BASIC PROPOSAL—AND VARIATIONS

No matter what kind of funder you apply to—whether a private or corporate foundation, a government agency, even an individual donor—some aspects of the proposal will remain the same. You will always include something like a mission statement, you'll always need to provide basic information about the project, and you'll always have to explain your qualifications to do the project. Nevertheless, you may need to work up a few different variations on these basic themes.

Some proposals can take a relatively free form, and some will have to follow rigid guidelines. Government agencies have the most strict and demanding requirements, while private foundations may offer more room for creativity. Corporate foundations and giving programs are probably the most flexible in what they'll accept as a proposal. You may need to fill out preprinted application forms for some grants or supply some combination of application form and supplementary pages. If you are applying under the sponsorship of an organization, it will have to provide additional information.

Whatever form your proposal takes, you must follow the printed guidelines of each funder. Guidelines may ask you to use special formats, address specific questions, or provide particular supplementary documents. Whatever the guidelines ask for, you must provide it, even if it means cutting, pasting, and restructuring the proposal you've been sending to other funders. Follow the guidelines to the letter; they are not negotiable.

If a funder's guidelines differ from the suggestions you find in this chapter, follow the guidelines. Funders have reasons for asking what they do, and it's best to provide them with exactly what they want.

Let's look at some of the different kinds of proposals that you may need to prepare.

THE FULL-BLOWN PROPOSAL

Many foundations will not specify the form of the proposal, except perhaps to mention certain topics that they would like you to address. In these cases, you may submit a formal three- to ten-page proposal.

You will normally use this kind of full-length proposal only if you are applying through a sponsor, but in some cases you might use it for an individual grant application. I recommend you read the section on the full proposal later in this chapter (pages 271–98), even if you will be applying as an individual and filling out application forms. Many of the topics addressed in the full proposal can appear in some form on application forms, so it will help you to think these through beforehand. And if you are going to meet with a funder, it will certainly help to have thought about these issues and to have made some notes.

For a full proposal, you should submit a *proposal package* that includes your written proposal, along with a cover letter, your résumé, and any supporting documentation or sample work. It should reach the funder by the indicated deadline for their next funding cycle. (There might be one or several funding cycles each year.) Let's look at the basic elements.

1. **Cover letter.** You should write a cover letter after you have finished your entire proposal. This can be very brief, introducing your proposal, providing your mission statement, and indicating how much money you are requesting. We will discuss the cover letter in greater detail later in this chapter.

2. **Title page.** This gives the title of your project, and basic information about who is submitting the proposal, whether an individual or an organization. See later in this chapter for the correct format.

3. **Table of contents.** If you have more than about five pages, the table of contents will list the various sections of the proposal.

4. **Project summary, or introduction.** On one page, you'll give all the important information about your project: your mission statement, the problem or need, who you are, what you want to do, your total budget, and how much you are asking for. Here you fill in more details than are in the cover letter. Foundation staff, board members, and grant officers will read the project summary to get a quick sense of your proposal.

5. **Statement of need.** In this section you'll discuss the need for your project and, if applicable, the kind of problem that your project will solve. Describe the community that will be served and the long-range goals that will be achieved.

6. **Objectives.** What are the specific, immediate objectives that you wish to accomplish with your project (as distinct from long-range goals)?

7. **Plan.** Here you'll outline the plan or method you'll use to accomplish those objectives. Give the details of your project— where it will take place, the steps you'll go through, and the schedule or timeline for those steps. You will base this on your project outline.

8. **Evaluation.** Foundations want to know whether the projects they invest in are successful; your proposal should indicate how you will report on your project and what evidence of its success you will provide.

9. **Personnel.** This is where you attach your résumé. If it's a larger project, you might include the résumés of two or three other key people as well.

10. **Budget.** A one- or two-page budget, broken down into major categories.

11. **Other funding received.** If you've already received any funding when you send out a proposal, list it here to strengthen your request.

12. **Future funding and support.** If you are planning a project that will extend beyond the initial grant period, you should give some indication here of how you might keep the project going in the future.

13. **Official certification and signatures.** If you are applying through a sponsoring organization, you may be asked to provide a copy of the sponsor's 501(c)3 Internal Revenue Service certification, and some indication of the sponsor's support.

14. **Supporting documentation.** This is where you can include a relevant article about the need for your project, one or two letters of endorsement, and any reviews or articles on your work.

Not every proposal needs each of these components. If you're writing a short proposal for individual funding, you won't need the table of contents, future funding, and official certification. But you should include all the other items, even if your statement of need, objectives, and evaluation sections are only a few sentences in length. For personnel in this case, you'd simply insert your résumé. Your cover letter and project summary might be combined, and you would go into a little more detail for your plan. A budget is always essential, even if it's half a page in length. And if you have one or two pieces of supporting documentation, that's all to the good.

Later in this chapter, we'll take a closer look at each of these sections; but for now, let's consider some other forms of proposal.

THE SIMPLE LETTER OF REQUEST

Some foundations will ask in their guidelines for a simple letter of request rather than a more elaborate proposal. This might be defined as a *letter of request,* or a *letter of intent.* It calls for a brief two- or three-page letter containing all the basic information about you and your project. Very small foundations often prefer this type of informal proposal because they simply do not have the staff to handle large stacks of paper.

If they read the letter and are interested in your project, they may fund you directly or ask for more details.

How to Write a Letter of Request.   Follow these steps:

1. In the first paragraph, use your mission statement to introduce your project and indicate how much money you are requesting.
2. In a paragraph or two, describe the problem your project will solve (if applicable), the need for the project, your specific objectives, and the population you will serve or reach out to.
3. Next, explain your plan, including the location of the project and the time frame in which you hope to accomplish it.
4. Explain why you are qualified to apply for funding to this foundation and how you meet their guidelines. Also describe your qualifications for doing the project.
5. Attach a budget of no longer than one page (unless you are specifically requested not to) and your résumé.
   See also the sample Letter of Request on page 253.

To write an effective letter of request, you must be clear and succinct. In a way, you are condensing all the elements of a full-blown proposal into a few pages. The letter of request is really a combination of the cover letter and project summary. If you haven't explored all the points listed above in your project outline, or haven't already done a full-blown proposal, read the section in this chapter on how to do a complete proposal (pages 271–98) and use this as a guide. Write a paragraph to address each topic of the full-blown proposal, and condense as necessary to fit the important information within two or three pages.

SAMPLE LETTER OF REQUEST

Ms. June Wentworth
XYZ Foundation
St. Louis, MO

Dear Ms. Wentworth:

I am writing to obtain funding for a photo-documentary project, called, simply, *Farmer*. This will be a portrait of Midwestern farm life as it once existed. The project will be presented both as a gallery exhibition and in book form.

A way of life is dying out in America. From the earliest European settlements throughout the nineteenth century, farm life was at the core of the American identity. To many, it now seems a romantic, idealized way of life, a simpler, more honest way, the extended family living on the homestead, children and adults living and working together, in touch with the land, the seasons, producing whatever they needed from the land itself. In many ways, this was a true portrait. Yet it could also be a dangerous, fragile existence, at the mercy of storms and drought, an existence earned by grinding daily labor. By the 1920s more of the population was living in urban areas than in rural ones. The 1930s gave us indelible images of the harsh lot of backward and drought-stricken rural communities. Yet the heaviest pressure would come from economic forces, as vast agribusinesses, using high-tech machinery to manage thousands of acres of land with just a few hired hands, began to drive family farms out of business. International competition, energy prices, land taxes, interest rates—all conspired to bring an end to the family farm, and to a way of life.

Farmer is a project intended to preserve and document the shape and history of this vanishing culture. Focusing on the Midwest, where the farming way of life has lingered longest, the project will combine oral history, photographic impressions of living farms, farm people, and farming communities, and a collection of historical photographs, borrowed from family collections, which will be reproduced for gallery and book presentation. The project will feature a selected number of farm families and communities that are emblematic of the vanishing way of life. Though the emphasis will be on the past, the project will lead us through the recent transformation of farming into agribusiness, and feature one of the vast, capital-intensive operations that have replaced many smaller farms.

The project will take one year to complete, including collecting the oral histories, taking photographs, making archival masters of family photographs, and preparing for exhibition. Subjects will be sought in Indiana, Illinois, Missouri, Iowa, Kansas, Nebraska, and neighboring states.

Upon completion of the project, selected photographs, and excerpts from the oral histories, will be presented at the Capitol Gallery in the I——state capitol building. (The I——State Arts Council has already expressed interest in supporting this exhibition—see letter enclosed.) During the year, we will also be exploring possibilities for touring the exhibition to other venues in the Midwest and throughout the country. We will also prepare an edited text of the oral histories, along with selected photographs, for publication in book form. The University of I——Press, which published my previous book, *Tobacco Land,* has expressed strong interest in *Farmer.* (See enclosed letter.)

As author of a successful photo-essay book, *Tobacco Land,* and as a native Midwesterner, I feel I have a special understanding of farm culture and the people. In fact, the concept for this project arose from the many comments that people offered during research for my earlier book.

Since the XYZ Foundation has supported projects in the visual arts and oral history in the past, I am pleased to submit this proposal, and to request a contribution of $15,000 toward realization of this project.

I have enclosed a budget, and additional materials about my earlier work, including a résumé, along with letters from the I——State Arts Council and the I——University Press in support of this project. If you have any questions or need additional materials, please do not hesitate to call me at 987-654-3210.

Sincerely,
Ruth Miller

Farmer—Project Budget: $33,800

Salaries

Project director—half-time, one year:	$18,000
Part-time assistant:	$ 8,000
Supplies, equipment:	$ 2,800
Telephone, office expenses:	$ 800
Bookkeeper:	$ 200
Travel:	$ 2,000
Promotion and development (including fund raising):	$ 2,000
Total expenditures:	$33,800

THE PRELIMINARY LETTER OF INQUIRY

After you've written for guidelines and an annual report, you'll find that some foundations may request a preliminary letter of inquiry that briefly outlines your project. They will ask you to identify yourself in the letter and describe your intent to apply. If the foundation is interested in your project, they will then invite you to submit a full-blown proposal. On rare occasions they may give you suggestions that will influence the writing of your proposal. (They will generally only do this for organizations, however, not individuals. And the larger foundations are usually too swamped with proposals to offer this kind of personalized attention even to groups.)

How to Write a Preliminary Letter of Inquiry. This is easy— the letter of inquiry will look exactly like the simple letter of request described above. You can use the same two- or three-page format. Make sure you observe any restrictions on the length of the letter, and include any specific information that the guidelines request. Send it in, then stand by to see if the funder invites you to submit a complete proposal.

APPLICATION FORMS

Some funders will want you to fill in an application form rather than write a proposal. College scholarships and fellowships often require application forms. These are fairly clear; you just fill in the blanks. You won't have to do the outlining and structuring yourself. Still, you will sometimes run into forms that have large boxes or lined pages for you to fill in with text. They may ask you to attach supplementary pages, so that you are really doing a combined application form and proposal.

The first thing you should do when you get any application form is to make a copy of it to use as a rough draft. This is really essential. Fill in the blanks in pencil. When you come to a tough question, or a large box, work on your answer on a separate piece of paper, until you are satisfied with the wording. Type it out and make sure it will fit in the space given. If supplementary pages are required, type out finished drafts with clear headings at the top, using the same wording as in the guidelines or the application form. Attach these pages to the application form in the appropriate order.

Some forms may ask questions that directly relate to some of the major topics of a proposal. Review the later sections of this chapter to get a sense of what kinds of answers they are looking for.

Following are two sample application forms, the first for a private foundation, the second for a government agency.

THE INGRAM MERRILL FOUNDATION
POST OFFICE BOX 202, VILLAGE STATION, NEW YORK CITY 10014

APPLICATION FOR AWARD OR GRANT

Must be typewritten

Name   Anne   Elizabeth   Josephs
         First   *Middle name or initial*   *Last name*

Address   132 West 28th Street, New York, NY 10010

Telephone no.   (212) 555-1379

I. PERSONAL HISTORY

Present occupation   Design Consultant

Place of birth   Yonkers, New York   Date of birth   4/27/49

Are you an American citizen?   Yes   If you are a naturalized citizen give date and place of naturalization.

If you are not an American citizen, give country of which you are a citizen, subject, or national.

Are you now, or will you be at any time falling within the period of your project, a representative, agent, or employee of any foreign nation or political subdivision, or political party thereof? If so, give details.

No

Number of dependents, other than yourself.   None

What is your estimated income from other sources in the year or years in which you will be working on your project? A detailed answer is necessary.

Consultant in decorative arts and textiles - $20,000

Teaching - $2,000

II. ACADEMIC AND OCCUPATIONAL BACKGROUND

Summarize your academic background, listing colleges, universities, or other institutions of learning attended, with degrees, diplomas, and certificates held.

Syracuse University, School of Visual and Performing Arts

— B.F.A. Degree 1970

Summarize your occupational background, indicating employer, position held, and dates of tenure.

Lawson Houston, Ltd.   Design Consultant and Writer
Aug. 1986-present

Cohama Riverdale   Director of Design
Oct. 1980-July 1986

Parsons School of Design   Part-time Instructor
Sept. 1983-present

Waverly Fabrics div./Schumacher   Design Director
Dec. 1974-Oct. 1980

List all fellowships, grants, and scholarships you have received, giving full details of each, including name of grantor, amount of stipend, and studies or work carried on thereunder.

None

List your publications, giving title, publisher, and date of publication of each. Submit copies of all of this work with your application, unless it is totally irrelevant to the present project. One copy of each is sufficient. Painters and sculptors should supply representative slides of their work. All applicants must enclose a stamped, self-addressed envelope for the return of materials submitted.

III. DESCRIPTION OF PROJECT

Concise statement of project ___We are writing a book on historical___

interiors and residences (18th—early 20th century) that com-

bines both Eastern and Western styles of design, becoming

hybrids of both worlds. It would be of significant interest to

design students, professionals, and decorative arts historians.

A more detailed statement of your project and of your plans for work may be attached.

When do you wish to begin your project? ___January 1991___

Give your best estimate of time required for its completion. ___1 year___

Give an estimate of the sum which you feel you will require from this Foundation in order to carry out your project.

$7,500

When do you desire payment? Keep in mind that funds are available once a year only; approximately the first of the year. Your application must be received by the 15th of August for consideration in that year.

January 1991

Have you applied elsewhere for a fellowship, grant, or scholarship for the same project or for another project for the same period of time? If so, give details.

John Simon Guggenheim Memorial Foundation, Rockefeller

Foundation Humanities Fellowships, Marguerite Ever Wilbur

Foundation, Graham Foundation for Advanced Study in the

Fine Arts

IV. REFERENCES

Give names of three or more persons who can supply further information with regard to your qualifications, and (if your project is of a scholarly nature) who can give expert opinion concerning the value of this project as a contribution to knowledge; ask them to write on your behalf as soon as you submit your application.

Mr. David Smith	Curator, Cooper-Hewitt Museum
Mr. Samuel Foley	Retired (1986) Dean of Continuing Education Parsons School of Design, Consult. to New York School of Interior Design
Ms. Katherine Johns	Editor, Simon & Schuster
Ms. Sarah Pickens	Professor, University of California at Davis
Mr. David Levy	Vice-President, Waverly/Schumacher

(If in any of the foregoing items sufficient space is not allowed for a full and complete answer, it is requested that the information called for be stated in a separate paper securely attached to this application form. Each such separate paper should be signed and dated by the applicant. The application, which must be typed, should be mailed to The Ingram Merrill Foundation, Post Office Box 202, Village Station, New York, NY 10014.)

Anne Josephe
Signature

September 12, 1990
Date

NOTE: Any false, misleading, or incomplete answer or statement in any of the items above shall be ground for the immediate termination of any scholarship or fellowship that may be awarded on this application.

Please note that the foundation does not grant personal interviews; applications are to be submitted by mail only.

Individual Grant Application National Endowment for the Arts	Visual Arts Program
Applications must be submitted in trip-licate and mailed with other required materials to the address indicated under "Application procedures" for your category.	Category under which support is requested: COLLABORATIVE PROJECTS

Name (last, first, middle initial) Brown, Joseph	U.S. Citizenship Yes X No Visa Number
Present mailing address/phone 123 Main Street New York, NY 12345 (212) 555-1111	Professional field or discipline Artist, Preparator (see background) Birth Date Place of Birth 1-1-53 Raleigh, N.C.

Permanent mailing address/phone
123 Main Street
New York, NY 12345
 	
(212) 555-1111
	Period of support requested
	Starting October 1, 1991
	            month day year
	Ending October 1, 1992
	            month day year

Career summary or background

Matthew Smith and Joseph Brown met while undergraduates at New York University in 1972. Their past collaborations include "REAPER-CUSSION," a musical performance for the Todd Ensemble at the Picasso Art Gallery in Rochester, New York, in June 1990, and, most recently, "Hyper-Space," a performance and instal-lation at the Rosen-Fox Gallery in Buffalo, New York, in September 1990.

Matthew Smith is currently teaching drawing and painting at the State University of New York at Buffalo and is preparing for the "Albright-Knox Invitational" this March. Please see attached résumé.

Joseph Brown is working as a full-time artist and is a preparator at the West Museum in New York City. Please see attached résumé.

Amount requested from National Endowment for the Arts $5,000.00

Education			
Name of institution	Major area of study	Inclusive dates	Degree
New York University	drawing/printmaking	1972-1976	BFA
Yale University	drawing/sculpture	1976-1978	MFA

Fellowships or grants previously awarded			
Name of award	Area of study	Inclusive dates	Amount

Present employment		
Employer	Position / Occupation	Total income last calendar year
West Museum	Preparator, installationist	$7,200.00

Prizes / Honors received	Membership professional societies
Permanent collection—Missouri Art Center, 1977 Mural—Trade Center Observation Deck, 1979	

Description of proposed activity

(Do not complete this section if you are applying for an Artists', Craftmen's, or Photographers' Fellowship)

The goal of our collaboration is to produce a lively and harmonious relationship between the organic and inorganic aspects of our natural world.

Matthew Smith has created a series of drawings and musical pieces that express the atomic stucture of four elements taken from the Periodic Table of Elements (which is a mathematical inventory of the natural elements). The series is enhanced by the clean technical feel of the drawings and the "architectural" feel of the music, achieved by using Moog synthesizer and an electric piano in the building and reduction of tones.

Conversely, Joseph Brown's work projects the earthy textural resonance of animals as they interact among themselves.

The collaboration will involve the building of a scale environment (details are attached to the slide sheet). Through music, abstract depictions of animals will "interact" in the environment. The music will blend electronically synthesized sound with live recordings of animals, previously recorded on site in the Peruvian jungles. The drawings will be developed using the same methods as Matthew Smith's earlier works (using the Periodic Tables), by systematically scoring the pieces using the animals' spatial placement. The result will be a euphonious conversation between the living and nonliving world.

The interdisciplinary focus of the proposed installation will be amplified through the use of drawings, sculpture, and sound. The result will be a completely enveloping and engrossing environment.

Certification: I certify that the foregoing statements are true and complete to the best of my knowledge.

Signature of applicant _Joseph Brown_ Date _7/12/90_

PROPOSALS BY SPONSORING ORGANIZATIONS

If you are working with a sponsor, they will be submitting the proposal, and the format will be somewhat different from that of a proposal you would submit as an individual. There will be no application form, as a general rule, and you'll be applying as a project of an institution. The nonprofit organization will have to supply information about its history, its past funders, its current operating budget, and more. If it's a small nonprofit, and they haven't done much of this before, you may need to get very involved and educate yourself on how to prepare this kind of proposal. You can refer to the books mentioned in Chapter 4 (page 160), and in the Appendix, for help.

Usually, though, there will be a development officer or other member of the organization who has done proposals before and is quite familiar with the process. This person will tell you what you need to supply, and you should work quite closely with them. In general, if you can supply all the sections that you would normally put in your own proposal, that will give them enough material to work with. Go ahead and write these up, from project summary through budget, and show them to the development officer. Ask if you should type or prepare things in any special way. Usually, the more you give an organization to work with, the easier it is for them to generate a strong proposal. After all, you are the one who knows and cares the most about your project. Don't leave a development officer guessing how to present it.

HOW TO PLAN AND PREPARE YOUR PROPOSAL

There are some general considerations that apply to any proposal, from a simple letter of request to a ten-page monster. It *is* important that you plan the proposal-writing process. You will need to think through issues of style and tone, and to adjust your basic proposal for different funders. You'll need to prepare for proofreading and typing or word processing and to organize the physical preparation of your proposal package. You'll need to plan ahead to do all your preparation in time to meet important deadlines.

STYLE AND LENGTH—KEEP IT SIMPLE!

Follow the "Three-C" rule: be Clear, Concise, and Convincing. You don't need to write like a professional, you just need to explain your project in clear, simple language. Use short sentences, and a basic vocabulary. You are not trying to impress anyone with your style, just getting the information across. Don't be too vivid, don't use purple prose, don't try to tug at the emotions. If your project does have a moving, emotional side, just tell the story and let the facts back you up. If you are dealing with a technical subject, don't use professional jargon; this may confuse readers rather than impress them. Translate any technical terms into ordinary language, and remember, what is clear to you as a specialist may be obscure to a program officer who is a generalist.

Quality of writing is important, but you should be able to do an effective draft of a proposal even if you are not an experienced writer. Imagine that you are writing a letter to a friend, explaining your project to someone who is eager to listen. Try to be brief, clear, and to the point. Follow the proposal outline given in this chapter, step by step. If you get stuck, use wording from the sample letters and proposals in this book, substituting your own specifics.

If you are concerned about your writing, get help. Show or read your draft proposal to a friend and ask them if there's anything that they don't understand, or if it sounds like you are repeating yourself. Rephrase until they understand the material clearly, and cut out the repetitions. If you know you have real problems with writing, hire a freelance editor or consultant to help you. Or go through a local college or university and hire an English major or graduate student to do a second draft of your proposal.

Be sure to proofread your work for proper grammar and spelling. Your final proposal should look as perfect as a magazine article or professional brochure. This is a crucial test of your professionalism, and program officers will be turned off by substandard grammar or spelling. Even though writing may have nothing to do with your project, it is still the medium through which you must reach out for funds. Top executives in business don't have to be good writers, but they know they have to put out good writing to represent their company well. You don't have to do the proofreading yourself. You may be able to write effectively but have trouble with rules of grammar or spelling.

If this is the case, it's essential that you get a freelancer, secretarial service, or college student to do the proofreading for you.

- **TIP:** If you are a little unsure about your writing skills, you may find the following book helpful. It's one of the best and shortest books on writing style, and one that's been a standard for years: *The Elements of Style,* by William Strunk, Jr., and E. B. White. 3rd edition, New York: Macmillan, 1979.

Your proposal does not have to be a massive document. An effective proposal, again, can be anywhere from three to ten pages in length. It's impossible to be more specific, since the length will depend on your project and on what a funder asks you for. As a rule, anything over ten pages is too long. Foundations actually prefer shorter proposals, because they must sift through thousands every year.

In fact, I've seen more often than not that foundation officers will turn down proposals that are too long and wordy. Again, to make the strongest case for your project, be clear, brief, and to the point. Of course, if you are working on a full-blown proposal, this does not mean that you can just write up a few paragraphs and expect to get funding. You do have to cover all the points on the outline and answer any specific questions that the funder may pose in the guidelines. But strive for the simplest, clearest way to make each essential point.

When you are through writing your proposal, show it to a friend or adviser and get their response. Ask for positive criticism or feedback. Ask if all the points are clear, if there's any repetition, if there is a logical development from one section to the next. Go back and rewrite as many times as you have to until you think that you have the best possible presentation.

STRIKING THE RIGHT TONE

Funders who read your proposal will naturally begin to form a judgment about you as a person. It's important to strike the right tone in your proposal, so that you come across as a qualified, committed person who cares deeply about your project. It's okay to give a sense of your personal connection to the work, but your main goal should be an objective description of your project, the need for it, and your qualifications. It's good to write vividly, but avoid purple prose. Avoid overdramatizing needs, or appealing too baldly to emotions. Your passion and enthusiasm are important, but don't get carried away in describing your objectives and what you hope to accomplish. You need to have specific, achievable goals. Don't make grandiose promises that you might not be able to keep.

You may have a strong political perspective that motivates you to do your project, but try to keep this out of the description. Describe your mission, needs, and objectives in terms that don't have an obvious political slant—many proposals are rejected for doing this. Don't start blaming a corrupt or unjust political system in your community, or the country, for the problems you are trying to solve. Just describe the problem and say how you are going to solve it. If you are targeting a funder that clearly indicates a sympathetic political interest in their mission statement or interest areas, this is all the better for your project. But you should still avoid making politically based appeals.

Emphasize the positive. In your mission statement, project summary, and objectives, try to turn negative statements into positive ones. If you are proposing a television series, don't go on about the banal, predictable, condescending programming that already exists. Say that you want to create fresh, original, challenging programming that is unlike anything currently on the broadcast spectrum. If you want to start a day-care center, don't say that no one in the community is willing to contribute to this. Say that your project represents a great opportunity for the funder to do something in a financially strapped community. Don't say, "I can't go on without funding," but rather, "Look at all that I could do with funding!"

It helps to think positively about the foundation that you are addressing your proposal to, even if you've had no personal contact with them. Envision an individual who is going to take interest in your ideas and consider them seriously. Since you may not have much personal contact with a funder at the initial stages, it's easy to fall into the feeling that you are dealing with a large bureaucracy, where no one really cares. Since the funder has the power to approve or deny your request, you can also begin to imagine that you are in an adversarial relationship. Remember, people have gotten involved in the nonprofit sector because they want to make good things happen. They are trying to select worthy projects that fit their mission and overall funding strategy. And they are dealing with a great number of submissions. As an individual making a first-time application, you probably won't receive the kind of attention that an organization with a track record might get. But be assured that even at the largest foundations some individual, and maybe several, will be taking a close look at your proposal.

PHYSICAL PRESENTATION—MAKE IT LOOK GOOD!

Because foundations are swamped with proposals, you want yours to stand out from the pack. Readers will probably give your proposal a quick overall scan when they receive it, and their first impressions begin there. So make your proposal visually appealing. If you have it typed by a word-processing service, you can use large or boldface type for headings, use bullet points for lists, and emphasize key concepts with underlining or italics. If you are hand-typing your proposal, aim for a clean, uncluttered look. Double-space and use headings. Number the pages, and use page headings that identify your proposal by name. Don't go overboard with this, however; you don't need fancy covers with pictures, cute typefaces, colored paper or color graphics. The most important part of a proposal is the content, not the packaging. Your writing should speak for itself. The most important thing is still to express yourself clearly.

Read carefully any guidelines on packaging your proposal and note how many copies are requested. Don't use any bindings that can't be easily unfastened—a program officer may want to take out some pages to pass around or want to make extra copies of your proposal. For the same reason, never use staples—it really is annoying to have to remove them. Instead, fasten your pages with paperclips or binder clips.

It is essential to present your proposal in a neatly typed form with no handwritten corrections. Nothing, I repeat, nothing can be hand-written. This includes application forms. If you can't type, hire a typist. The physical form of your proposal must be near-perfect. Whatever its other merits, bad typing and rampant errors can single-handedly ruin a proposal's chances. You may not catch every last typo, but it's crucial to go through your final draft several times and check for errors.

If you have support documentation, make good, clear photocopies and attach these at the end of your proposal. Don't submit original letters or newspaper clippings. If an article doesn't fit easily on a page, do some cutting and pasting and set it up on letter-sized paper for photocopying. If you're asked to send in other kinds of documentation—slides, photographs, videotapes—make sure that everything is clearly labeled with your name and the project title. If you're submitting slides or photos, use plastic mounting pages that you can attach directly to your proposal. You should never submit originals; things do get lost, and foundations may not always return your materials.

FUNDER FOCUS—ADJUST YOUR PROPOSAL FOR DIFFERENT FUNDERS

Every funder will assume that you are applying to several sources. But even though they understand this necessity, you'll need to adjust your proposal slightly to focus on each funder's particular mission and interests. This doesn't mean that you are going to change your own mission or project in any way. You only want to show how they fit and could further the mission of each funder. This is why you should give each version of your proposal a special focus.

For example, say you've invented a process that will remove certain hazardous chemicals from water. There are several ways you could slant your description of this. For foundations that support scientific research in your region, you can stress that most of the R&D will be locally based. If you approach a foundation that supports environmental projects, highlight your project's ability to help clean up ponds or streams. For a funder interested in scientific education, explain that you will employ chemistry majors at the local university to help monitor trials of your process. Your basic plan remains the same, but you should adjust your statement of need and objectives to reflect the aspect of your project that each funder will be most interested in.

It's much better to integrate the funder focus into the body of your proposal in this way. Some grant seekers try to do this just in the cover letter, but I think this is the easy way out, and not as effective. You don't want to try to second-guess the foundation by making your project sound like something it isn't—there should be nothing manipulative or insincere about this process. What you want to do is put yourself in the funder's shoes and think about your project from the point of view of their mission and criteria. Write your proposal with an eye to making it clear why they in particular should give you a grant.

For example, I was recently working on a proposal for a public television series about books. Now, there are many directions one could go in with this kind of project, but I was targeting a foundation that is primarily interested in literacy programs, including media literacy programs. When writing the proposal for them, I directly addressed the concerns in the foundation's own mission statement. I talked about how this was a creative use of the television medium to get people motivated to read and make books seem more accessible. And it worked—we got the grant! (By the way, you should never tailor a proposal to make your project resemble other projects that have been funded by an organization. You should focus your writing only toward their mission statement.)

DEADLINES AND TIMING

Meeting deadlines is essential. Funders are extremely strict about this, and if you miss the deadline, you miss the chance for the grant. It really is that simple. You have to get your proposal into the funder's hands—a postmark by the deadline is usually not good enough. You can ask for an extension only if you have a history with the foundation, and even then they don't like to do this. Unless you have applied many times and have gotten grants from a foundation, forget about an extension.

In fact, it's best to send your proposal in advance; the early bird does get the worm. If you get your proposal in early, the staff will have time to make copies and distribute them to board members. Program officers and board members will have time to look over your proposal and think about it. It will already be in the back of their minds when they are looking at new proposals and thinking about priorities. And if the staff or a program officer wants to get in touch with you to clear up any questions, or to look at additional material, there's plenty of time.

So you shouldn't be trying to hammer proposals together at the last minute. You can't write an effective proposal the night before a deadline, though people have tried. Allow time for research, writing, and just carefully thinking through how you want to present yourself. Not to mention the time it takes to type up clean copies, or get work to a typist and back. If you are a first-time grant seeker, working on your first proposal, expect to spend ten or fifteen hours on it, perhaps over the course of a week. This takes into account writing time as well as thinking time. You need to let your ideas simmer.

Planning ahead to meet deadlines is a sign of professionalism in fund raising. I once knew of a small nonprofit organization that did very interesting work in the cultural field. Their principal funder was a state arts council. They had a unique program, but it seemed that every year they were sending someone to the post office at the very last minute to get their proposal in to their principal funder. This was emblematic of their approach to fund raising, and this is one organization that is not around anymore. You should not be coming in at the eleventh hour.

I find the best way to effectively meet deadlines is to do a wall chart, as we discussed in Chapter 2. If you are applying to eight foundations, list all of them on the chart, list their deadlines, and designate a column for each section of the application. Mark your own deadlines for getting supplementary documentation and collecting résumés. Mark your personal deadlines for completing the basic proposal and having the budget done. Keep your deadlines well ahead of the funder's final deadline, so you have time for contingencies and can still get the proposal in early.

Now that you know some of the general considerations that apply to any proposal, let's take a closer look at the components of the full proposal package.

HOW TO PREPARE THE FULL PROPOSAL PACKAGE

If you are going to write up a full proposal, you can follow this outline in most cases. It is a standard approach that most funders are familiar with. Remember, though, that you *must* follow the funder's printed guidelines to the letter. If these differ in any way from this outline, don't worry; just follow the funder's guidelines.

The average proposal for an individual project will probably run from three to five pages in length, not counting the cover letter, the table of contents, or your résumé and supporting documentation. Keep it simple. The summary should never be longer than one page; the other sections each might run from a paragraph up to a page or two at most. Shorter is fine. If it starts to get too long, program officers will feel oppressed by all the verbiage, and this is not good for you. Of course, if you are proposing a complex, long-term project, the proposal will have to run a little longer. Explicate your ideas and plans, and don't lose sleep over the length.

1. COVER LETTER

This is where funders get their first impression of you and your project. It goes without saying that the cover letter is important. Be sure that you address it to the appropriate person—whether the head of the foundation, a program officer, or another contact person. You have double-checked that you have the right name (and spelling!), and that this person is still with the funder.

Say you're pleased to submit a proposal, and give the name of your project or organization. Your mission statement and the amount you are requesting should appear right in the first paragraph. Explain that you are writing "to obtain funding for . . ." and follow up with your mission statement. Next, state how much money you are requesting and what it would do. Your mission statement should really tell the whole story in a nutshell. Make sure it's clear and not too wordy. If you want, go back to Chapter 1 and review some of the samples of mission statements.

You can add a sentence here explaining where the project will take place and in what time frame. Say that you'll be happy to answer any questions or provide any further information. Thank the reader for their time and consideration, say you look forward to hearing from them, and leave it at that.

2. TITLE PAGE

The title page states your project title, your name, and the name of the funding source you are applying to. Center the project title and funding source near the top of the page. Think carefully about the title you give your project—and make it sound interesting.

Instead of simply:

PROPOSAL FOR FUNDING OF A DAY-CARE CENTER
Presented to the XYZ Foundation

you might call it:

THE FREEDOM TO WORK
A Request to the XYZ Foundation

In the lower right-hand corner of the page, include your full name, your address, your telephone number, and the date. If you have a sponsor or institutional affiliation, add the sponsor's name, address, and phone number under your own.

A catchy title might attract the reader's eye and pique some interest in your project, but it is not essential. What really matters in a proposal is the content of the project summary and the rest of the proposal. On a full-length proposal, I often include the mission statement and the amount requested on the title page.

3. TABLE OF CONTENTS

If your proposal runs five pages or longer, you should include a table of contents immediately following the title page. This would list the major sections, including Project Summary, Statement of Need, Objectives, Plan, Evaluation, Personnel, Budget, Future Support, and Supplementary Documentation. List the separate items that you are including under the Supplementary Documentation heading. If you are including more than one résumé, list the individual names in this section as well.

Even if you have a shorter proposal, you might include a simple List of Enclosures, itemizing such components as Project Summary, Proposal, Résumés, Budget, and Supplementary Materials.

4. PROJECT SUMMARY

Immediately following the cover letter or table of contents, you should provide a project summary. On a single page, outline your mission statement, the need for your project, your objectives, and your plan, and briefly describe yourself and your qualifications for receiving the grant. The project summary will give the funder's staff a quick sense of your project and tell them whether they want to read on.

Because it serves this important function, the project summary needs to arouse the reader's interest and provoke them to read further. It must also quickly convey all the essential facts about your project. Get as much information as you can into the first sentence. Again, begin with your request for funds and your mission statement: "This is a request to the XYZ Foundation from Jane Smith for a grant of $50,000 to enlist its support for the financing of her college education," or: "This is a request for a three-year grant totaling $110,000 to create a unique theater in Rapids City, South Dakota." Quickly describe the need for and the essential features of the project. You should be able to get most of the essential information into one paragraph. The project summary should never be longer than 250 words or one page.

In a new paragraph, explain why supporting your project is a good opportunity for the funder you are applying to. Make them feel that yours is a good cause. Explain how your project will have a positive impact, solve a problem, or satisfy a need. You can briefly provide some background on the community or context in which the project will take place, describe the outreach you will do, and tell why this will be important. If you are proposing to answer a need that no one else is addressing, you should stress this.

Finally, you can provide some background information on yourself and your qualifications. You might briefly describe your personal history if it is relevant to the project. If you are applying through a sponsor or institution, introduce them here. Mention anything about the past or present work or activities of the organization that relates directly to your project.

Try to come up with one or two key details that give evidence of your competence, or your unique qualifications to receive the grant. You should definitely mention any significant awards you have won, past funding, or any other outstanding accomplishments. Keep it short—this is not a résumé, and the whole project summary has to fit on one page. If you are a professional with much experience in the field, just say that, and let the reader flip to your résumé for more. If you're worried that you don't have much directly relevant experience, mention one or two positive facts that will indirectly support your case. If you're starting that day-care center, mention that you've done community volunteer work for your church, or been an officer in a Parent-Teacher Association.

Program officers will have a pretty good idea whether your project is feasible for them within a few minutes of reading your project summary. So keep it short, strong, and thought-provoking. If it's clear and to the point, your introduction will pique interest and induce the reader to read on. In the sections that follow you will be able to explain the needs, your objectives, and your plans in more detail.

5. STATEMENT OF NEED—PROBLEM STATEMENT

The body of your proposal begins with your statement of need. Keep this section, too, as concise as possible. The funder wants to know why you need the money, and whom the grant will help—whether an organization, a community, or you as an individual. It could be all three. The funder who sponsors you will want to know that they are having an impact upon a unique and urgent need. It could be your need as an individual or an opportunity for your community. Make the funder feel that you are a good "investment," that they will solve a problem or do good for society by giving you a grant.

Do emphasize the urgency of your need, and why your case may be unique. The need statement should be factual but it can help to dramatize a bit. Aim to have an emotional impact upon your reader, but don't overdo it. You need to find that delicate line between tugging on the heartstrings and presenting facts that speak for themselves.

Inject a sense of urgency. Show the funder that the problem you are addressing needs special attention and can be solved with *their* help. If current resources for dealing with the problem are inadequate, you should explain this. For an individual project, let them know if you don't have any alternative sources to turn to. For a community project, let them know if there are no other organizations or services addressing the need.

As you write your need statement, bear the following points in mind:

- Keep your need statement clearly connected to your mission statement. You are describing the need that the mission is designed to fulfill.
- Keep your need statement specific—localize it in time and space. You don't want to end up describing a huge social problem that your one project is helpless to solve by itself.
- The need statement is a good place to connect your project to the mission of each particular funder. Describe the need in a way that associates it as closely as possible with the kind of need the funder wants to address. Your project might in reality answer several needs, but emphasize the one that falls closest to the funder's interests.
- Emphasize the social need more than the strictly financial need. If an idea has integrity, the money will follow. So don't get as carried away with money as you do with your passion for the project.
- Don't focus on your personal life or personal need unless it relates directly to the larger problem. Try to cast personal need more in terms of positive opportunities than negative lacks. If you are applying for a scholarship, don't say that you are poor and don't have the money. Say that you have an incredible chance to enter this degree program, and that it's special because no one from your family, or your community, has ever had such an opportunity.
- You can mention some evidence to support your need statement, but you shouldn't go overboard on this. Just explain in an overview. Outline the causes or origins of the problem, and the current conditions or repercussions. You can briefly cite some statistics that support your need, if any are available.
- If applicable, mention the funding and support climate for your project. Is this a kind of project that has been neglected because resources have gone elsewhere? Is the need now becoming even more urgent because of the neglect?

- Don't overwrite. As long as it includes the necessary information, the shortest, clearest statement of need will be the strongest.

A strong statement of need will interest the funder in the next section of the proposal, which describes how you are going to fulfill the need.

6. OBJECTIVES

This section explains how your project meets the need you've just described. Here you want to list the goals you expect to achieve—the development of an invention to the point where it can be marketed, the completion of your college education, etc.

Your objectives will be unique to your project. Your objective may be personal and individual or it may reach out to the community. If you are going to do a research project, your objectives might include showing whether there's a clear correlation between two variables, publishing the results of your research, and establishing what the next course of research should be. If you are a performing artist, your objectives might be achieving a new level of skill in your craft, developing a new piece to perform at a certain theater, or developing new audiences for your work. A project may have one narrowly defined objective, or several related ones.

It's fine to itemize several objectives, as long as they develop in a logical, step-by-step way. Don't use this section to try to be all things to all funders. Stay focused, and be sure your objectives follow naturally and logically from your mission statement and statement of need.

Always go back to your mission statement. Your objectives are really a more detailed version of your mission. The mission statement gives a long-range, global vision of what you want to do. The objectives section goes into the specifics. I worked with one client whose mission was to bring free theater to children who normally don't have the opportunity to see it. When the client applied for funding, one of his specific objectives was to purchase a property for offices and performance space; another was to put on a particular show.

Above all, present your objectives in a positive way, as something that a funder should want to help you achieve. Don't just say you want to complete a series of twelve paintings for a public show; say you want to make twelve paintings that will grapple with a specific artistic problem, or will present the history of an oppressed community. Foundations want to know that something will change for the better because of their funding.

As you work on your objectives, keep the following in mind:

- Always include some kind of outreach among your objectives. You will bring people to the project, bring the project to people, or publish or disseminate results. If it's a community project, note how many people you hope to reach. If you are a filmmaker, explain that you will try to have your work screened at five festivals.

- If the need you describe is not being addressed by anyone else in the community, or the profession, be sure to mention this. This means that your project will have a special impact, and the funder will make a real contribution by giving you a grant.

- Regardless of your field or need, try to be as detailed and specific as you can. Show the foundation that you've thoroughly researched and thought through your project.

- Strike a positive note as you list your objectives. Convey the feeling that they can really be achieved. Include any information or evidence that will support this. If you have a community project, mention that you've done outreach in the community before and know what response to expect. If you're an artist, mention that you've completed commissions successfully.

- Your objectives should answer the needs you've described in specific, well-defined ways. In the need statement, you can talk about broad, long-standing needs. In the objectives section, discuss the short-term, readily achievable goals that you want to accomplish. In the need statement you can address the need for jobs and sophisticated work training for youth in your community. In your objectives, say that you'll provide fifty paying internships in high-tech local companies within the first year of your project.

- Don't confuse objectives with steps of your plan itself. Conducting a series of dance workshops with junior-high students in different inner-city schools is a method—part of a plan. Putting on a public performance of a new dance work with some of those students is an objective. Renting a space and hiring teachers to care for children are two steps in a plan. Providing day care for twenty children during a specific calendar year is an objective.

- As with the statement of need, be clear, concise, and to the point. You shouldn't have a huge number of objectives, and you don't have to write at length about each one to get your point across. A sentence or two of explanation for each will do the trick.

Outlining your objectives will lead directly to the next sections of the proposal—plan and evaluation. Once you have described your specific objectives, you'll be able to lay out the methods by which you'll achieve them. And if your objectives are clear, it will be easy to evaluate your success at the end of the project.

7. PLAN—PLACE, METHODS, SCHEDULE

In this section, you should really dig into the details of your project. This will probably be the longest section of the proposal. It will be based on the project outline that you've been developing from the start. There are three major areas you will clarify in the plan. You'll explain where the project will take place; you'll describe the steps in the process, from start to finish; and you'll provide a schedule for accomplishing those steps.

You don't have to be creative about the writing, appeal to emotions, or explain how you chose your methods. Just write down exactly what you plan to do, clearly and in detail. The length of this section will depend on how complicated your project is. You don't have to belabor the obvious, but do explain any aspects of your plan that a funder might be curious about. In fact, this is a good way to proceed: Imagine that someone who knows nothing about you or your project is asking you specific questions, and answer them. If you've discussed the project with others, and some good questions have come up, be sure to answer them in this section.

As always, be organized, proceed step by step, and avoid lengthy discussions. The form of this section will be determined by the steps of your project, from start to finish. As you write this section, be sure to cover the following five aspects:

- **Place:** Where will you be doing the project? If you want a fellowship, explain where. If you want to travel, detail your itinerary. If you are working in a community, identify it by location, ethnicity, shared interest—whatever applies. If you are going to be doing scientific research at an institution, describe the facilities. If you are doing an artistic project, identify the studio where you'll be working, or the theater where you'll be rehearsing.

- **Method:** Go through the different stages of your project in step-by-step fashion.

  If your project is large, explain how you will administer, operate, and keep records on it. Discuss any special aspects of financial administration and bookkeeping.

- **Personnel:** If your project will involve other key people, identify them (if you know who they are) and the jobs they will be doing. This won't be a separate section—just explain what the others will be doing at each stage of the project. If you will be hiring an assistant or a staff, working with professional consultants, or hiring a specialist, explain all this here. You don't have to say who they will be, or, if you know, go on at length about them. Just attach their résumés.

- **Outreach:** Be sure to lay out the details of how you will bring people to the project, bring the project to people, or publish or disseminate the results.

- **Time:** Indicate the starting and completion dates for the project as a whole. If it's a complex or long-term project, indicate expected starting and completion dates for each stage. It may help to provide a chart or diagram showing when each stage of a longer project will take place. Include outreach and evaluation in your schedule.

8. EVALUATION

This may be the section you've thought least about, but it's important to funders. They want to have some means of getting feedback from you and of knowing that their dollars were well spent, that the project succeeded as planned, that their grant made a difference. For a simple project, the evaluation process might be as straightforward as writing up a short report for the funder. For a large or complex project, an evaluation might involve supplying progress reports, compiling figures or statistics, or receiving visits by independent observers. Funders may request specific evaluation procedures in their guidelines, or work these out with you once they've given you a grant. If the guidelines give any clues, write this section accordingly.

Be creative in thinking of ways to help the funder evaluate your project. At the very least, you should offer to write a report for the funder upon completion of the project. If you are doing any outreach, try to measure the impact of your project on the community. You can keep track of the number of people you've reached—through attendance records at your theater performance or enrollment records at your day-care center. You can record the number of young people who get full-time jobs after your internship program. If you will need ongoing feedback about your project, you might be planning to make up questionnaires or have an open discussion period. If your work is going to be publicized, you may be able to offer reviews or articles.

Some points to keep in mind as you write this section:

- For many projects, the evaluation will naturally be more subjective. If you've gotten a scholarship or a fellowship, you will simply have to describe your own understanding of the impact of your education on your life. If there will be any public presentation or publication of your work, do mention this, but it may be sufficient for you to write up a report.
- You can always base the evaluation on your original objectives—at the end of the project you should be able to tell whether or not you accomplished them. (Even if your methods of achieving them changed!)
- For some projects, having third parties evaluate your work will be a normal part of the process. If you are presenting a play, you'll naturally want reviewers to see it. If you are doing scientific research, you will certainly want to present your findings to a professional journal, which will review your work for publication.
- Think of a way to determine whether beneficial changes came about as a result of your project, and to identify any changes that might have had other causes. Remember, though, outside factors from the weather to the economic or political climate affect how well your project succeeds.
- If appropriate, discuss the kinds of conclusions you will be able to draw at the end of your project. If you are doing research, what should you be able to find out? If you are doing an experimental program working with young people, what

might the success of this program imply for other projects? You may be able to show that a new direction in research or social work will be especially fruitful for others.

9. PERSONNEL

If you are doing a small, individual project, this section is easy: just attach your résumé. Some funders will ask that you give them a biographical sketch instead of a résumé. (See page 282 for more on these.) If your project is larger, you should include the résumés of the other key people who will be involved. You've already introduced these people and explained what they will be doing in your plan, so here you just attach their résumés. You only need résumés for the most important people; three or four is probably the maximum.

If you've talked to some people about your project and already have a tentative commitment, ask them for copies of their résumés. If they aren't sure about this, ask if they mind your mentioning their names as possibilities. As long as this is okay with them, write up brief biographical sketches of the people you've contacted. Make it clear that these are only tentative commitments, and *never*, ever use anyone's name whom you haven't spoken to or who has said no. A funder may check up on this, word will get out, and your credibility will be zero.

On Résumés and Bios.   There are plenty of references available to help you work up a good résumé. If you already have a résumé, or if you're starting one from scratch, it is a good idea to give it a slant so that it better supports the project you are proposing. (Many people make up two or three versions for different purposes.) Emphasize and expand on the education or experience that relates most directly to your project.

Don't worry if you can't show a lot of professional experience that is directly related to your project. You don't necessarily need special qualifications if you can build your résumé to emphasize experience that indirectly supports your case. Even if you've worked in a completely different field, you can describe your duties and activities so as to feature general skills and experience that would also be useful in the project area. Maybe you've managed construction projects with complicated schedules and many independent contractors. This is the kind of management experience that can carry over to almost any other kind of work. Remember, you don't have to list only job experience on your résumé. You may have done volunteer work for a church, or an organization that involved community outreach. Maybe you've been very active in a school PTA, and have special understanding of some relevant educational issues.

On the other side, if you have substantial professional experience, don't go in for overkill. In the academic world it may be effective to have a fifteen-page résumé that lists every article you've ever published, but funders get weary of this. They don't want to wade through a résumé that's longer than your whole proposal. Summarize your accomplishments and list only the essentials and highlights. Funders will get the picture.

If you are including résumés of other people, take a close look at them to see if they will support your project. As project director, you must make this evaluation. Sometimes you'll get a résumé that is simply not well done or is slanted in the wrong direction. In such cases, you should consider rewriting the résumé to give it the spin that will help make your case.

- **TIP:** For help with preparing a résumé, take a look at:
  The Only Job Hunting Guide You'll Ever Need, by Kathryn and Ross Petras. New York: Poseidon Press, 1989.
  Writing a Job-Winning Resume, by John E. McLaughlin and Stephen K. Merman. Englewood Cliffs, NJ: Prentice-Hall, 1986.

Biographical sketches, or "bios," are a peculiar format, and not everyone is used to writing them. They generally convey the same information as a résumé, but in condensed, third-person prose. You normally structure them chronologically, to give a sense of the story of your life. Start with your name, and continue writing about yourself in the third person. Begin with your birthplace, summarize your education, then move on to your professional career, honors, and accomplishments. You might mention significant experiences that relate directly or even indirectly to your career or project. Bios can have more of a personal feel than résumés, but you don't want to take this too far. Avoid cuteness and melodrama, and focus on your professional career. Guidelines may tell you how long the bio should be, but they are usually shorter than résumés. One page is a maximum, and you may be asked for something even shorter. Writing a bio is a useful exercise, because it forces you to pick out the highlights of your career, your most significant experiences and accomplishments.

10. THE BUDGET—YOUR REALITY CHECK

Your budget is probably the most important part of your proposal, after the mission statement. It is going to tell funders whether you are being realistic or fanciful about your needs. The only time you shouldn't submit a budget with your proposal is when a funder specifically asks you not to. This will rarely happen. If there's no mention of a budget in a funder's guidelines, submit one.

Program officers will often turn to your budget immediately after reading your mission statement, to see how savvy and realistic you are. It's not hard to do a good budget—common sense is the rule of thumb. But you do need to prepare carefully.

You will normally prepare your budget after writing the rest of the proposal. Everything in the budget must be consistent with the objectives and plan you've laid out. Essentially, you will be breaking down your expenses into major categories. (We'll talk about these categories below.) However, the actual figures must be based on real research into costs and prices. You can't just estimate them. You need to collect price lists, make phone calls, get quotes, sit down with a calculator and start adding things up. You will not be able to put down exact figures for every item. Don't worry about this—just make an informed estimate. Funders know that you will probably need to modify your budget slightly as you get into the project. But do get as many exact figures as you can and make your estimates as accurate as possible.

The budget must be clear and concise. One or two pages at the most will be sufficient. Much of the research and thinking you do to construct a budget will not appear in the final form. You'll simply list the total figures for the various categories.

Nonetheless, it is important to do the detailed research. First, because you want to present an accurate budget that will seem realistic to funders. Second, because you want to be able to justify your figures if a funder should ask you for more details. And finally, because by putting together an accurate budget, you will be bringing your project that much closer to reality, and you will know that if you get the money you will really be able to make it work.

Some foundations will study your budget closely and compare it with your project summary, your objectives, and the steps listed in your plan. Be sure any major budget items are mentioned in your plan. If your plan is not specific enough and does not mention, for example, that you will need to rent or purchase office equipment, the funder may find no clear reason why you need this equipment. Finally, be sure that your expenses are clearly related to specific objectives. If you list a budget item that doesn't seem to support your objectives, funders will question this. You may not get a chance to justify your need for an expense if it's not clearly supported in your proposal.

Budget Format.   To keep things clear, use a simple format for your budget. Put a title on your budget page, such as "Budget for the 'Make a Difference' Project," and use a two-column format. List the expense categories and items in the left-hand column and dollar amounts in the right-hand column. Round off to the nearest $10, $50, or $100. Make sure to line up all the figures in neat columns and subtotal each category that contains more than one amount. If you have just a few expense items in your budget, you can list each item by category. If you have a large budget that includes many individual items, just list the categories. As always, if the funder requests a specific budget format in the guidelines, follow their instructions. Below is a sample set of budget categories you can use to get started if the funder doesn't request a particular format.

- *Personnel*   Includes salaries and wages. If you are putting someone on salary, you normally have to include fringe benefits, like unemployment insurance and health insurance. If you have an individual project, you can get around this by simply paying a professional fee to yourself or others involved in the project, as below. (For help with fringe benefits, see the references on pages 286–87.)

- *Consultants and professional services*   Fees for professionals and contracted services. You can pay most of the people who work for a project on a fee basis. They will simply report this as self-employment income on their IRS returns.

  If a development consultant or program consultant is getting a percentage of monies raised, this must be listed with a dollar amount.

- *Living expenses or per diem expenses*   For a student on a scholarship, or a researcher who is traveling.

- *Expendable supplies*   Supplies that will be used in the course of your project. These could involve anything from office supplies to a scientist's glassware to a sculptor's clay.

- *Special contracted services* Word processing, bookkeeping, film or photo laboratories, photocopying. If you think you'll be managing a lot of expenditures (or even income) once your project gets started, you might want to include a budget item for bookkeeping services. This doesn't have to be a big amount. You probably can get away with $100 or $150 monthly or quarterly, depending on how much needs to be done.

- *Space or facilities* Rental of office space, studio space, etc.

- *Equipment* Purchase and rental. Be aware, though, that some funders specifically bar the use of their funds for purchase of equipment.

- *Travel* Foreign, domestic, local.

- *Communications* Telephone installation or service, toll calls, faxes, messengers, postage, shipping.

- *Publicity and publications* Advertising, printing of flyers, reports, programs, catalogues.

- *Promotion* Special public relations events, receptions, dinners, entertainment.

- *Other costs* Lump together any miscellaneous expenses that don't seem to rate a category of their own.

These are only sample categories. Feel free to use others if they apply to your project and to drop any that don't apply. Also see the sample budgets on pages 255 and 296.

How long should a budget be? One page is usually sufficient—or two for a large project. I like to flesh out the budget and give funders a little more detail, so that they can see what some of the important line items are. (*Line items* is budget jargon for one item on one line of a budget.) Have a few line items under each category. If you're paying three major professional or consultant's fees, list these under Personnel. List the major types or items of equipment. List the major categories of expendable supplies. You don't have to list every single supply or subcategory, but a budget with some detail shows funders that you have done your homework. They'll be able to judge whether you are being realistic financially.

If someone has offered you in-kind services, or will donate time to your project, and the commitment is really solid, you should show this in your budget. Just list the item under the appropriate category, and on the dollar side write "Donated" or "In-Kind." If you are going to donate your own equipment or facilities, enter this in the same way. Some funders might ask that you do this differently. They might want you to list the dollar value of the donated services, mark the items that are donated, and then subtract the total value of donated services from your budget total. Just follow their guidelines.

When you come up with your total, go back and adjust figures slightly to make your total a nice, round figure. Shave an amount here, supplement one there. A round figure will stick in funders' minds better—and will seem more realistic, since your budget does include some estimates. Make your budget total $7,500, not $7,350, $30,000 instead of $28,000.

DIRECT AND INDIRECT COSTS

If you are applying through a sponsor, many funders like you to break down your budget into two major categories: direct costs and indirect costs. Direct costs are those clearly connected with the actual project, such as salaries, fees, equipment, travel expenses, and publications. Indirect costs generally apply only to organizations and institutions and are a percentage of their overhead or general operating expenses. Indirect costs include items like rent and upkeep on facilities, administrative costs, a percentage of the salaries of the organization's officers, heat and electricity, and telephones and office supplies. Government applications and others for institutions usually ask for a breakdown of indirect and direct costs. They also may want you to break down some expenses into great detail—who exactly is being hired, what are their titles, job descriptions, etc.

If you are applying as an individual, you will have only direct costs. If you need to rent space, or include a budget line for telephone expenses, list these as direct costs. If you are applying through a sponsor, budgeting can get much more complicated, but there is usually someone on staff at the organization who can help you through the process. If there is no one experienced with this, you will need to do some research. See the books listed below for help with institutional budgets.

- *A Nonprofit Organization Operating Manual: Planning for Survival and Growth,* by Arnold J. Olenick and Philip R. Olenick. New York: The Foundation Center, 1991.

- *Raise More Money for Your Nonprofit Organization: A Guide to Evaluating and Improving Your Fund-Raising,* by Anne L. New. New York: The Foundation Center, 1991.
- *Securing Your Organization's Future: A Complete Guide to Fund-Raising Strategies,* by Michael Seltzer. New York: The Foundation Center, 1987.
- *Grants: How to Find Out About Them and What to Do Next,* by Virginia P. White. New York: Plenum Press, 1975.
- *Grants for the Arts,* by Virginia P. White. New York: Plenum Press, 1980.

Unless you are applying both as an individual and through an affiliate, you should be able to submit the same budget to most funders. Some, especially government agencies, may require special breakdowns. They may want you to itemize travel expenses in a certain way, or group together some categories and split others apart. In these cases, just read the guidelines and follow the instructions. For the most part, though, you'll be able to present the budget in the generic format that I've detailed in this section.

HOW TO MAKE BUDGETING EASIER

If you are not used to working with budgets, the process can seem a little daunting. A good way to proceed is to go to your stationery store, get a journal or ledger, and assign separate pages to different categories. Then you can enter in each expense as you research it. Many expenses will be linked to the projected time of your project. You'll have to estimate daily, weekly or monthly costs for certain items, and multiply to get totals.

If you have a personal computer, there are several simple money management programs available that will help you prepare quite elaborate budgets and do all the calculations automatically. If you're still at a loss, see if there is a service organization in your field that has a book or pamphlet on budgeting. Better yet, you might get someone from the organization to sit down with you for a consultation. As a last resort, you can hire a freelance consultant to prepare the budget. Look again at Chapter 2 for suggestions on how to do this. For the most part, though, preparing a budget simply requires common sense. Anyone who has done a household budget or prepared an income tax return should be able to do it.

How Fat or How Lean?

One question that grant seekers often fret over is just how big the budget should be. Can you fill it out with all kinds of perks and extras that would make life easier, or do you need to pare it down to the bare essentials? There's no easy answer to this. It depends on the funding climate in your subject area, on how innovative your project is, and on your personal qualifications. It helps to have some sense of what other projects in your area cost, though you can't simply reproduce someone else's budget request.

One of the problems in preparing a budget is the sometimes long lead time between the fund raising and start-up of a project. You have to be prepared for unexpected contingencies and cost increases. One way to factor this in is to pad each budget line a little. Don't base your budget lines on the most rock-bottom discount price you could find. Program officers expect a little bit of padding in a budget. Many organizations pad their budgets by 10 to 30 percent. This is not cheating—it's just being realistic. Everyone knows that prices can change by the time you have received all your funding and are ready to start up your project. You may need to take into account higher postage costs, higher rentals, higher personnel costs. On the other hand, program officers can spot excessive padding in two seconds. They are not stupid, and they'll throw out your budget, and your proposal.

Some guidelines will ask you to put down an amount for contingencies, and they may suggest a figure of up to 5 percent of your total budget. Do as they suggest, but you still shouldn't put down the rock-bottom price for each line item. Even if you like to work on a shoestring budget, make your costs look realistic.

If your fund raising stretches out over a long time, you may want to double-check your budget figures periodically. If some basic costs have gone up, factor this in, and adjust the total accordingly.

Program officers will be skeptical if your budget seems too low. They may suspect that you are not being realistic and conclude that you will never accomplish your project for this amount of money. They will worry that if they do give you money, it will be thrown away. So while it's good to be economical, don't underestimate your needs. Be honest with yourself, list all necessary expenses, and don't tell yourself that you'll solve that problem when you come to it, or that you can count on somebody to donate services. Even if you are used to working on shoestring budgets, use figures that reflect the going rate for goods and services. If you think you can do your project for less, you'll just have that much more flexibility.

Many grant seekers wonder about the issue of salary and compensation. You may be so excited about your project that you almost feel you'd like to do it without any compensation; but realistically, you probably need to support yourself. If it's a project with a limited time frame or scope, you can budget a professional fee for yourself, based on your estimate of the number of hours you'll be working on the project. If you will be managing a big project for a year and it will be your full-time job, put down a salary for the year. If this is the case, you'll probably be working through a sponsor, and you can get their help in figuring out fringe benefits.

When you are figuring salaries or professional fees, use the going professional rate, not the minimum wage that you might find somebody to work for. Remember, though, that the going rate in most parts of the nonprofit world, except at the very top, is somewhat lower than in the business world. It's not unusual for a project director of a cultural community project to earn between $25,000 and $35,000 annually. However, if you do have access to someone who is impassioned about the project and will work for union scale instead of their usual fee, or if you have someone who will volunteer time, by all means document this. The more money you can save, the stronger your chances of success.

If you are applying for travel grants, or there is a travel section in your budget, you will usually use a per diem figure that indicates basic daily expenses for lodging, meals, local transportation, etc. (This is exclusive of plane tickets and other intercity travel.) The per diem really depends on where you're going and what you consider a reasonable amount of money. A usual per diem is about $100 a day. The U.S. State Department lists the per diem it pays its employees in different cities in the world, so you might use this as a basis for budgeting international travel.

If you have one or two very expensive items in your budget, you don't have to explain or annotate them, as long as they are justified in your plan. If something is very unusual, you should explain in your plan why you are doing things this way. You should have good reasons for all your budget lines. If you get a meeting with a funder, they may well ask. You will not be turned down for a questionable item, but you may be questioned. If you do have a meeting, bring notes on how you arrived at your figures, so that you can answer such questions.

If you can get hold of some sample budgets for projects in your field, this may help you think through your own, and remind you of items that you might have overlooked. Of course, you can't copy someone else's budget format exactly, or base the size of your budget on someone else's. You have to build up your own budget from scratch, based on the needs of your particular project.

Similarly, you can't use a funder's grant guidelines or giving patterns to determine how big your budget should be. You will probably have to go to several funders to raise all the money for your project, and giving patterns can only help you decide how much of this sum to ask for from each funder.

11. OTHER FUNDING RECEIVED

If you have already received some funding at the time you send in a proposal, list it after the budget. Indicate the name of the funder and the amount of the grant. List any in-kind services or materials you've been offered here, too. This will help build your credibility—it shows that someone has already placed their confidence in you and that you are one big step toward getting your project done. Sometimes a funder will ask you to list other foundations or programs you are currently applying to, and you can list these after the budget as well, with an explanatory heading. Do this only if you are asked to—there is no need to volunteer this information.

12. FUTURE FUNDING AND SUPPORT

This is another optional section that usually only applies to institutional proposals. If you have an individual project with a definite completion point, you can skip it. If you are planning an ongoing, open-ended project, this is where you lay out any ideas you have about generating income to support the project, whether selling tickets, charging fees, or whatever. If this is a pilot project, you might discuss the stage at which you will start to do additional fund raising to continue the project, and how the results of the pilot will affect future fund raising. If you have an individual project that will continue after the initial grant period, you might plan to become part of an existing nonprofit organization, or to encourage your community to adopt the project.

You cannot usually go back to the same funder year after year. You have to go after a number of different sources and alternate them year to year. Some government agencies and large foundations will fund

projects on an ongoing basis, but generally only for nonprofit organizations and institutions.

13. CERTIFICATIONS

If you're applying under an umbrella organization, you will usually be
asked to supply a copy of its 501(c)3 IRS certificate of exemption.
Some funders may also want an official statement of affiliation signed
by officers of the organization or institution you are working with.

14. SUPPORTING DOCUMENTATION

Your supporting documentation might include one or two letters of
endorsement (as discussed in Chapter 2), statistical evidence, a press
release, a newspaper article about the problem or need, an article
about you, or a review of your work. If you've been funded before,
and this doesn't appear on your résumé, list it here.

Keep these documents to a minimum, and choose material that
very directly supports your proposal. Don't pad this section. Many
foundations are understaffed, program officers are overworked, and
they can't wade through pages and pages to find the one or two telling
documents. This is an area that many grant seekers abuse. As with
the rest of the proposal, short and to the point makes the strongest
impression.

If the guidelines address documentation, follow them very carefully. Funders may make very specific requests, or limit documentation.
Do include anything they ask for. Most corporate and private foundations leave to you the judgment of what will best support your
proposal. Government agencies may place very strict limits on what
you can send them; don't send them anything but what they ask for,
and send it in the form they request.

If you're applying under an umbrella organization, you normally
add documentation about the organization itself. This will typically
include a list of their supporters, major contributors, and past funders.
The organization will supply these. Insert any reports, brochures, or
other literature about your sponsor that is relevant to your project.
Again, don't bloat your proposal with every piece of publicity material
that your funder has produced.

If you get an expression of interest from a funder, or a meeting,
they may request certain documentation. For a recent project, a funder
asked to see very specific support documentation on how television
influences individuals in their book-buying habits. I had to do some

research to come up with material on this. But even when asked for something, don't go overboard.

Especially if you are doing creative work, funders may want to see samples of your work. If you want your work returned, they'll usually ask you to include a mailer with postage. But be warned: Over the years, I've raised a lot of money for visual artists, authors, and film-makers, and I'd say you should expect that your samples may not be returned. Even funders with good systems and fine intentions slip up. Never send original material, your only set of slides, or your only copy of something. Again, include only what's asked for. Less is more. Funders will ask for additional material if they need it.

SAMPLE PROPOSAL

This sample proposal comes from a nonprofit organization, but it will be equally instructive for individuals who are submitting full-blown proposals. It has several components: a cover letter; an introduction that includes the project summary, statement of need, and objectives; a plan of events that lays out the details of the project; a section on how the project's success will be evaluated; a summary; a list of the supporting documentation that would be attached to the proposal, including a list of personnel and information on other funding received; and the all-important budget. The title page and the table of contents are self-explanatory and thus are omitted here, but you should certainly include them in your proposal package—they'll make it both more professional-looking and more accessible.

Ms. Patricia Harrington
ZDF Corporate Foundation
Metropolis, NY

Dear Ms. Harrington:

We are honored to submit this proposal to the ZDF Corporate Foundation on behalf of VISIONQUEST, a nonprofit educational organization.

We are writing to obtain funding for the OPEN DOORS Career Conference and Workshop, a special one-week program designed to introduce minority and disadvantaged young people to career options in financial, service, manufacturing and media industries in the greater Metropolitan region. We are requesting a contribution of $10,000 to support this project.

If you should have any questions, need anything further, or would like to schedule a visit to any of our current programs, please don't hesitate to contact me.

Thank you again for your consideration.

Very truly yours,

Dr. Mara Lewis
Program Director
VISIONQUEST

I. INTRODUCTION [INCLUDES PROJECT SUMMARY, STATEMENT OF NEED, OBJECTIVES]

There are a number of thriving industries in the greater Metropolitan region, yet studies show that young people from minority and disadvantaged homes do not easily make their way into these industries, even at entry-level positions. Part of the reason has to do with expectations on the part of young people themselves, part with difficulties that many young people have in adjusting to the behavioral norms of the world of work. VISIONQUEST has addressed these issues in several of its programs, yet one hidden obstacle often remains: simple lack of information about the business world. While young people from middle-class or educated environments may know quite a bit about the career options open to them, as part of their general knowledge, the same cannot be assumed for many disadvantaged and minority young people.

These young people are in many ways cut off from information about the kinds of careers available, and they perceive limited options based on what they see in their neighborhoods, what they know of through friends and family members, and what they see on television. They may only know of jobs that seem either insecure and exploitive, or simply out of reach, and are thus unable to develop concrete goals and aspirations that would help motivate school study and personal development. With no information about challenging, rewarding work, many young people become increasingly alienated from the world of work, turning to dangerous, illegal activities, or simply giving up hope.

This is the need that the OPEN DOORS Career Conference and Workshop is intended to address. OPEN DOORS has three principal goals:

1. To introduce young people to the variety of occupations and careers that are available in the major industries of the region—financial, service, manufacturing, and media.
2. To provide each participant with a thorough understanding of how a selected one of these industries functions by the end of the one-week workshop experience.
3. To offer each participant individual counseling and information about further education, training, mentoring, and financial aid that might support their career goals or explorations. This would include information about the ongoing OPEN DOORS workshops in workplace habits and behavior.

VISIONQUEST is a ten-year-old educational organization, with experience in bringing together educators and businesspeople to enrich the educational process in the Metropolitan area. It began by forging links between specific high schools and colleges and the business community, bringing professionals into the schools to offer presentations on career options, and offering work-study mentoring and counseling on an individual basis. For five years it has successfully operated the OPEN DOOR Training Program, which is a rigorous training program for minority young people and adults in the culture, expectations, language, dress and behavior patterns of the workplace. Graduates of the Program are supported in active job searches, most of them successful. The OPEN DOORS Career Conference and Workshop is a natural expansion of VISIONQUEST's mission and activities.

II. Plan of Events

The OPEN DOORS workshop will be hosted by Metropolitan University, at its central campus, and will begin with a "Career Fair," including exhibits, introductory presentations by academics and industry professionals, and counseling. This will be followed by three days of intensive exploration of an industry that each participant will select, including counseling focused on that industry. Participants will be able to meet and learn directly from prominent and successful professionals in various fields. They will visit active business locations: banks, law offices, factories, television stations, graphic design studios.

Young people of high school or college age will be able to register through their educational institutions or community groups, or directly through VISIONQUEST. Scholarship stipends will cover such costs as lunch and dinner each day in the Metropolitan University dining hall; chartered bus transportation, counselor supervision and guidance; college and career counseling provided by experienced Metropolitan University faculty; all program activities and seminar materials.

III. EVALUATION AND CONTINUATION OF PROJECT

It is anticipated that after initial funding, the OPEN DOORS Career Conference will be an annual event and will be continued for years to come.

Measurable results of the program will include an outreach campaign and an overall recruitment effort geared toward attracting disadvantaged and minority young people with potential. VISIONQUEST will disseminate news of the conference in various ways, including brochures and program materials; liaison with area schools, colleges, and community groups; and publicity/recruitment stories carried by the media, as well as through VISIONQUEST public relations efforts.

VISIONQUEST will maintain annual records documenting the numbers of young people participating in the program. A specific evaluation form will be designed for participants, and will induce individual appraisals of the program in the following areas: (1) if they feel the program enhanced their basic understanding of how the various industries work; (2) whether they are likely to pursue careers in those areas; (3) specifically what was of most interest to them; (4) what educational and career value they received from the program; and (5) their recommendations for improving the program to enhance the experience for future participants.

VISIONQUEST will also conduct follow-up surveys one, two, and three years after the program to identify any specific correlations between conference participation and educational or career choices.

IV. Summary

Over the years, VISIONQUEST has received strong support from the Metropolitan educational and business communities. This support has been continued for the OPEN DOORS Career Conference, with Metropolitan University offering facilities and personnel and with members of the local business community offering their time and expertise, as well as financial support. We see this as an opportunity to make a real difference in the often-difficult lives of our young people, a way to offer them challenges and goals and to help bring them into the mainstream world of work.

List of Attachments (Supporting Documentation)

a. Budget for OPEN DOORS Career Conference and Workshop
b. Organizational budget for current and upcoming fiscal years
c. Copy of most recent financial statements
d. Proof of tax-exempt status
e. List of current supporting organizations (other funding received)
f. OPEN DOORS Training Program brochure
g. *Metropolitan Daily News* article on OPEN DOORS
h. Youth underemployment studies
i. OPEN DOORS Career Conference schedule of events
j. VISIONQUEST's Board of Directors (personnel)

OPEN DOORS Career Conference Budget

Salaries:

Conference director	$ 6,000
Administrative assistant	$ 4,000
Conference Week counselors	$ 6,000
Consultants	$ 3,000

Fringe benefits	$ 1,500
Administrative Overhead:	
Office expenses, telephone	$ 800
Bookkeeping	$ 300
Outreach, Advertising and Promotion:	
Fund raising, printing, postage, publicity	$ 3,000
Liability Insurance Rider:	$ 600
Fees:	
Metropolitan College facilities	$ 4,000
Food service and catering	$ 4,000
Transportation (buses)	$ 800
Program Materials and Surveys:	$ 1,000
TOTAL EXPENSES	$35,000

THE BIG PICTURE

When you've finished a draft of your proposal, look over the whole package to see how the various parts work together. Make sure there is a genuine progression. See that the needs or problems that you've described in your statement of need are clearly connected to your mission statement. Make sure the statement of need connects to the mission and interests of the funder as well. See if the objectives clearly answer the needs, and that your plan includes specific steps to achieve each objective. Make sure your plan justifies whatever will appear in your budget. Ask yourself if the evaluation will give the funder a sense of whether you will have achieved your objectives. Make sure résumés or bios seem relevant to your project, and put supporting documentation to the same test. Also take the following six final steps:

1. Look over your cover letter, and your statement of need, to be sure that you haven't been too emotional or melodramatic in stating the need for your project. Make sure that you've avoided leaning on political arguments or taking a political position. A simple statement of facts will be the strongest support for your project.

2. Look again at your objectives, and check that they are clear and attainable, not vague, long-term goals that simply restate your mission. Make sure, too, that you are not merely listing steps in your plan.

3. Make sure your plan includes the three basic elements: location of the project or activity, steps for accomplishing the objectives, and a timeline or schedule.

4. Make sure that your résumé clearly conveys your qualifications to do the project. Check your supporting documentation. Don't pad this section—use relevant documents only.

5. Look again at your budget, and be sure you have followed any guidelines from the funder about budget items or format. Make sure the need or use for line items has been clearly stated or implied in your plan. Make sure you've added all your figures correctly!

6. Look over the whole proposal once more and make sure that you are giving the funder all the information that they need to make a decision. Make sure that you've included outreach ideas wherever they fit. You can discuss outreach in the statement of need, objectives, plan, or evaluation. Depending on your project, outreach might even be part of your mission statement.

Don't do this right before sending out a proposal, but as you're working on the draft, you might want to show it to one or two *experienced* people for constructive criticism or response. "Experienced" means someone familiar with proposal writing and the nonprofit field. You might also want to have a freelance consultant look over your work. (See Chapter 2 for more on this.) Don't wait till the last minute—you don't want someone to devastate you with criticism the day before you have to send out your proposal.

A SPECIAL CASE: GOVERNMENT APPLICATIONS

Government applications are quite a bit different from private and corporate-style proposals. Instead of supplying the agency with your basic proposal, you'll have to fill in the blanks on complicated application forms. These often ask you to separate out and break down information in very specific and seemingly peculiar ways. You may have to do a lot of cutting and pasting and rework the material from your basic proposal to fit the government requirements. You may also have to do some additional research.

The forms can be quite long, require detailed information, and include specific requests and limitations. You may have to make multiple photocopies and add several attachments. Some of these intricacies can be intimidating even to the seasoned professional. But don't worry. Just follow the instructions in a step-by-step way and you won't have any problems.

It's a good idea to make your own photocopies of the blank forms, so that you can do rough drafts before typing up the final versions. Just go along, following the instructions and filling in the blanks. You *must* fill all of them in. If a question is not applicable, type N/A in the blank.

Government forms are usually broken down into sections. They may follow the format of the generic proposal, with boxes or blank lines for a project summary, objectives, timeline, budget, future funding, or other funders applied to. Or they may use different headings. Break up your proposal into the parts they ask for. This is almost like filling out a tax form, although the results may be more pleasant. The application may give you less space than you'd like to respond to a question. You really have to boil down your information into the clearest, briefest, strongest statements. Tinker with the wording of your responses until you get the best version you can.

There may be boxes that you can fill in with a paragraph or two, or just a few lines. You can type up a response on a blank page or a word processor, and cut it out to see if it will fit in the space provided. Cut and reword until you make it fit. The application guidelines will often warn you in dire terms not to go outside the allotted space, so do be careful. Sometimes you'll have the opportunity to attach a page in support of a particular entry on the form. If you do this, make sure you head the page with exactly the same entry name and number that appear on the application form. Type "See attached" on the form. Put your name and the agency to which you are applying on each separate attached page, in case it gets lost or separated from the rest of the application.

Government budget forms can be extremely detailed and may require you to enter information in ways that seem awkward and nonintuitive. You may have to rework your budget quite a bit to get it into the required form. Government budget forms demand extreme precision, requiring you to calculate all costs down to the last penny (though some will ask you to round off figures). You'll have to break down any travel expenses on a per diem basis.

You'll find that government application guidelines are usually very specific about what kind of support documentation is required or permitted. You may be asked to submit testimonials, endorsements, press clippings, photos, videos, artwork, etc. Send in only what's requested or specifically allowed, and in the specified format.

When you are ready to do the final draft of the application, type carefully, neatly correct any errors, and proofread for typos. You'll usually be asked to submit the application in duplicate or triplicate. You should also make copies of everything you are submitting for your own files. Carefully follow any guidelines on the physical format of the application. Use a removable binder if permitted, or just use paperclips or binder clips for each set of copies. Send the entire application in one folder or with a big binder clip to keep it together. Address it as the guidelines indicate.

The forms and guidelines aren't always clear, and you may be stumped by something as you are filling out an application or getting ready to submit one. You can try calling up the agency to see if there is someone on the staff who can help you. Some of the larger agencies can seem very impersonal and you may find it difficult to get anyone to listen to your questions. Be persistent if you truly have a question that you cannot answer yourself. You can also get in touch with someone at a nonprofit or service organization that is familiar with this program and ask them for advice.

WRAPPING IT ALL UP AND SENDING IT IN

So you've finally put all the pieces together and you have your complete proposal ready to send out. Before you send it, do some last-minute checking, as every good development officer does. Look at the checklist below, and make sure you have included every element that you need.

1. *Cover Letter.* Double-check that you have addressed this to the right person. If it's been three or four weeks since you got their name, call right before submitting your proposal. The contact person might have changed in the meantime.
2. *Title page*
3. *Table of contents*
4. *Project summary*—maximum one page!

5. *Statement of need*
6. *Objectives*
7. *Plan*—location, steps, timeline
8. *Evaluation*
9. *Personnel*—your résumé or bio and any others
10. *Budget*
11. *Other funding received*—if applicable
12. *Future funding and support*—if applicable
13. *Official certification and signatures*—if applicable
14. *Supporting documentation.* Don't pad—include relevant items only.

If all the components are there, proofread the proposal one last time for spelling and typos. Check for general neatness and retype pages if you have to. If the funder has asked for additional copies, make them, and *always* make one for your files. Be sure you have a copy of each piece of supporting documentation as well. Put your copy in the file you are keeping for this funder, and note on the file folder the date you send the proposal out. If you are using a wall chart or calendar, mark the date on that as well.

I had a personal experience that demonstrates exactly why you must make a copy of each proposal you send out. Some years ago, a client of mine was up for a major grant. The foundation was interested in the project but couldn't find their copy of the proposal we had sent them. We were close to the deadline, we had to get them a copy of the proposal, and it turned out that somebody in my office had sent it to them without making a copy. I went nuts. Luckily, the foundation found it, or we would have lost the grant. So foundations can misplace things; you *must* make copies of proposals.

Your proposal is ready. Now you look at your wall chart or calendar and see that you still have time before the deadline. You can send it by regular first-class mail, or perhaps U.S. Priority Mail. I don't like to send proposals certified—return receipt requested or not—because I think it annoys the funder. The nonprofit world is still a little bit in the nineteenth century, and you need to follow different rules than in normal business. If you're down to the wire, you could send your proposal by U.S. Express Mail, or by Federal Express, but you shouldn't be pushing the deadline like this. Don't send the proposal by messenger, or hand-deliver it, unless you are at the eleventh hour. It's best just to send it through the regular first-class mail, well in advance of the deadline. The low-key, low-pressure approach works best with funders, and sending your proposal in early shows that you've got your act together.

THE WAITING GAME

You've put a lot of time, care, and consideration into writing your proposal. Once you have submitted it, though, there's nothing to do but wait. Some foundations will send you a reply card or form letter to let you know that your proposal has been received and that you will be notified of its status shortly. If a foundation has not contacted you after twelve weeks, you should call them, just to make sure they have received the proposal. Making one follow-up call shows that you are on top of things; if you start making too many calls, you'll be seen as pushy and overly eager. Do not make more than one, unless a funder has given you the go-ahead to call them.

Sometimes funders will contact you if they have questions about your project, or if they want to meet with you about it. If you have the opportunity to meet with a grant officer, this is a chance to create a good personal impression and to explain your project in detail. You should prepare for such a meeting carefully and bring any supporting materials that might be useful, including more detailed budget notes.

On the other hand, many funders will advise you not to call them but to wait until their Board of Trustees meets and makes its decision. The larger foundations in particular are so inundated with proposals that they do not want to be bothered with any questions. Their guidelines will usually specifically instruct individuals not to contact them until a few months after the submission of the proposal. If a funder's guidelines state, "No personal calls whatsoever," you should respect this. If it seems that the decision period has passed and you've heard nothing, you could send them a brief note, saying that you sent them a proposal on such-and-such a date and you just want to confirm that they received it. If you never do hear from a funder, just assume that they weren't for you and go on to the next one. This is why you send proposals to a number of different funding sources.

Don't feel discouraged if funders seem remote and unavailable. This is the way they must operate in order to be able to process the vast number of proposals they get. Also, don't feel discouraged if they don't contact you about your application. Most people who get grants simply send in their proposals, wait until the funder makes a decision, and receive notice of their grant at that time.

The waiting game requires patience. If you have been thorough in working up your mission statement and your plan, if you've been careful about selecting the right funders to apply to, if you've written the best proposal you can, then you have a good chance of getting a grant. When you're notified whether you got the grant or not, take a look at the next chapter to consider how to proceed.

10

FOLLOW-UP

YOU ARE AWARDED A GRANT!

Congratulations! You may receive the news through the mail or, more informally, over the telephone. If it's by telephone, wait for your formal notification letter before beginning your project. And hang on to that letter. Put it in the funder's file, which has just advanced from potential to actual status.

Your notification letter should indicate the amount you've been granted and the schedule of payment. The grant check may be enclosed with the notification letter, or it may follow close behind (usually through the mail). If you are working with a sponsor organization, the check will probably be made out and mailed to them. In any case, don't spend your own money on the project before receiving the promised grant funds. Wait until all the details are settled before moving ahead.

Once you have received formal notification of funding, you should write a brief thank-you letter to the funder. Expressing your gratitude will help you build a positive relationship with the funder. You want to stay on good terms not only for the funding period but afterward, in case you later seek additional funding from the same source, or referrals to other funding sources. If you receive the check some time after the notification, write again just to let them know it has arrived.

LITTLE GRANTS AND BIG: THEY ALL ADD UP

You may have been fortunate enough to be awarded a grant but still feel discouraged because it wasn't as much as you requested, or isn't enough to fund your whole project. Do understand, most funders do not expect to underwrite an entire project. The only time a funder will pay for your whole project, and do so exclusively, is when they want to take full credit for it. A perfect example is Mobil Oil's single-handed support of *Masterpiece Theater.*

Usually, though, grant amounts are based on what funders feel they can give, or want to give, to your project. So if you requested $10,000 and they only give you $5,000, don't be disappointed. It is simply that they want to make awards to a certain number of different applicants. Getting any grant is an honor, and you should be pleased to be one of the recipients.

If you can't complete your project with what you have been given, I advise you to accept the partial funding and pursue additional funding elsewhere. Yes, it is tough to keep on trying to raise money, but it's not impossible. Receiving one grant makes your case stronger for other funders. If you have raised a good percentage of the funding, chances are good that you will raise the rest of the money—as long as you keep trying.

I once worked with a television producer who had a very timely project, which we had to find support for quickly. She had a budget of $120,000; after quite a bit of hard work I managed to raise $70,000 for her, but it was time to start production. She was so discouraged by not having raised the whole sum that she seriously suggested returning all the money, thinking she just couldn't do it for that amount. I couldn't believe it. Fortunately, I was able to line up additional in-kind services that made it possible for her to finish the project. The point is: if you get a substantial part of the funding you need, there is usually a way to go ahead with your project, even if it's on a smaller scale.

ARE THERE STRINGS ATTACHED?

Before you start spending the grant money, establish where there are special restrictions or requirements regarding expenditures. Usually these will be very carefully spelled out in your award letter, or have already been announced in the guidelines. If you're not sure about a restriction, ask the funder for clarification. Many of the points below will apply only to complex, sponsored projects, but some may come into play for the individual.

Be sure you understand *any restrictions on the types of expenditures* you are allowed to make with the grant money. For example, some foundations will not let their funds be used for administrative salaries, or to purchase equipment. Others may forbid use of their funds for advertising or press releases.

There may be *time* restrictions on the grant. You may be expected to use all the funds within a certain period. If you've been awarded a challenge grant, or another kind of restricted grant, you may not be able to use the money immediately. (See Chapter 2 for more on challenge grants and matching grants.)

Content restriction is a special problem that has been much in the news, and the debate continues. In the past few years, a few artists and arts organizations awarded government grants were asked to sign a statement that they would not produce or present work that might be considered obscene. Some signed and some did not; eventually the requirement was removed. Recently, subject restrictions have started to appear in the humanities and scientific fields as well.

Some funders have *operating* restrictions that apply to the way scientists can do research or the kinds of materials they can use. Usually, though, these come into play when the funding decision is made, and recipients are not always required to sign agreements.

People have different views about some of these restrictions. Some feel that if you are going to accept money from a patron, whether public or private, it's realistic to expect to accept any restrictions they might impose. Others feel that the principle of freedom of speech should apply to government funding. They draw an analogy to academic freedom in colleges and universities. This is very much a matter of personal opinion.

You should be aware, though, that if you refuse to accept content or operating restrictions, you may have to give up the grant. This may also affect your future funding possibilities, though in unpredictable ways. It could jeopardize your future funding with the particular agency, or with other agencies. On the other hand, some people who have turned down grants on this basis have suddenly found themselves offered awards from private sources.

If you do have problems with this issue and want to talk to others who are concerned with it, you can contact:

- People for the American Way
  2000 M Street, N.W., Suite 400
  Washington, DC 20036
  202-467-4999

Even when project content is not an issue, you will on rare occasions be asked to sign an *agreement* with the funder. Usually this simply means agreeing to whatever restrictions or requirements are listed in the guidelines. If you don't understand all the terms, talk to someone at the program or foundation. This is a very civilized business, and dialogue is welcome at this point of the process. If you're still unsure, do have a lawyer, or someone knowledgeable in the field, look at it.

Check on the *method of payment*. Will the funder send you one lump-sum check or pay out the grant in installments? Are installments keyed to the calendar or to stages of your project? If a sponsor is acting as your fiscal agent, they may receive the grant as a lump sum and dole out limited amounts to you. You should clarify this with your sponsor.

Financial recordkeeping is another important matter to clarify. What kinds of records will the funder require? If you have a sponsor, they may be responsible for keeping these records—but don't assume so. Discuss this point with your sponsor, as well as with your funder.

If you have a sponsor, you should set up a meeting to discuss *accounting procedures*. There may be some grant-related details to take into account, details not anticipated when you drew up and signed your formal letter of agreement. The person you should meet with at this point is the sponsor organization's fiscal officer (i.e., business manager), rather than the individual(s) with whom you arranged the sponsorship.

Find out whether or not the funder requires you to make regular *progress reports*, and if so, how often. How formal must these reports be? Is there a recommended or required format, or specific topics you must address? Get all the details you can—if you know beforehand about special requirements, you can keep appropriate notes as you go along and use these to create the progress reports.

Check on how your project will be *evaluated*. Does the funder require or prefer any specific type of evaluation process? Do they want to be involved, or will you be solely responsible for evaluating your success? When will you be expected to provide or participate in an evaluation?

USE YOUR FIRST GRANT TO GET MORE

One of the great benefits of getting the first grant is that it can help you raise more funds. If it's all right with the funder, you should certainly make public announcements about your grant in your field's local or professional papers. This may attract other funders, as well as increase your profile and credibility. And be sure to include this information in any new proposals you send out.

Can you ask for referrals to other funders after you've received a grant? Usually only if you are having a lot of dialogue with the funder and they broach the subject first. If a program officer is musing out loud, "This is the sort of thing that ABC likes to support," then you can definitely say, "Oh really, who should I approach over there?" But if you are having minimal contact with the funder, and they don't offer help first, don't bring it up yourself.

You also want to update any foundations or government agencies that are considering funding you. Send a brief letter of announcement to these funders, and add the information to your résumé as well.

There are occasions when a funder will not want you to announce your grant. This is rare, but you should always check with the funder before you publicize it or tell other funders. If your project receives any media attention, or if you plan to send out press releases (either announcing your grant award or just mentioning it in connection with a publicized opening or show), be sure to clear all public mention with the funder (and in some cases with the sponsor) beforehand. Many corporate foundations prefer that all their press coverage be coordinated through their own PR offices. Some funding sources avoid all media attention. Respect the wishes of the funder.

Likewise, if you are planning to use the funder's name in any brochures or programs, you should definitely get their approval first. Years ago, a client of mine got money from a major oil company for a series of symphony concerts. We printed up thousands of brochures, and then it turned out they did not want their name mentioned as underwriting the project. We were dumfounded (they had never minded before), but had to reprint the whole lot without their name. You don't have to clear all press releases and public information about your project with the funder, just those that mention them.

FORGING AHEAD—WORKING WITH THE FUNDER

After getting funded, it's important to maintain a good professional relationship with your funders. Keep them abreast of any new information about your project—send a brief note from time to time, telling of your progress. If you hold any kind of performance or public event, you should certainly invite them. If you are doing community outreach, send them a copy of any brochures or press releases. At the same time, remember that the funder's function is really to provide the support and then sit back and enjoy the results. Even if they've been helpful and cooperative, you shouldn't expect them to be interacting with you on a daily or weekly basis. If you encounter problems in doing your project, go to your sponsor, or try to get help through a service organization in your field. Don't ask a funder for more help than they've already given you.

With funding in hand, you are finally ready to forge ahead. As you devote your attention to the project itself, reserve some time for the paperwork and recordkeeping that funders, and perhaps the IRS, require. It's a good idea to set aside a specific time each week to do this.

FINANCIAL MANAGEMENT

It's extremely important to administer your grant in a professional, responsible manner. You have been privileged to receive grant money, and some responsibility comes along with it. You want to manage the finances professionally so that not only will your project succeed but you'll also be in a position to apply for further funding in the future.

Good financial management requires good recordkeeping. If the funder will ask for financial accounting, you need to keep records of all of your grant-related expenditures. Save receipts, make entries in a ledger book, do whatever it takes to create a complete and organized record of your grant spending. Behave as if you expect an audit. Your funder will appreciate accurate records of how their money was used. For smaller projects, though, the funder may expect only minimal accounting or none at all. Check your award announcement and guidelines carefully.

One way to keep good records is to get a ledger book with columns and use one column for each of your budget categories. Write checks, use credit cards, or keep receipts for your expenditures, and every week or two go through your receipts and checkbook, entering each expense in the appropriate column. Depending on your project, you may need to have a credit column (or columns) where you record funding received, or other income generated by your project.

- **TIP:** If you use a personal computer, a simple money management or checkbook program will help you keep track of your expenditures. You can set up an account or "check register" for your project and enter all expenses, dates, check numbers, and expense categories, and the program will automatically prepare reports with exact figures and category breakdowns.

If you received a very large grant and your project is complex, do set up a good, simple bookkeeping system such as any small business would use. For certain government grants, or a very large or long-term project, you will definitely be expected to provide detailed financial accounts. You might explore the possibilities of hiring a professional bookkeeper, which could cost from $100 to $150 a month, and which should be built into the budget. If you are working with a sponsor, they will already be taking care of most of this.

Do you have to worry about mingling grant monies with your other personal funds? Not necessarily. If you have received a small grant such as a scholarship, or several thousand dollars for a personal project, it isn't necessary to set up a separate bank account. You can deposit and write checks from your regular bank account as long as you keep separate records of your expenses.

If you're looking at more than a few thousand dollars in funding, you should consider setting up a separate bank account for the project. This can cost a little extra money, but you will have very clear records of all income and expenditures, and your balanced checkbook will itself be a good financial record.

TAXES

The bad news is that most grants, prizes, and awards to individuals are taxable, whether they come from private foundations, the government, or nonprofit organizations. This is another reason why you will want to keep careful records of all grant income and project-related expenses. The good news is that some of your grant expenditures may be deductible or even exempt.

The portion of the grant that covers your professional fee or salary is always taxable. If you are working on a career-related project, however, many of your expenditures may be deductible as business expenses. If you're a writer, a painter, or a researcher, and you sometimes earn money from your work—or plan to—you can deduct such expenses as the cost of materials, research expenses, tools and equipment, and project-related travel. The usual way to deduct these expenses is to file an IRS Schedule C form, on which you declare business income and expenses. However, detailed tax advice is really beyond the scope of this book. You should consult a qualified accountant or tax preparer, or do some research on your own. If you do decide to work with a professional, get someone who is familiar both with your field and with grants. There are also a number of printed references you can turn to for help with proper tax procedures. A few are listed below.

- *The Artist's Tax Guide and Financial Planner,* by Carla Messman. New York: Lyons and Burford.
- *J. K. Lasser's Your Income Tax.* New York: Simon & Schuster (published annually).
- *J. K. Lasser's Tax Guide for Small Business.* New York: Simon & Schuster (published annually).
- *Tax Guide for College Teachers.* College Park, MD: Academic Information Service (published annually).

If you are funded through a sponsor, you are shielded from some tax liabilities because the sponsor is the actual recipient of the grant and is a nonprofit organization. This can simplify your recordkeeping a great deal—you may not have to get involved with business deductions. Still, any fees or salaries paid you by the sponsor are taxable.

There are other complications for individuals receiving grants. There is a special place to list grants, prizes, and awards on the IRS 1040 form. Fellowships and awards are taxable as income but are not subject to Social Security tax. They cannot be used as part of earned income for IRAs. Fulbright fellowships are taxable, but foreign income tax credit can be used to offset some tax liability. You get the picture— it's a complex situation, and you need to either have help or do the research.

The tax rules for students and graduate degree candidates can get even more complicated. Grants for tuition and related instructional expenses such as fees, books, supplies, and equipment are generally tax-exempt. Tuition remission is tax-exempt. However, grants for room, board, and living expenses are considered taxable income. The rules are different for degree and nondegree candidates, and there are special rules regarding Social Security tax exemption. The definition of whether you are receiving a scholarship or a fellowship becomes important—fellowships and assistantships are considered taxable income. Gifts are tax-free, while grants, prizes, and awards are subject to tax rules. There are special places to report tax-free grants on a tax return, and ways to report scholarships and grants to minimize the chance of an audit. Again, there is much more to this than we can cover here. You should find a good tax reference guide, or consult a specialist, or perhaps someone in your school's financial aid office can help with these issues.

PROGRESS AND PROJECT REPORTS

If your project is not too big, you may be asked to write an informal report at the end or deliver some kind of material as evidence and record of what you did. If it's a larger, more complex project, you may be asked to file formal progress reports, which you would send to your funder at regular intervals during the course of your project. The grant guidelines will spell out the reporting requirements, or a program officer will explain them when you are awarded the grant. Reporting requirements vary from funder to funder. If you're asked to file reports, put a little time and effort into making them readable and informative. Turn them in promptly. Make your funders feel that you are pleased by their interest and eager to share news of your project. Remember, you and the funder are now in a working relationship. You need to hold up your end of the bargain—especially if you might have to request additional funding in the future, for this project or others.

Even if formal reports aren't required, you should still keep your funders up to date about your project. One or two informal phone calls a year is sufficient. You don't want to overwhelm funders with your enthusiasm or intrude on their time. Even if it's not a requirement, do invite funders to any performances, shows, or demonstrations related to your project. This lets them see firsthand what their money has enabled you to accomplish.

IF YOU RUN INTO PROBLEMS

The most usual problems you might run into are delay in getting your project started, perhaps because you are still raising funds, or delay in finishing your project. If reports or evaluations are due at a certain time and you're just not ready to submit them, do write to the funder, explain the reason for the delay, and ask for an extension. Give an interim summary of progress, explain what stage you're at, and give an estimated schedule for completion. If grant payments are tied to calendar dates, or to stages of your project, ask for an extension of the scheduled payments beyond your original schedule and explain in detail the reasons for the delay. (We're not talking about additional payments, just about making scheduled payments beyond an initial cut-off date.) If funders see that you are committed to the project, working at it, and delayed by circumstances beyond your control, they will usually continue to support you. They want to see the project completed successfully.

What happens if you get grant monies, you start a project, disaster strikes, and you can't continue? Should you offer to give back part of the money? Not unless it is required, but it depends on the circumstances. You have probably spent some of the money developing the project. If you don't raise the entire budget, do you have to return the money? No, with the caveat that you must use it toward the project; you can't use it to buy groceries or pay your mortgage. If the project doesn't fly, the project doesn't fly. If there is a balance remaining that you haven't spent, I would encourage you to return it. It's a sign of professional responsibility, and it will stand you in better stead if you ever want to raise funds again.

Remember, funders have placed a high degree of trust in you and made a real commitment. You must deal with your funding responsibly. I once knew of a highly respected but rather unpredictable artist who got a prestigious government grant, used the money somehow, but never seemed to have really pursued the project he got the grant for and never made any kind of final report to the granting agency. They gave him the money and never heard from him again. This was a serious, committed artist, who was certainly not getting rich off grants, but he was blacklisted in the funding world for years. So you do want to follow up on your reporting, even if you run into problems.

This raises another question: What if in the middle of the project you suddenly get hit with a massive, unanticipated expense, or something affects your budget? Should you tell the funder? Yes and no. Chances are the funder will not increase your funding. Continue anyway, even if you can't do the complete project. You're going to have to shave expenses. I've seen this happen to project after project. You can also try to raise more funds. People are always dealing with the unexpected when working on big projects. When one budget category balloons, you just have to cut back on another.

IF YOUR REQUEST IS TURNED DOWN

A rejection notice is always disappointing.

Worse, some foundations don't even notify unsuccessful applicants. They only contact those to whom they are making awards. This limits administrative costs, especially when they are swamped with applicants. In most cases, you can find notification policies listed in the funder's application guidelines. If you have heard nothing, but the decision should have been made by now, call the funder to check on the status of your request. Be prepared for bad news. Remain polite and thank the individual on the phone for helping you.

WHAT DOES THIS MEAN?

How should you respond to being rejected by a funder? It's important to be realistic and not be thrown off course. You must realize that this is not a personal slight on your project. Perhaps the funder was over-committed. Perhaps it just wasn't meant to be for this cycle. Instead of dwelling on negativity, look at your proposal and project and see if they can be made to work better, or if you just need to keep trying with other funders.

Often, you'll find that a corporation, or even a foundation, that can't give you cash will think about making an in-kind donation.

Still, there are some legitimate, logical reasons why a funder might turn you down:

1. **Funding area.** The most common reason given in a rejection notice is that your project doesn't fit the guidelines or granting areas of the funder. This is something you shouldn't be getting too much of, since you did your research and should have ruled out any inappropriate funders. Still, you may have interpreted guidelines or announcements to mean something different from the funder's intentions. There isn't much you can do about this one; there's no point in trying to argue with a funder about their guidelines. Pack your bags and move on. But you might want to look again at your proposal. Did your statement of need clearly fit with the funder's mission? Consider this carefully for your next proposal.

2. **Lack of affiliation.** Another common reason for rejection is that the funder does not accept proposals from unaffiliated individuals. Again, this is a problem that you should have avoided through research and screening. Still, you may have applied to a funder that didn't clearly state their restrictions. There's nothing you can do about this except to go back again through a sponsor.

3. **Proposal problems.** It may be that your proposal simply wasn't strong enough to sell the funder on your idea. If you think this might be the case, go back to Chapter 9 again and measure your proposal against its recommendations. Look again at "The Big Picture" on page 297 and evaluate your proposal in terms of these guidelines and potential problems. If you think you have a proposal problem, consider having a freelance consultant look it over. Remember, a proposal problem could reflect a problem with your mission statement or the plan itself. Make sure these are carefully thought through.

4. **Budget problems.** The funder may have had a problem with your budget or with the cost of your project. They may have felt your budget was unrealistically small, or not reflective of actual costs in the field. Or they may have felt your budget was excessively padded, too luxurious, too big for a person of your experience to handle, or just so big that it would be too difficult to raise all the funds you would need. They won't always tell you this, but if you suspect it might be the problem,

you can sometimes try to get the information out of the funder. (See the next section, Finding Out Why.) Some of these determinations simply represent a judgment call on the funder's part, and another funder might not have the same problem. If you think your budget might be the trouble, though, take a careful look at it.

5. **Your idea or approach.** A more unpredictable reason for rejection is that the funder may have some negative history with your type of project. They may know that other people have tried the idea or approach you are proposing and it hasn't worked. Or they may disagree philosophically with it. They may even have a similar project under consideration, from someone with more experience or better credentials.

There isn't much you can do about this, and it's hard to find out if it's the problem. All you can do is to research your field and make sure you know about the kinds of projects that other people have done. If you suspect that others may be proposing similar projects, be sure to present your unique insights and skills in your proposal. If you know that your idea has been tried before but was never successfully implemented, do try to clarify in your proposal and plan what will give it the edge to succeed. Never, however, directly compare your project to failed projects. You might end up scaring a funder that hadn't even heard of the failures.

6. **Your qualifications.** Another problem, and perhaps the most frustrating, is that the funder may like your idea and your approach but feel that you don't have the experience or qualifications to do it. You won't find it easy to learn if this is the problem, and it's not an easy one to solve. If lack of experience is indeed the case, you still may find another funder willing to take a chance on you. You can try to bring in a collaborator with more experience to back you up. If you are applying as an individual, you can consider going through a sponsor, which will add its credibility to yours.

7. **Your sponsor.** The funder may like your idea but feel that your sponsor is somehow not the right one. If the problem is the sponsor, this gets sticky, and it's hard to even find this out. A funder may think your sponsor is too inexperienced in your project area, or that your sponsor's mission doesn't really fit with your project. If you have done your research and selected

your sponsor carefully, you shouldn't run into such trouble. Don't be too quick to change a sponsor. You have spent some time building up this relationship, and there are many other reasons why a proposal can be rejected. Still, if you get some very clear feedback that there is a problem with your sponsor, and you feel that this could influence other potential funders, you should consider a change.

FINDING OUT WHY

It is not easy to get frank details on why you were turned down; in fact, usually it is just impossible. Sometimes, however, you can get hints or clues from a funder. You are in a stronger position to get information if a funder informed you that you were under consideration, and the board then didn't approve your project. In such a case, program officers may be willing to speak with you in some detail. Usually, though, finding out the reasons behind a rejection is very hit-or-miss. It may be more worthwhile for you to put your energies into pursuing other prospects.

Still, you may be able to glean something that will help you. If you are informed by telephone that your proposal has been rejected, gently try to find out why. Make it clear that you aren't trying to change anyone's mind, but you would like some constructive criticism to improve your chances next time.

If you get a form letter turning you down, the letter itself may give you a clue. If it tells you that the funder doesn't give to individuals, or that your project isn't in the funder's area of interest, just fold up your tent and move on. And be more careful in evaluating future potential funders. If the letter says that they "had many fine proposals and just couldn't fund all of them," it may be impossible to find out more.

Again, the only time I really recommend that you talk to a program officer is if you were told that you were being considered for funding and you then got turned down by committee. In this case it's appropriate to call the funder and try to find out more information. If you got a simple rejection letter at the outset, do not call the foundation. If you were under consideration, call up and ask for the program officer who signed your rejection letter. Very briefly ask if there was something you could have done, or should do in your next application, to improve your chances. Don't be defensive, don't argue points, just take it all in. Write down notes as you're talking, so you don't miss anything because of an emotional response to what you are hearing. Be sure to tell the program officer that you appreciate their taking the time to talk to you.

If you are dealing with a government agency, especially if it's a huge bureaucracy, it can be difficult to get any response. However, if your project reached a certain level of consideration, and you were in touch with officials about it, you may be able to get some feedback. If you were dealing with a state or local agency, such as an arts council, it may be easier. Try calling up and speaking to a staff person. Ask if they can give you the gist of a panel's assessment of your project. Explain that you are just trying to glean any information that might help you proceed with the project.

REFERRALS AND RESUBMISSIONS

There are cases when you should consider reapplying to a funder. This depends on the funder's reason for rejecting your application. If your project was outside their mission or area of interest, just move on to other funders. If your project was recommended to the Board of Trustees or Directors for consideration but not approved, then it's worth resubmitting.

Don't just send the proposal back immediately; wait until the next grant cycle. If you do plan to reapply, ask the funder if a resubmission of the same idea is allowed in the next funding cycle. (Some foundations prohibit this.) Make any revisions that you think might improve the proposal and add any new information about funding received. Many people do get funding on the second or third application. The funder sees that you are serious about the project, and if they've been considering other projects before yours, yours has now moved to the head of the line.

Depending on the reasons for rejection, you might be able to ask for referrals to other (perhaps more appropriate) funding sources. The nonprofit world has its own intricate interconnections. One funding organization may be able to direct you to several other organizations— organizations not known to much of the general public. Again, you should only ask about this if your proposal was under serious consideration, made it through the initial screening, and was up for a decision by the board. If you are a first-time grant seeker and just got a standard form letter, don't bother the foundation about this.

On rare occasions, you may be rejected for being outside the funding criteria, but it seems that you really do fit in, according to all that you read in the guidelines. If this is an initial turndown, it did not go to committee, and you were not considered by the board, you might consider reapplying. It may be that a staff member took a quick look at your proposal and misread or misunderstood it. Do look again at the guidelines, make sure you understand them clearly, and make sure your proposal and cover letter clearly state how you fit within the funder's mission and criteria. Don't bother calling program officers about this, but rework your proposal as needed and try again for the next funding cycle.

Some government agencies and private foundations convene special panels, sometimes called *peer panels*, to make their funding decisions. Very often some of the panelists change from funding cycle to funding cycle. You can usually find out about this by reading guidelines or reports. If you're rejected by a panel for one cycle, it may be worth reapplying for the next. New panelists may have a different and more positive view of your project. Sometimes, though, depending on how panelists are chosen, a panel can develop a character or perspective that persists even though the individuals rotate. Still, you might get lucky and have an individual panelist really support your case. So it can be worthwhile to reapply two or three times to some funders.

What to Do Next

Failing to get a grant does not make your idea worthless. As we've discussed in this chapter, there are many factors that can cause a funder to turn down a proposal. Sometimes ideas are timely and sometimes they are not. Luck definitely plays a part in getting a grant. I often light candles.

If you do get turned down, you may feel anger and self-doubt, but you cannot let this get to you. You have to focus again on the worth of your project and your passion for it, and this will keep you going.

What should you do next? Look again at the possible reasons for a turndown listed in this chapter. See if you think any of these apply to you and whether you can adjust your proposal and fund-raising campaign. If you can get any reasons at all, try to apply them. If it seems appropriate, ask for referrals or revise and resubmit your proposal.

You may also want to revise or adapt your idea to the current funding climate—that is, to the kinds of issues that funders are currently concerned with. It may be that you can refocus your statement of need, or find a new application for your idea. I remember my client with the low-cost shelters, who shifted from the need for international disaster relief, which had little funding interest, to the need for shelter for the homeless, which was a timely problem. Or the client who got funding for hiring personnel by focusing on hiring recovering alcoholics. Or the client with the water-purifying filter who tied his project to environmental concerns. See if you can connect your idea to a need that funders want to support.

One of the toughest problems to solve is the funders' perception that your qualifications or experience are not adequate to the project. If you are passionate enough, and do enough good planning and preparation, you may be able to overcome this. It may help to work as an intern in your field, building up contacts and experience. You can also consider teaming up with more experienced collaborators.

If you are just getting started in a field, you may simply need to develop your work and ideas further and build stronger evidence of your abilities. You may want to try doing something on a low-budget, speculative, or volunteer basis to get more experience, or to create work that shows your abilities. If you are an artist, painter, or choreographer, you may have to develop a greater body of work, a record of shows and performances, or stronger samples. It can sometimes be very refreshing to step back from the grant-application grind and really focus on what you want to do, on a smaller scale and a more independent basis.

If you are rejected by all the funders you apply to, should you give up? It depends on how passionate you are about the project. Independent filmmakers confront this issue all the time. Some will never work on a project if they don't have the money up front; others will work on smaller projects, or plunge in and try to get a film started even without all the funding in place. Many have spent years raising money for their projects, and have kept on working at them without any idea where the rest of the money would come from. Sometimes the films have been completed and sometimes they haven't. It all depends on the extent of your commitment and your passion, on your willingness to take certain risks. I think of Julie Dash, an African American independent filmmaker who took seven years to complete her first feature, *Daughters of the Dust.* Along the way, she enlisted support from all kinds of people who believed in the project, and she finally got the completion funding from American Playhouse, which permitted her to go ahead and finish the film. If you believe in your project, and you do have a good one, you should eventually get funding. It just may take a while.

APPENDIX: BOOKS AND RESOURCES

GUIDES TO FUNDERS—GENERAL GUIDES

Annual Register of Grant Support 1996, edited by R. R. Bowker. Wilmette, IL: National Register Publishing Co., 1965 (published annually).

GUIDES TO FUNDERS—BY FUNDER TYPE

FOUNDATIONS

Directory of New and Emerging Foundations. New York: The Foundation Center, 1994, 3rd edition.

Foundation Giving: Yearbook on Facts and Figures on Private, Corporate and Community Foundations. New York: The Foundation Center, 1994.

The Foundation Directory. New York: The Foundation Center, 1995, 17th edition.

The Foundation Directory, Part 2: A Guide to Grant Programs $25,000–$100,000. New York: The Foundation Center, 1995, 17th edition.

Foundation Grants to Individuals. New York: The Foundation Center, 1995, 9th edition.

National Data Book of Foundations: A Comprehensive Guide to Grantmaking Foundations. New York: The Foundation Center, 1995.

Public Media Center's Index of Progressive Funders. San Francisco, CA: Public Media Center, 1985.

Selected Grant Guides by Subject. New York: The Foundation Center, published annually. A series of thirty guides to foundation giving. Each guide covers one subject or population. Contact the Foundation Center for specific titles.

Source Book Profiles. New York: The Foundation Center, 1995.

CORPORATIONS

Corporate 500: The Directory of Corporate Philanthropy. San Francisco, CA: Public Management Institute, 1995 (latest edition).

Corporate Giving Directory. Rockville, MD: The Taft Group, 1995 (latest edition).

National Directory of Corporate Giving. New York: The Foundation Center, 1993, 3rd edition.

GOVERNMENT

Catalog of Federal Domestic Assistance. Washington, DC: Government Printing Office, 1995, published annually.

Free Money® from the Federal Government, by Laurie Blum. New York: John Wiley & Sons, Inc., 1996.

The United States Government Manual. The Office of the Federal Register. This describes the broad responsibilities of all the major federal government departments and agencies. It doesn't list grant programs specifically, but does list various publications that are offered by each agency. If you know that an agency gives grants—and many do—you can find useful information about it in some of these publications. You can contact the relevant agencies to have your name put on their mailing lists for program information.

Government Assistance Almanac 1995–96, by J. Robert Dumouchel. Detroit, MI: Omnigraphics, Inc., and Washington, DC: Foggy Bottom Publications, 1995.

Guide to Federal Grants & Financial Aid: For Individuals and Nonprofit Organizations, edited by Calvin Fenton and Charles Edwards. Dubuque, IA: Kendall/Hunt Publishing Co., 1985, 2nd edition.

1992 Guide to Federal Funding for Governments and Nonprofits, edited by Charles Edwards. Vols. 1 and 2. Arlington, VA: Government Information Services, 1992.

To find your local U.S. Government Bookstore, call 202-512-0132.

To order U.S. Government publications by mail, write:
U.S. Government Printing Office
Superintendent of Documents
Washington, DC 20402

For general information about U.S. government programs, contact the Federal Information Center nearest you. The main office is
Federal Information Center
P.O. Box 600
Cumberland, MD 21501
Tel.: 301-722-9000

Federal Assistance Programs Retrieval System (FAPRS). There are designated access points in each state where you can ask for a computer search of the database. You can also access the database through some commercial computer-network companies.

For more information, contact:

Federal Domestic Assistance Catalog Staff
General Services Administration
Reporters Building, Room 101
300 7th Street, S.W.
Washington, DC 20407
Tel.: 800-669-8331, 202-708-5126

For literature on federal business loans, write or call:
The Director
Loan Policy and Procedures Branch
Small Business Administration
409 Third Street, S.W.
Washington, DC 20416
Tel.: 202-205-6490

SMALL ORGANIZATIONS, PRIZES, AWARDS

Awards, Honors and Prizes, edited by Gita Siegman. Vol. 1: *United States and Canada.* Vol. 2: *International & Foreign.* Detroit: Gale Research, 1994, 11th edition.

INDIVIDUAL DONORS

Biographical Dictionaries Master Index. This gives information on fifty-three different biographical references to living individuals.
Current Biography. New York: Wilson Company, monthly and annual.
Martindale-Hubbel Law Directory.
Medical Specialists Directory.
"The Richest People in America, The Forbes Four Hundred," *Forbes.*
The Social Register 1996. New York: Social Register Association, two-volume set, 1996 (annually). This lists prominent families, with names and addresses, clubs, organizations, and affiliations.
Standard & Poor's Register for corporate executives.
Trustees of Wealth. Washington, DC: Taft Corporation.
Who's Who. Various volumes, by profession, population, and region. Consider which volumes might best lead you to potential donors.

GUIDES TO FUNDERS—BY SUBJECT AND POPULATION GROUP

THE ARTS

General

ARIS Funding Messenger: Creative Arts and Humanities Report. San Francisco, CA: Academic Research Information System. Special rates for individuals, eight issues per year.

Artist's Market: Where and How to Sell Your Artwork, edited by Lauri Miller. Cincinnati, OH: Writer's Digest Books, 1991.

The Business of Art, edited by Lee Evan Caplin. Englewood Cliffs, NJ: Prentice-Hall, 1989, 2nd edition.

Free Money® for People in the Arts, by Laurie Blum. New York: Applause Books, 1996.

Grants for the Arts, by Virginia P. White. New York: Plenum Press, 1980.

Guide to Funding for Emerging Artists and Scholars, by Jennifer Sarbacher. Washington, DC: President's Committee on the Arts and the Humanities, 1991.

The National Directory of Grants and Aid to Individuals in the Arts, by Nancy A. Fandel. Arts Patronage Series, no. 15. Des Moines, IA: Arts Letters, 1989.

National Guide to Funding in Arts and Culture. New York: The Foundation Center, 1994, 3rd edition.

1992 Guide to Funding for Arts & Culture, edited by James Marshall. Virginia: Educational Funding Research Council, 1992.

Performing Arts

Dramatists Sourcebooks: Complete Opportunities to Playwrights, Translators, Composers, Lyricists and Librettists, edited by Angela E. Mitchell and Gillian Richards. New York: Theatre Communications Group, 1989.

Money for Performing Artists, edited by Suzanne Niemeyer. New York: American Council for the Arts, 1991.

Money for Performing Artists: A Guide to Grants, Awards, Fellowships, Artists Residencies, and More, edited by Suzanne Niemeyer. New York: American Council for the Arts, 1991.

Film and Video

The Independent Film and Videomaker's Guide, by Michael Wiese. Studio City, CA: Michael Wiese Productions, 1990, revised edition.

Money for Film and Video Artists, edited by Suzanne Niemeyer. New York: American Council for the Arts, 1991.

Museums and Collections

Funding for Museums, Archives and Special Collections, by Denise Wallen and Karen Cantrel. Phoenix, AZ: Oryx Press, 1988.

Official Museum Directory, by American Association of Museums. Wilmette, IL: National Register Publishing Co., 1988.

Music

Musical America: International Directory of the Performing Arts. New York: ABC Leisure Magazines, 1995.

Visual Arts

Money for Visual Artists, edited by Suzanne Niemeyer. New York: American Council for the Arts, 1991.

Writers

Grants and Awards Available to American Writers 1994–1995, edited by John Morrone. New York: PEN American Center, 1994.

Publication Grants for Writers & Publishers: How to Find Them, Win Them, and Manage Them!, by Karin R. Park and Beth Luey. Phoenix, AZ: Oryx Press, 1991.

BUSINESS

Computer Grants Directory. San Francisco, CA: The Public Management Institute, 1991, 4th edition.

Free Money® for Small Business & Entrepreneurs, by Laurie Blum. New York: John Wiley & Sons, 1994, 4th edition.

How to Invest in Real Estate Using Free Money®, by Laurie Blum. New York: John Wiley & Sons, 1991.

Pratt's Guide to Venture Capital Sources, edited by Jane Morris. Wellesley Hills, MA: Venture Economics, 1989, 13th edition.

Venture Capital, Where to Find It. Membership Directory. Washington, DC: National Association of Small Business Investment Companies, 1985.

EDUCATION

General and Undergraduate

College Financial Aid Annual, edited by John Schwartz. New York: ARCO Publishing, Inc., 1995 (latest edition).

Chronicle Student Aid Annual: For 1990–91 Schoolyear. Moravia, NY: Chronicle Guidance Publications.

College Blue Book. New York: Macmillan, 1995, 25th edition.

Financing a College Education: The Essential Guide for the 90s, by Judith B. Margolin. New York: Plenum Press, 1989.

Free Money® for College, by Laurie Blum. New York: Facts on File, 1994.

Free Money® for Foreign Studies, by Laurie Blum. New York: Facts on File, 1991.

Free Money® for Private Schools, by Laurie Blum. New York: Simon & Schuster, 1992.

National Guide to Funding for Elementary and Secondary Education. New York: The Foundation Center, 1995, 3rd edition.

1992 Guide to Funding for Education, edited by James Marshall. Virginia: Educational Funding Research Council, 1992.

Peterson's Guide to Four-Year Colleges 1996. Princeton, NJ: Peterson's Guides, 1995, 26th edition.

Scholarships, Fellowships and Loans 1994–95. Detroit, MI: Gale Research, 1993.

Graduate, Postgraduate, and Research

The Directory of Research Grants. Phoenix, AZ: Oryx Press, annual.

Graduate Scholarship Directory: The Complete Guide to Scholarships, Fellowships, Grants and Loans for Graduate and Professional Study, by Daniel J. Cassidy. Englewood Cliffs, NJ: Career Press, 1993, 3rd edition.

The Grants Register. New York: St. Martin's Press, published twice a year.

U.S. Government Support

Free Money® from the Federal Government, by Laurie Blum. New York: John Wiley & Sons, Inc., 1996.

ENVIRONMENT

The National Guide to Funding for the Environment and Animal Welfare. New York: The Foundation Center, 1994, 2nd edition.

Environmental Grantmaking Foundations 1992 Directory. Rochester, NY: Environmental Data Research Institute, 1992.

Environmental Grants: A Guide to Grants for the Environment from Government, Companies and Charitable Trusts, by Susan Forrester. London: Directory of Social Change, 1989.

HEALTH

AIDS Funding: A Guide to Giving by Foundations and Charitable Organizations. New York: The Foundation Center, 1993, 3rd edition.

Directory of Biomedical and Health Grants 1996. Phoenix, AZ: Oryx Press, 1995, 10th edition.

Free Money® for Diseases of Aging, by Laurie Blum. New York: Simon & Schuster, 1992.

Free Money® for Heart Disease and Cancer Care, by Laurie Blum. New York: Simon & Schuster, 1992.

Handicapped Funding Directory, by Richard M. Eckstein. Margate, FL: Research Grant Guides, 1990, 7th edition.

National Guide to Funding in Aging. New York: The Foundation Center, 1992, 3rd edition.

National Guide to Funding in Health. New York: The Foundation Center, 1993, 3rd edition.

Scholarships and Loans for Nursing Education. New York: National League for Nursing, 1990.

HUMANITIES

Directory of Grants in the Humanities 1995–96. Phoenix, AZ: Oryx Press, 1995, 9th edition.

National Endowment for the Humanities Annual Report. Washington, DC: National Endowment for the Humanities, 1995.

HUMAN SERVICES

Free Money® for Day Care, by Laurie Blum. New York: Simon & Schuster, 1992.

Fundraiser's Guide to Human Service Funding, by Susan E. Elnicki. Rockville, MD: Taft Information, 1992, 3rd edition.

Towards a Solution to Homelessness: An Annotated Funding Directory. San Francisco, CA: HomeBase, 1990.

MINORITIES

Black Americans Information Directory, edited by Julia C. Furtaw. Detroit, MI: Gale Research, 1993, 3rd edition.

Directory of Financial Aids for Minorities 1993–95, by Gail Ann Schlachter. San Carlos, CA: Reference Service Press, 1993, 5th edition.

Guide to Multicultural Resources, edited by Charles Taylor. Madison, WI: Praxis Publications, 1989.

RELIGION

Fundraiser's Guide to Religious Philanthropy 1996, edited by Bernard Jankowski. Rockville, MD: The Taft Group, 1995, 96th edition.

Foundation Guide for Religious Grantseekers, edited by Kerry A. Robinson. Atlanta, GA: Scholars Press, 1992.

RESEARCH AND SCHOLARSHIPS

Annual Register of Grant Support 1996, edited by R. R. Bowker. Illinois: National Register Publishing Co., 1995.

Directory of Research Grants 1996. Phoenix, AZ: Oryx Press, 1995.

Fiscal Year 1989 Awards by State and National Science Foundation Directorate. Washington, DC: National Science Foundation, 1990.

Graduate Scholarship Directory: The Complete Guide to Scholarships, Fellowships, Grants and Loans for Graduate and Professional Study, by Daniel J. Cassidy. Englewood Cliffs, NJ: Career Press, 1993, 3rd edition.

Research Centers Directory, edited by Karen Hill. 2 vols. Detroit, MI: Gale Research, 1995.

SCIENCE

Directory of Biomedical and Health Care Grants 1996. Phoenix, AZ: Oryx Press, 1995, 10th edition.

Fellowships and Grants for Training and Research: To Be Offered in 1991–1992. New York: Social Science Research Council, 1991.

Grants for Science and Technology Programs. New York: The Foundation Center, 1994.

TRAVEL

Financial Aid for Research and Creative Activites Abroad 1994–1995, by Gail Ann Schlachter and R. David Weber. San Carlos, CA: Reference Service Press, 1994.

Financial Resources for International Study: A Definitive Guide to Organizations Offering Awards for Overseas Study, by the Institute of International Education. Princeton, NJ: Peterson's Guides, 1989.

Free Money® for Foreign Studies, by Laurie Blum. New York: Facts on File, 1991.

Fulbright and Other Grants for Graduate Study Abroad 1992–1993. New York: Institute of International Education, 1991.

International Scholarship Directory: The Complete Guide to Financial Aid for Study Abroad, by Daniel J. Cassidy. Englewood Cliffs, NJ: Career Press, 1993, 3rd edition.

WOMEN

Directory of Financial Aids for Women 1993–1995, by Gail Ann Schlachter. San Carlos, CA: Reference Service Press, 1993.

A Directory of Selected Research and Policy Centers Working on Women's Issues, compiled by Mary Anne Jorgensen. Washington, DC: Women's Research and Education Institute, 1989.

Grants for Women and Girls. New York: The Foundation Center, 1994.

FUNDER GUIDES—BY GEOGRAPHY

ALABAMA

Alabama Foundation Directory. Birmingham Public Library, 1990.

ARIZONA

Arizona Foundation Directory. Phoenix: Junior League of Phoenix, 1991.

ARKANSAS

The Guide to Arkansas Funding Sources, edited by Earl Anthes and Jerry Cronin. West Memphis: Independent Community Consultants, 1990.

CALIFORNIA

Guide to California Foundations, by Carol Fanning. San Francisco: Northern California Grantmakers, 1988, 7th edition.
San Diego County Foundation Directory. San Diego Community Foundation, 1989.

COLORADO

Colorado Foundation Directory. Denver: Junior League of Denver, 1990.

CONNECTICUT

The Connecticut Foundation Directory, edited by Michael Burns. Hartford: Development and Technical Assistance Center, 1990, 6th edition.

DELAWARE

Directory of Delaware Grantmakers: 1990. Wilmington: Delaware Community Foundation, 1990.

DISTRICT OF COLUMBIA

Directory of Foundations of the Greater Washington Area. Washington, DC: Community Foundation of Greater Washington, 1991.

FLORIDA

The Complete Guide to Florida Foundations, edited by Lonna J. Myers Hord. Miami: John L. Adams, 1991, 4th edition.
Foundation Guide: N.E. Florida. Jacksonville: Volunteer Jacksonville, 1990.

GEORGIA

Foundation Profiles of the Southeast: Georgia, by James H. Taylor. Williamsburg, KY: James H. Taylor Associates, 1983.

HAWAII

Directory of Charitable Trusts and Foundations for Hawaii's Non-Profit Organizations, compiled by Marcie Hanson. Honolulu: Volunteer, Information and Referral Service, 1990, 2nd edition.

IDAHO

Directory of Idaho Foundations. Caldwell, ID: Caldwell Public Library, 1990, 5th edition.

ILLINOIS

The Directory of Illinois Foundations, edited by Marty Bowes. Chicago: Donors Forum of Chicago, 1990, 2nd edition.

Chicago's Corporate Foundations: A Directory of Chicago Area and Illinois Corporate Foundations, by Ellen Dick. Oak Park, IL: Ellen Dick, 1990, 2nd edition.

INDIANA

Directory of Indiana Donors. Indianapolis: Indiana Donors Alliance, 1989.

IOWA

Iowa Directory of Foundations, by Daniel Holm. Dubuque: Trumpet Associates, 1984.

KANSAS

The Directory of Kansas Foundations, edited by James Rhodes. Topeka: Topeka Public Library, 1991, 3rd edition.

KENTUCKY

A Guide to Kentucky Grantmakers, edited by Nancy Dougherty. Louisville: Louisville Foundation, 1982.

LOUISIANA

Citizen's Handbook of Private Foundations in New Orleans, compiled by Joseph Lazaro. New Orleans: Greater New Orleans Foundation, 1987.

MAINE

Directory of Maine Foundations. Portland: University of Southern Maine, 1990.

MARYLAND

Index of Private Foundations, 1989. Baltimore: Attorney General's Office, 1990.

MASSACHUSETTS

Massachusetts Grantmakers. Boston: Associated Grantmakers of Massachusetts, 1990.

Worcester County Funding Directory, edited by Jane Peck and Charlene Sokal. Worcester, MA: Worcester Public Library, 1991.

MICHIGAN

The Michigan Foundation Directory. Grand Haven, MI: Council of Michigan Foundations, 1991, 7th edition.

MINNESOTA

Guide to Minnesota Foundations and Corporate Giving Programs: 1991–92. Minneapolis, Minnesota Council on Foundations, 1991, 6th edition.

MISSOURI

The Directory of Missouri Foundations, compiled and edited by Wilda Swift. St. Louis: Swift Associates, 1991, 3rd edition.

The Directory of Greater Kansas City Foundations, edited by Linda Talbott. Kansas City: Clearinghouse for Midcontinent Foundations, 1990.

MONTANA

Montana and Wyoming Foundations Directory, compiled by Travis Grossman and edited by JoAnn Meide. Billings, MT: Eastern Montana College Library, Grants Information Center, 1991.

NEBRASKA

Nebraska Foundation Directory. Omaha: Junior League of Omaha, 1989.

NEVADA

Nevada Foundation Directory, compiled by Vlasta Honsa and Mark Stackpole. Las Vegas: Las Vegas—Clark County Library District, 1989.

NEW HAMPSHIRE

Corporate Philanthropy in New England: New Hampshire, edited by Michael Burns. Vol. 2. Hartford: D.A.T.A., 1987.

NEW JERSEY

The Mitchell Guide to Foundations, Corporations, and Their Managers, edited by Wendy Littman. Belle Mead, NJ: Littman Associates, 1990.

NEW MEXICO

The New Mexico Funding Directory, edited by Denise Wallen. Albuquerque: University of New Mexico, 1990, 2nd edition.

NEW YORK

New York State Foundations: A Comprehensive Directory. New York: The Foundation Center, 1992, 2nd edition.

NORTH CAROLINA

North Carolina Giving: The Directory of the State's Foundations, by Anita Gunn Shirley. Raleigh: Capital Consortium, 1990.

OHIO

Charitable Foundations Directory of Ohio, by Lee Fisher. Columbus: Attorney General's Office, 1991, 9th edition.
The Cincinnati Foundation Directory, by Frances Martindale and Cynthia Roy. Cincinnati: MR & Co., 1989.

OKLAHOMA

The Directory of Oklahoma Foundations, compiled by Mary Deane Streich. Oklahoma City, OK: Foundation Research Project, 1990, 3rd edition.

OREGON

Guide to Oregon Foundations, by Marc Smiley and Nancy Bridgeford. Portland, OR: United Way of Columbia—Wilmette, 1991.

PENNSYLVANIA

Directory of Pennsylvania Foundations, compiled by Damon Kletzien. Springfield, PA: Triadvocates Press, 1990, 4th edition.

RHODE ISLAND

Directory of Grant-Making Foundations in Rhode Island. Providence: Council for Community Services, 1983.

SOUTH CAROLINA

South Carolina Foundation Directory, edited by Guynell Williams. Columbia, SC: South Carolina State Library, 1990, 4th edition.

SOUTH DAKOTA

The South Dakota Grant Directory. Pierre, SD: South Dakota State Library, 1992.

TENNESSEE

The Tennessee Directory of Foundations and Corporate Philanthropy. Memphis: City of Memphis Bureau of Intergovernmental Management, 1985, 3rd edition.

TEXAS

Directory of Texas Foundations, edited by Mary Elizabeth Webb. San Antonio: Funding Information Center of Texas, 1990, 11th edition.

VERMONT

Vermont Directory of Foundations, edited by Christine Graham. Shaftsbury, VT: CPG Enterprises, 1991, 4th edition.

VIRGINIA

Directory of Virginia Private Foundations. Hampton, VA: Hampton Public Library, 1991.

WASHINGTON

Washington Foundation Directory: How to Get Your Slice of the Pie, by Mardell Moore and Charna Klein. Seattle: Consultant Services Northwest, 1991.

WISCONSIN

Foundations in Wisconsin: A Directory, edited by Susan Hopwood. Milwaukee: Marquette University Memorial Library, 1990, 10th edition.

WEST VIRGINIA

West Virginia Foundation Directory. Charleston, WV: Kanhawha County Public Library, 1987, 2nd edition.

SERVICE ORGANIZATIONS—DIRECTORIES AND PUBLICATIONS

GENERAL DIRECTORIES

American Library Directory 1996–97. New York: R. R. Bowker, 1996.

Directory of Special Libraries, Vol. 1: A Guide to Special Libraries, Research Libraries, Information Centers, Archives & Data Centers, 2 vols. Detroit, MI: Gale Research, 1993, 17th edition.

Encyclopedia of Associations, edited by Deborah Burek. Vols. 1–3. Detroit, MI: Gale Research, 1993, 28th edition.

National Directory of Nonprofit Organizations. Rockville, MD: The Taft Group, 1996.

Online Database Search Services Directory, edited by Martin Connors. Detroit, MI: Gale Research, 1987, 2nd edition.

DIRECTORIES BY SUBJECT AREAS

Audiovisual Market Place, R. R. Bowker Company, 121 Chanlon Road, New Providence, NJ 07974-1541. Tel.: 908-665-2881.

Dance Magazine—Summer Dance Calendar Issue, Dance Magazine, 33 W. 60th Street, New York, NY 10023. Tel.: 212-245-9050.

Religious Organizations Directory, American Business Directories, Inc., 5711 South 86th Circle, Box 27347, Omaha, NE 68127-4146. Tel.: 402-593-4600.

Fine Arts Marketplace, American Business Directories, Inc., 5711 South 86th Circle, Box 27347, Omaha, NE 68127-4146. Tel.: 402-593-4600.

Photomarket, PhotoSource International, Pine Lake Farm, Osceola, WI 54020. Tel.: 715-248-3800.

Scientific Directory & Annual Bibliography, National Institutes of Health, Department of Health and Human Services, Building 31, Room 2B03, Bethesda, MD 20892. Tel.: 301-496-4143.

Stern's Performing Arts Directory, Dance Magazine, 33 W. 60th Street, New York, NY 10023. Tel.: 212-245-8937.

Who's Who in Finance and Industry, Marquis Who's Who, 121 Chanlon Road, New Providence, NJ 07974. Tel.: 908-464-6800.

Writer's Digest Books, 1507 Dana Avenue, Cincinnati, OH 45207. Tel.: 513-531-2222.

JOURNALS AND PERIODICALS

BCA News
(quarterly)
Business Committee for the Arts
1775 Broadway, Suite 510
New York, NY 10019-1942
Tel.: 212-664-0600

The Chronicle of Higher Education
(weekly)
1255 Twenty-third Street, N.W.
Washington, DC 20037
Tel.: 202-466-1212

Crain's New York Business
(weekly)
Crain Communications Inc.
220 East 42nd Street
New York, NY 10017-5846
Tel.: 800-678-9595

Currents
(monthly)
Council for Advancement and
Support of Education
11 Dupont Circle, Suite 400
Washington, DC 20036
Tel.: 202-328-5900

Forbes
(biweekly)
Forbes Inc.
60 Fifth Avenue
New York, NY 10011
Tel.: 800-888-9896

Fortune
(weekly)
Time Inc.
Time-Life Building
Rockefeller Center
New York, NY 10020-1393
Tel.: 800-621-8000

F[or]. Y[our]. I[nformation].
(quarterly)
New York Foundation for the Arts
155 Avenue of the Americas
New York, NY 10013
Tel.: 212-366-6900

Health Funds Development Letter
(monthly)
Sharing Information on Federal
and Foundation Fund Services
Health Resources Publishing
Brinley Professional Plaza
3100 Highway 138
Wall Township, NJ 07719-1442
Tel.: 908-681-1133

The Independent Film & Video
    Monthly
(monthly)
Foundation for Independent Video
    and Film
304 Hudson Street, Sixth Floor
New York, NY 10013
Tel.: 212-807-1400

National Science Bulletin
(monthly)
National Science Foundation
4201 Wilson Boulevard
Arlington, VA 22230
Tel.: 703-306-1234

Poets & Writers Magazine
(bi-monthly)
72 Spring Street
New York, NY 10012
Tel.: 212-226-3586

Dance Magazine
33 West 60th Street
New York, NY 10023
Tel.: 212-245-9050

SERVICE ORGANIZATIONS—BY SUBJECT AREA

THE ARTS

American Council for the Arts
1 East 53rd Street
New York, NY 10022
Tel.: 212-223-2787

Art Information Center
280 Broadway, Suite 412
New York, NY 10007
Tel.: 212-227-0282

Business Committee for the Arts
1775 Broadway, Suite 510
New York, NY 10019
Tel.: 212-664-0600

People for the American Way
2000 M Street, N.W.
Suite 400
Washington, DC 20036
Tel.: 202-467-4999

Volunteer Lawyers for the Arts
1 East 53rd Street, Sixth Floor
New York, NY 10022
Tel.: 212-319-2787

See also:
*Volunteer Lawyers for the Arts
National Directory*, New York:
VLA.

BUSINESS

American Business Association
292 Madison Avenue
New York, NY 10017
Tel.: 212-949-5900

National Association for the Self-
Employed
2121 Precinct Lion Road
Hurst, TX 76054
Tel.: 800-232-6273

National Business Association
5151 Beltline Road, Suite 1150
Dallas, TX 75240
Tel.: 214-458-0900

Patent Research Associates
8826 Washington Boulevard
Jessup, MD 20794
Tel.: 800-548-3721

EDUCATION

American Council on Education
One Dupont Circle, N.W.

Suite 800
Washington, DC 20036
Tel.: 202-939-9300

Council for Advancement and
Support of Education
11 Dupont Circle, N.W.
Washington, DC 20036
Tel.: 202-328-5900

Council for Aid to Education
342 Madison Avenue
Suite 1532
New York, NY 10173
Tel.: 212-661-5800

National Association of
Independent Schools
1620 L Street, N.W.
Suite 1100
Washington, DC 20036
Tel.: 202-973-9700

ENVIRONMENT

Americans for the Environment
1400 Sixteenth Street, N.W.
Washington, DC 20036
Tel.: 202-797-6665

FEDERAL GOVERNMENT

Federal Information Center
P.O. Box 600
Cumberland, MD 21501
Tel.: 301-722-9000

HEALTH

Association for Healthcare
Philanthropy
(formerly National Association for
Hospital Development)
313 Park Avenue, Suite 400
Falls Church, VA 22046
Tel.: 703-532-6243

National Health Council
1730 H Street, N.W.
Suite 500
Washington, DC 20036
Tel.: 202-785-3913

HUMANITIES

American Council of Learned
    Societies
228 East 45th Street, 16th Floor
New York, NY 10017
Tel.: 212-697-1505

Council for International
    Exchange of Scholars
3400 International Drive, N.W.
Suite M500
Washington, DC 20008
Tel.: 202-686-4000

National Humanities Center
7 Alexander Drive
P.O. Box 12256
Research Triangle Park, NC
    27709
Tel.: 919-549-0661

INVENTORS

Patent Research Associates
8826 Washington Boulevard
Jessup, MD 20794
Tel.: 800-548-3721

MINORITIES

Minority Business Information
    Institute
130 Fifth Avenue, 10th Floor
New York, NY 10011
Tel.: 212-242-8000

National Association of Minority
    Women in Business
906 Grand Avenue, Suite 200

Kansas City, MO 64106
Tel.: 816-421-3335

RELIGION

Global Congress of the World's
    Religions
10 Dock Road
Barrytown, NY 12507
Tel.:914-758-6881

The Interchurch Center
475 Riverside Drive, Room 253
New York, NY 10115
Tel.: 212-870-2932

SCIENCES

National Research Council
2001 Wisconsin Avenue, N.W.
Washington, DC 20418
Tel.: 202-334-2000

SENIOR CITIZENS

American Association of Retired
    Persons
1909 K Street, N.W.
Washington, DC 20049
Tel.: 202-872-4700

TRAVEL

Academic Travel Abroad
3210 Grand Street, N.W., First
    Floor
Washington, DC 20007
Tel.: 202-333-3355

Council on International
    Educational Exchange
205 East 42nd Street
New York, NY 10017
Tel.: 212-661-1414

WOMEN

Ms. Foundation for Women
120 Wall Street, Suite 6-S
New York, NY 10010
Tel.: 212-742-2300

FUND-RAISING RESOURCES

FOUNDATION CENTER OFFICES

The Foundation Center
79 Fifth Avenue, 8th Floor
New York, NY 10003
Tel.: 212-620-4230

The Foundation Center
1001 Connecticut Avenue, N.W.
Washington, DC 20036
Tel.: 202-331-1400

The Foundation Center
312 Sutter Street, Room 312
San Francisco, CA 94108
Tel.: 415-387-0902

The Foundation Center
Kent H. Smith Library
1422 Euclid, Suite 1356
Cleveland, OH 44115
Tel.: 216-861-1933

The Foundation Center
Grand Lobby Hurt Building
50 Hurt Plaza, Suite 150
Atlanta, GA 30303
Tel.: 404-880-0094

FOUNDATION CENTER AFFILIATES

See above for a list of the phone
numbers of regional affiliates.

ALABAMA

Birmingham Public Library
Government Document
2100 Park Place
Birmingham, AL 35203
Tel.: 205-226-3600

Huntsville Public Library
915 Monroe Street
Huntsville, AL 35801
Tel.: 205-532-5940

University of South Alabama
Library Reference Department
Mobile, AL 36688
Tel.: 205-460-7025

Auburn University at
   Montgomery Library
7300 University Drive
Montgomery, AL 36117-3596
Tel.: 205-244-3653

ALASKA

University of Alaska Anchorage
Consortium Library
3211 Providence Drive
Anchorage, AK 99508
Tel.: 907-786-1848

Juneau Public Library
292 Marine Way
Juneau, AK 99801
Tel.: 907-586-5249

ARIZONA

Phoenix Public Library
1221 North Central Avenue

Phoenix, AZ 85004
Tel.: 602-262-4636

Tucson Public Library
101 N. Stone Avenue
Tucson, AZ 85726-7470
Tel.: 602-791-4393

ARKANSAS

Westark Community College
    Library
5210 Grand Avenue
Fort Smith, AR 72913
Tel.: 501-785-7000

Central Arkansas Library
System References Services
700 Louisiana Street
Little Rock, AR 72201
Tel.: 501-370-5950

Pine Bluff-Jefferson County
    Library System
200 East Eighth
Pine Bluff, AR 71601
Tel.: 501-543-2159

CALIFORNIA

Ventura County Community
    Foundation
Community Resource Center
1355 Del Norte Road
Camarillo, CA 93010
Tel.: 805-988-0196

California Community Foundation
Funding Information Center
606 South Olive Street, Suite
    2400
Los Angeles, CA 90014-1526
Tel.: 213-413-4042

Community Foundation for
    Monterey County

177 Van Buren Street
Monterey, CA 93940

Riverside Public Library
3581 Mission Inn Avenue
Riverside, CA 92501
Tel.: 909-782-5202

California State Library
Reference Services, Room 301
914 Capitol Mall
Sacramento, CA 94237-0001
Tel.: 916-654-0261

Non Profit Resource Center
Sacramento Central Library
828 I Street
Sacramento, CA 95814
Tel.: 916-264-2700

San Diego Community
    Foundation
101 West Broadway, Suite 1120
San Diego, CA 92101
Tel.: 619-239-8815

Non Profit Development Center
1922 The Alameda, Suite 212
San Jose, CA 95126
Tel.: 408-248-9505

Peninsula Community Foundation
1700 South El Camino Real
San Mateo, CA 94402-3049
Tel.: 415-358-9392

Volunteer Center Resource
    Library
1000 East Santa Ana Boulevard
Santa Ana, CA 92701
Tel.: 714-953-1655

Santa Barbara Public Library
40 East Anapamu Street
Santa Barbara, CA 93101-1603
Tel.: 805-962-7653

Santa Monica Public Library
1343 Sixth Street
Santa Monica, CA 90401-1603
Tel.: 310-458-8600

COLORADO

Pikes Peak Library District
20 North Cascade Avenue
Colorado Springs, CO 80903
Tel.: 719-531-6333

Denver Public Library
Reference Division
1357 Broadway
Denver, CO 80203
Tel.: 303-640-6200

CONNECTICUT

Danbury Public Library
170 Main Street
Danbury, CT 06810
Tel.: 203-797-4527

Hartford Public Library
Reference Department
500 Main Street
Hartford, CT 06103
Tel.: 203-293-6000

D.A.T.A.
70 Audubon Street
New Haven, CT 06510
Tel.: 203-772-1345

DELAWARE

University of Delaware
Hugh Morris Library
Newark, DE 19717-5267
Tel.: 302-451-2432

FLORIDA

Volusia County Library Center
City Island

Daytona Beach, FL 32014-4484
Tel.: 904-255-3765

Nova University–Einstein Library
Foundation Resource Collection
3301 College Avenue
Fort Lauderdale, FL 33314
Tel.: 305-475-7497

Indian River Community College
Learning Resources Center
3209 Virginia Avenue
Fort Pierce, FL 34981-5599
Tel.: 407-468-4757

Jacksonville Public Library
Business, Science and Documents
122 North Ocean Street
Jacksonville, FL 32206
Tel.: 904-630-2665

Miami-Dade Public Library
Humanities Department
101 West Flagler Street
Miami, FL 33130
Tel.: 305-375-5575

Orlando Public Library
Orange County Library System
101 East Central Boulevard
Orlando, FL 32801
Tel.: 407-425-4694

Selby Public Library
1001 Boulevard of the Arts
Sarasota, FL 34236
Tel.: 813-951-5501

Tampa Hillsborough County
Public Library System
900 North Ashley Drive
Tampa, FL 33602
Tel.: 813-223-8865

Community Foundation of Palm
Beach and Martin Counties

324 Datura Street
West Palm Beach, FL 33401
Tel.: 407-659-6800

GEORGIA

Atlanta-Fulton Public Library
Foundation Collection
Ivan Allen Department
1 Margaret Mitchell Square
Atlanta, GA 30303-1089
Tel.: 404-730-1900

HAWAII

Hawaii Community Foundation
900 Fort Street, Suite 1300
Honolulu, HI 96813
Tel.: 808-537-6333

University of Hawaii
Thomas Hale Hamilton Library
2550 The Mall
Honolulu, HI 96822
Tel.: 808-956-7214

IDAHO

Boise Public Library
715 South Capitol Boulevard
Boise, ID 83702
Tel.: 208-384-4024

Caldwell Public Library
1010 Dearborn Street
Caldwell, ID 83605
Tel.: 208-459-3242

ILLINOIS

Donors Forum of Chicago
53 West Jackson Boulevard
Room 430
Chicago, IL 60604
Tel.: 312-431-0265

Evanston Public Library
1703 Orrington Avenue
Evanston, IL 60201
Tel.: 708-866-0305

Sangamon State University
Library
Shepard Road
Springfield, IL 62794-9243
Tel.: 217-786-6633

INDIANA

Allen County Public Library
900 Webster Street
Fort Wayne, IN 46802
Tel.: 219-424-7241

Indiana University Northwest
Library
3400 Broadway
Gary, IN 46408
Tel.: 219-980-6582

Indianapolis-Marion County
Public Library
40 East St. Clair Street
Indianapolis, IN 46206
Tel.: 317-269-1733

IOWA

Cedar Rapids Public Library
Funding Information Center
500 First Street, S.E.
Cedar Rapids, IA 52401
Tel.: 319-398-5123

Southwestern Community College
Learning Resource Center
1501 West Townline Road
Creston, IA 50801
Tel.: 515-782-7081, Ext. 262

Public Library of Des Moines
100 Locust Street
Des Moines, IA 50308
Tel.: 515-283-4152

KANSAS

Topeka Public Library
1515 West Tenth Street
Topeka, KS 66604
Tel.: 913-233-2040

Wichita Public Library
223 South Main
Wichita, KS 67202
Tel.: 316-262-0611

KENTUCKY

Western Kentucky University
Helm-Cravens Library
Bowling Green, KY 42101-3576
Tel.: 502-745-6125

Louisville Free Public Library
301 York Street
Louisville, KY 40203
Tel.: 502-574-1617

LOUISIANA

East Baton Rouge Parish Library
Centroplex Branch
120 St. Louis Street
Baton Rouge, LA 70802
Tel.: 504-389-4960

Beauregard Parish Library
205 South Washington Avenue
De Ridder, LA 70634
Tel.: 318-463-6217

New Orleans Public Library
Business and Science Division
219 Loyola Avenue
New Orleans, LA 70140
Tel.: 504-596-2600

Shreve Memorial Library
424 Texas Street
Shreveport, LA 71101
Tel.: 318-226-5894

MAINE

University of Southern Maine
Office of Sponsored Research
246 Deering Avenue, Room 628
Portland, ME 04103
Tel.: 207-780-5029

MARYLAND

Enoch Pratt Free Library
Social Science and History
   Department
400 Cathedral Street
Baltimore, MD 21201
Tel.: 410-396-5320

MASSACHUSETTS

Associated Grantmakers of
   Massachusetts
294 Washington Street, Suite 840
Boston, MA 02108
Tel.: 617-426-2606

Boston Public Library
666 Boylston Street
Boston, MA 02117
Tel.: 617-536-5400

Western Massachusetts Funding
   Resource Center
Campaign for Human
   Development
65 Elliot Street
Springfield, MA 01101-1730
Tel.: 413-732-3175

Worcester Public Library
Grants Resource Center
Salem Square
Worcester, MA 01608
Tel.: 508-799-1655

MICHIGAN

Alpena County Library
211 North First Avenue
Alpena, MI 49707
Tel.: 517-356-6188

University of Michigan–Ann
  Arbor
209 Hatcher Graduate Library
Ann Arbor, MI 48109-1205
Tel.: 313-763-1539

Battle Creek Community
  Foundation
One Riverwalk Centre
34 West Jackson Street
Battle Creek, MI 49017
Tel.: 616-962-2181

Henry Ford Centennial Library
16301 Michigan Avenue
Dearborn, MI 48126
Tel.: 313-943-2330

Wayne State University
Purdy-Kresge Library
5265 Cass Avenue
Detroit, MI 48202
Tel.: 313-577-4042

Michigan State University
  Libraries
Reference Library
East Lansing, MI 48824-1048
Tel.: 517-353-8818

Farmington Community Library
32737 West 12 Mile Road
Farmington Hills, MI 48334
Tel.: 810-553-0300

University of Michigan–Flint
  Library
Reference Department
Flint, MI 48502-2186
Tel.: 313-762-3408

Grand Rapids Public Library
Business Department
60 Library Plaza, N.E.
Grand Rapids, MI 49503-3093
Tel.: 616-456-3600

Michigan Technological
  University
Van Pelt Library
1400 Townsend Drive
Houghton, MI 49931
Tel.: 906-487-2507

Sault Ste. Marie Area Public
  Schools
Office of Academic Services
460 West Spruce Street
Sault Ste. Marie, MI 49783-1874
Tel.: 906-635-6618

Northwestern Michigan College
Mark & Helen Osterin Library
1701 East Front Street
Traverse City, MI 49684
Tel.: 616-922-1060

MINNESOTA

Duluth Public Library
520 West Superior Street
Duluth, MN 55802
Tel.: 218-723-3802

Southwest State University
  Library
Marshall, MN 56258
Tel.: 507-537-7278

Minneapolis Public Library
Sociology Department
300 Nicollet Mall
Minneapolis, MN 55401
Tel.: 612-372-6555

Rochester Public Library
101 Second Street, S.E.

Rochester, MN 55904-3776
Tel.: 507-285-8000

St. Paul Public Library
90 West Fourth Street
St. Paul, MN 55102
Tel.: 612-292-6307

MISSISSIPPI

Jackson-Hinds Library System
300 North State Street
Jackson, MS 39201
Tel.: 601-968-5803

MISSOURI

Clearinghouse for Midcontinent
  Foundations
University of Missouri
Block School of Business
5110 Cherry Street, Suite 310
Kansas City, MO 64112
Tel.: 816-235-1176

Kansas City Public Library
311 East 12th Street
Kansas City, MO 64106
Tel.: 816-221-9650

Metropolitan Association of
  Philanthropy
5615 Pershing Avenue, Suite 20
St. Louis, MO 63112
Tel.: 314-361-3900

Springfield-Greene County Library
397 East Central Street
Springfield, MO 65801
Tel.: 417-869-4621

MONTANA

Montana State University
Billings Library
1500 North 30th Street

Billings, MT 59101-0298
Tel.: 406-657-1662

Bozeman Public Library
220 East Lamme
Bozeman, MT 59715-3579
Tel.: 406-586-4787

Montana State Library
Reference Department
1515 East 6th Avenue
Helena, MT 59620
Tel.: 406-444-3004

NEBRASKA

University of Nebraska
106 Love Library
14th and R Streets
Lincoln, NE 68588-0410
Tel.: 402-472-2848

W. Dale Clark Library
Social Sciences Department
215 South 15th Street
Omaha, NE 68102
Tel.: 402-444-4826

NEVADA

Las Vegas–Clark County Library
  District
1401 East Flamingo Road
Las Vegas, NV 89119-6160
Tel.: 702-733-7810

Washoe County Library
301 South Center Street
Reno, NV 89501
Tel.: 702-785-4010

NEW HAMPSHIRE

New Hampshire Charitable Fund
37 Pleasant Street
Concord, NH 03301-4605
Tel.: 603-225-6641

Plymouth State College
Herbert H. Lamson Library
Plymouth, NH 03264
Tel.: 603-535-2258

NEW JERSEY

Cumberland County Library
800 East Commerce Street
Bridgeton, NJ 08302-2295
Tel.: 609-453-2210

Free Public Library of Elizabeth
11 South Broad Street
Elizabeth, NJ 07202
Tel.: 908-354-6060

The Support Center
17 Academy Street, Suite 1101
Newark, NJ 07102
Tel.: 201-643-5774

County College of Morris
Sherman H. Masten Learning
    Resource Center
214 Center Grove Road
Randolph, NJ 07869
Tel.: 201-328-5296

New Jersey State Library
Governmental Reference
185 West State Street
Trenton, NJ 08625-0520
Tel.: 609-292-6220

NEW MEXICO

Albuquerque Community
    Foundation
3301 Menual, N.E.
Suite 30
Albuquerque, NM 87107
Tel.: 505-883-6240

New Mexico State Library
325 Don Gaspar Street

Santa Fe, NM 87503
Tel.: 505-827-3824

NEW YORK

New York State Library
Cultural Education Center
Humanities Section
Empire State Plaza
Albany, NY 12230
Tel.: 518-474-5355

Suffolk Cooperative Library
    System
627 North Sunrise Service Road
Bellport, NY 11713
Tel.: 516-286-1600

New York Public Library
Bronx Reference Center
2556 Bainbridge Avenue
Bronx, NY 10458
Tel.: 718-220-6576

Brooklyn in Touch
One Hanson Place, Room 2504
Brooklyn, NY 11243
Tel.: 718-230-3200

Buffalo and Erie County Public
    Library
Lafayette Square
Buffalo, NY 14202
Tel.: 716-858-7103

Huntington Public Library
338 Main Street
Huntington, NY 11743
Tel.: 516-427-5165

Queens Borough Public Library
89-11 Merrick Boulevard
Jamaica, NY 11432
Tel.: 718-990-0700

Levittown Public Library
One Bluegrass Lane

Levittown, NY 11756
Tel.: 516-731-5728

SUNY/College at Old Westbury
    Library
Box 229
Old Westbury, NY 11568
Tel.: 516-876-3151

Adriance Memorial Library
93 Market Street
Poughkeepsie, NY 12601
Tel.: 914-485-3445

Rochester Public Library
Business Division
115 South Avenue
Rochester, NY 14604
Tel.: 716-428-7328

Onondaga County Public Library
    at the Galleries
447 South Salina Street
Syracuse, NY 13202-2494
Tel.: 315-469-8442

Utica Public Library
303 Genessee Street
Utica, NY 13501
Tel.: 315-735-2279

White Plains Public Library
100 Martine Avenue
White Plains, NY 10601
Tel.: 914-422-1480

NORTH CAROLINA

Asheville-Buncomb Technical
    Community College
Learning Resources Center
340 Victoria Road
Asheville, NC 28802
Tel.: 704-254-1921, Ext. 300

The Duke Endowment
200 South Tryon Street

Suite 1100
Charlotte, NC 28202
Tel.: 704-376-0291

Durham County Library
300 North Roxboro Street
Durham, NC 27701
Tel.: 919-560-0100

North Carolina State Library
109 East Jones Street
Raleigh, NC 27611
Tel.: 919-733-3270

The Winston-Salem Foundation
310 West 4th Street, Suite 229
Winston-Salem, NC 27101-2889
Tel.: 910-725-2382

NORTH DAKOTA

North Dakota State University
The Library
Fargo, ND 58105
Tel.: 701-231-8886

OHIO

Stark County District Library
715 Market Avenue North
Canton, OH 44702-1080
Tel.: 216-452-0665

Public Library of Cincinnati and
    Hamilton County
Education Department
800 Vine Street
Cincinnati, OH 45202-2071
Tel.: 513-369-6940

Columbus Metropolitan Library
96 South Grant Avenue
Columbus, OH 43215
Tel.: 614-645-2590

Dayton and Montgomery County
    Public Library
Grants Information Center

215 East Third Street
Dayton, OH 45402-2103
Tel.: 513-227-9500, Ext. 211

Toledo-Lucas County Public
    Library
Social Science Department
325 Michigan Street
Toledo, OH 43623-1614
Tel.: 419-259-5245

Ohio University—Zanesville
Community Education and
    Development
1425 Newark Road
Zanesville, OH 43701
Tel.: 614-453-0762

OKLAHOMA

Oklahoma City University Library
2501 North Blackwelder
Oklahoma City, OK 73106
Tel.: 405-521-5072

Tulsa City–County Library
    System
400 Civic Center
Tulsa, OK 74103
Tel.: 918-596-7944

OREGON

Oregon Institute of Technology
    Library
3201 Campus Drive
Klamath Falls, OR 97601-8801
Tel.: 503-885-1772

Pacific Non-Profit Network
Grantsmanship Resource Library
33 North Central, Suite 211
Medford, OR 97501
Tel.: 503-779-6044

Multnomah County Library
Government Documents Room

1407 S.W. 4th Avenue
Portland, OR 97201
Tel.: 503-248-5123

Oregon State Library
State Library Building
Salem, OR 97310
Tel.: 503-378-4277

PENNSYLVANIA

Northampton Community College
Learning Resources Center
3835 Green Pond Road
Bethlehem, PA 18017
Tel.: 610-861-5360

Erie County Public Library
27 South Park Row
Erie, PA 16501
Tel.: 814-451-6927

Dauphin County Library System
101 Walnut Street
Harrisburg, PA 17101
Tel.: 717-234-4976

Lancaster County Public Library
125 North Duke Street
Lancaster, PA 17602
Tel.: 717-394-2651

The Free Library of Philadelphia
Logan Square
1901 Vine Street #201
Philadelphia, PA 19103
Tel.: 215-686-5423

University of Pittsburgh
Hillman Library
Pittsburgh, PA 15260
Tel.: 412-648-7722

Pocono Northeast Development
    Fund
1151 Oak Street

Pittston, PA 18640-3795
Tel.: 717-655-5581

PUERTO RICO

University of Puerto Rico
Ponce Technological College
  Library
Box 7186
Ponce, PR 00731
Tel.: 809-844-8181

Biblioteca Madre Maria Teresa
  Guevara
Universidad del Sagrado Corazón
Apdo 12383
Correo Calle Loiza
Santurce, PR 00914
Tel.: 809-728-1515, Ext. 357

RHODE ISLAND

Providence Public Library
Reference Department
2205 Washington Street
Providence, RI 02903
Tel.: 401-455-8005

SOUTH CAROLINA

Charleston County Library
404 King Street
Charleston, SC 29403
Tel.: 803-723-1645

South Carolina State Library
Reference Department
1500 Senate Street
Columbia, SC 29211
Tel.: 803-734-8666

SOUTH DAKOTA

Non Profit Grants Assistance
  Center
Business and Education Institute,
  East Hall
Dakota State University

Madison, SD 57042
Tel.: 605-256-5555

South Dakota State Library
800 Governors Drive
Pierre, SD 57501-2294
Tel.: 605-773-3131
Tel.: 800-423-6665 (SD
  Residents)

Sioux Falls Area Foundation
141 North Main Avenue, Suite
  310
Sioux Falls, SD 57102
Tel.: 605-336-7055

TENNESSEE

Knox County Public Library
500 West Church Avenue
Knoxville, TN 37902
Tel.: 615-544-5750

Memphis-Shelby County Public
  Library and Information
  Center
1850 Peabody Avenue
Memphis, TN 38104-4021
Tel.: 901-725-8855

Public Library of Nashville and
  Davidson County
225 Polk Avenue
Nashville, TN 37203
Tel.: 615-862-5843

TEXAS

Community Foundation of
  Abilene
Funding Information Library
500 North Chestnut, Suite 1509
P.O. Box 1001
Abilene, TX 79604
Tel.: 915-676-3883

Amarillo Area Foundation, Inc.
700 First National Place One
800 South Fillmore
Amarillo, TX 79101
Tel.: 806-376-4521

Corpus Christi State University
Library
6300 Ocean Drive
Corpus Christ, TX 78412-5501
Tel.: 512-994-2643

Dallas Public Library
Grants Information Service
1515 Young Street
Dallas, TX 75201-5499
Tel.: 214-670-1716

El Paso Community Foundation
201 East Main, Suite 1616
El Paso, TX 79901
Tel.: 915-533-4020

Texas Christian University Library
Funding Information Center
P.O. Box 32904
Fort Worth, TX 76129-0001
Tel.: 817-921-7106

Houston Public Library
Bibliographic Information Center
500 McKinney Avenue
Houston, TX 77002-2534
Tel.: 713-247-2700

Lubbock Area Foundation, Inc.
1208 14th Street #502
Lubbock, TX 79401
Tel.: 806-762-8061

UTAH

Salt Lake City Public Library
Business and Science Department
209 East Fifth South
Salt Lake City, UT 84111-3280
Tel.: 801-524-8200

VERMONT

Vermont Department of Libraries
Reference Services

111 State Street
Montpelier, VT 05609
Tel.: 802-828-3268

VIRGINIA

Hampton Public Library
Grants Resources Collection
4207 Victoria Boulevard
Hampton, VA 23669-4243
Tel.: 804-727-1153

Richmond Public Library
Business, Science & Technology
101 East Franklin Street
Richmond, VA 23219-2193
Tel.: 804-780-4256

Roanoke City Public Library
System
Central Library
706 South Jefferson Street
Roanoke, VA 24016-5191
Tel.: 703-981-2473

WASHINGTON

Mid-Columbia Library
405 South Dayton
Kennewick, WA 99336
Tel.: 509-586-3156

Seattle Public Library
1000 Fourth Avenue
Seattle, WA 98104-1193
Tel.: 206-386-4100

Spokane Public Library
Funding Information Center
West 906 Main Avenue
Spokane, WA 99201-0976
Tel.: 509-838-3361

Greater Wenatchee Community
Foundation at the Wenatchee
Public Library

310 Douglas Street
Wenatchee, WA 98807
Tel.: 509-662-5021

WEST VIRGINIA

Kanawha County Public Library
123 Capital Street
Charleston, WV 25301
Tel.: 304-343-4646

WISCONSIN

University of Wisconsin–Madison
Memorial Library
600 North Park Street
Madison, WI 53706
Tel.: 608-262-3193

Marquette University Memorial
Library
1415 West Wisconsin Avenue
Milwaukee, WI 53233
Tel.: 414-288-7214

WYOMING

Natrona County Public Library
307 East Second Street
Casper, WY 82601-2598
Tel.: 307-237-4935

Laramie County Community
College Library
1400 East College Drive
Cheyenne, WY 82007
Tel.: 307-778-1205

Teton County Library
Community Resource Library
320 South King Street
Jackson, WY 83001
Tel.: 307-733-2164

INTERNATIONAL

AUSTRALIA

ANZ Executors & Trustees Co.
Ltd.
91 William Street, 7th Floor
Melbourne, VIC 3000
Australia
Tel.: 03-648-5764

CANADA

Canadian Centre for Philanthropy
1329 Bay Street, Suite 200
Toronto, Ontario M5R 2C4
Canada
Tel.: 416-515-0764

GREAT BRITAIN

Charities Aid Foundation
114/118 Southampton Row
London WC18 5AA
England
Tel.: 71-831-7798

JAPAN

Foundation Library Center of
Japan
Elements Shinjuku Bldg. 3F
2-1-14 Shinjuku, Shinjuku-ku
Tokyo 160
Japan
Tel.: 03-350-1857

MEXICO

Biblioteca Benjamin Franklin
United States Information Service
American Embassy, USICA
Londres 16
Mexico City 6, D.F. 06600
Mexico
Tel.: 905-553-63-69

THE SUPPORT CENTERS OF AMERICA

The Support Center of New York
305 Seventh Avenue
New York, NY 10001
Tel.: 212-924-6744

REGIONAL PHONE NUMBERS OF FOUNDATION CENTER AFFILIATES

CALIFORNIA

Palo Alto, CA
Tel.: 415-323-0873

San Diego, CA
Tel.: 619-292-5702

San Francisco, CA
Tel.: 415-552-7584

COLORADO

Denver, CO
Applied Research and
    Development Institute
Tel.: 303-691-6076

DISTRICT OF COLUMBIA

Washington, DC
Tel.: 202-331-1401

National/International
Tel.: 202-296-3900

GEORGIA

Atlanta, GA
Tel.: 404-688-4845

ILLINOIS

Chicago, IL
Tel.: 312-606-1530

MASSACHUSETTS

Boston, MA
Tel.: 617-338-1331

NEW JERSEY

Newark, NJ
Tel.: 201-643-5774

NEW MEXICO

Santa Fe, NM
National AIDS Support Center
Tel.: 505-986-8337

NEW YORK

New York, NY
Tel.: 212-620-4230

OKLAHOMA

Oklahoma City, OK
Tel.: 405-236-8133

Tulsa, OK
Tel.: 405-236-8133

RHODE ISLAND

Warwick, RI
Tel.: 401-781-3338

TEXAS

Houston, TX
Tel.: 713-739-1211

OTHER ORGANIZATIONS

AAFRC Trust for Philanthropy
25 West 43rd Street
Suite 1519
New York, NY 10036
Tel.: 212-354-5799

Council on Foundations
1828 L Street, N.W.
Suite 300
Washington, DC 20036
Tel.: 202-466-6512

Sponsors meetings for grantmakers, trustees, officers, and executives to keep abreast of current trends in the various fields of philanthropy.

The Grantsmanship Center
1125 West 6th Street, Fifth Floor
P.O. Box 17220
Los Angeles, CA 90017
Tel.: 213-482-9860
Fax: 213-482-9863

Independent Sector
1828 L Street, N.W.
Suite 1200
Washington, DC 20036
Tel.: 202-223-8100
Conducts research and educates the public about the role of the independent nonprofit sector and its usefulness to society.

National Charities Information Bureau
19 Union Square West, 6th Floor
New York, NY 10003-3395
Tel.: 212-929-6300
Seeks to maintain sound standards in the field of philanthropy and to aid wise giving through advisory reports to contributors.

National Society of Fund Raising Executives
1101 King Street, Suite 700
Alexandria, VA 22314
Tel.: 703-684-0410
Holds periodic workshops and seminars dealing with all phases of fund-raising.

Points of Light Foundation
(formerly National Volunteer Center)
1737 H Street, N.W.
Washington, DC 20006
Tel.: 202-223-9186
Assists communities and organizations to reinforce, expand, and improve the effectiveness of volunteer activities.

FUND RAISING—PUBLICATIONS AND REFERENCES

GENERAL REFERENCE BOOKS

The Foundation Center's User-Friendly Guide: Grantseeker's Guide to Resources, by Judith B. Margolin. The Foundation Center, 1994, 3rd edition.
Foundation Fundamentals: A Guide for Grantseekers, edited by Judith B. Margolin. New York: The Foundation Center, 1994, 5th edition.
Grants for the Arts, by Virginia P. White. New York: Plenum Press, 1980.
Grants: How to Find Out About Them and What to Do Next, by Virginia P. White. New York: Plenum Press, 1975.
The Individual's Guide to Grants, by Judith B. Margolin. New York: Plenum Press, 1983.

REFERENCE BOOKS—FOR NONPROFIT ORGANIZATIONS

Careers for Dreamers and Doers: A Guide to Management Careers in the Nonprofit Sector, by Lilly Cohen and Dennis R. Young. New York: The Foundation Center, 1989.

"How to Apply For and Retain Exempt Status for Your Organization." IRS Publication 557. This is published by the U.S. Government Printing Office in Washington, DC, and you can order it through your local IRS office.

A Nonprofit Organization Operating Manual: Planning for Survival and Growth, by Arnold J. Olenick and Philip R. Olenick. New York: The Foundation Center, 1991.

Raise More Money for Your Nonprofit Organization: A Guide to Evaluating and Improving Your Fundraising, by Anne L. New. New York: The Foundation Center, 1991.

Securing Your Organization's Future: A Complete Guide to Fund-Raising Strategies, by Michael Seltzer. New York: The Foundation Center, 1987.

To Be or Not to Be: An Artist's Guide to Not-for-Profit Incorporation. New York: Volunteer Lawyers for the Arts, 1986.

JOURNALS IN THE NONPROFIT FIELD

The Chronicle of Philanthropy
Chronicle of Higher Education, Inc.
1255 Twenty-third Street, N.W.
Suite 775
Washington, DC 20037-1190
Tel.: 202-466-1200

Corporate Philanthropy Report
Craig Smith, Editor
2727 Fairview Avenue East
Suite D
Seattle, WA 98102-3147
Tel.: 206-329-0422

Foundation News & Commentary
1828 L Street, N.W., Suite 300
Washington, DC 20036-5168
Tel.: 202-466-6512

Fund Raising Management
Hoke Communications, Inc.
224 Seventh Street
Garden City, NY 11530-5771
Tel.: 516-746-6700

Giving-USA (Annual and Update)
American Association of Fund-Raising
Counsel Trust for Philanthropy
25 West 43rd Street, Suite 820
New York, NY 10036-7406
Tel.: 212-354-5799

Non-Profit Times
Davis Information Group, Inc.
190 Tamaback Circle
Skillman, NJ 08558-2021
Tel.: 609-466-4600

PERSONAL DEVELOPMENT AND ORGANIZATION

The Seven Habits of Highly Effective People, by Stephen R. Covey. New York: Simon & Schuster, 1990.

Flow: The Psychology of Optimal Experience, by Mihaly Csikszentmihalyi. New York: Harper & Row, 1990.

Learned Optimism: How to Change Your Mind and Your Life, by Martin Seligman. New York: Alfred A. Knopf, 1991.

Wishcraft: How to Get What You Really Want, by Barbara Sher and Annie Gottlieb. New York: Ballantine Books, 1983.

Copyright, Patent, Licensing and Legal Issues

A Writer's Guide to Copyright, New York: Poets and Writers, 1990.

How to Be a Successful Inventor, by Gordon D. Griffin. New York: John Wiley & Sons, 1991.

Licensing Art & Design, by Caryn R. Leland. New York: Allworth Press, 1990.

Protecting Your Songs and Yourself, by Kent J. Klevens. Cincinnati: Writer's Digest Books, 1989.

Trademark and the Arts, by William M. Borchard. New York: Center for Law and the Arts, Columbia University School of Law, 1988.

VLA Guide to Copyright for Musicians and Composers, 1987.

VLA Guide to Copyright for the Performing Arts, 1987.

VLA Guide to Copyright for Visual Artists.

Volunteer Lawyers for the Arts National Directory.

To order VLA publications, contact:
Lynn E. Richardson
Volunteer Lawyers for the Arts
1 East 53rd Street, Sixth Floor
New York, NY 10022
Tel.: 212-319-ARTS, Ext. 25

Jobs and Résumés

Internships: On-the-Job Training Opportunities for All Types of Careers, by Kathy Jobst. Cincinnati: Writer's Digest Books.

What Color Is Your Parachute?, by Richard Nelson Bolles.

The Only Job Hunting Guide You'll Ever Need: The Most Comprehensive Guide for Job Hunters and Career Switchers, by Kathryn and Ross Petras. New York: Simon & Schuster, 1995.

Writing a Job-Winning Résumé, by John E. McLaughlin and Stephen K. Merman. Englewood Cliffs, NJ: Prentice-Hall, 1986.

Personal Computers

Introduction to Personal Computers, by Peter Stephenson. New York: John Wiley & Sons, 1991.

Personal Computers for the Computer Illiterate, by Barry Owen. New York: HarperCollins, 1991.

Your First Computer, by Alan Simpson. Alameda, CA: Sybex, 1992.

Tax Assistance

The Artist's Tax Guide and Financial Planner, by Carla Messman. New York: Lyons and Burford.

J. K. Lasser's Your Income Tax. New York: Simon & Schuster, annual.

J. K. Lasser's Tax Guide for Small Business. New York: Simon & Schuster, annual.

Tax Guide for College Teachers. College Park, MD: Academic Information Service, annual.

INDEX